1992

Spanish Imperialism
and the Political Imagination

1.   Giambattista Tiepolo, *The Triumph of Spain*, Royal Palace, Madrid (photo: Arxiu Mas).

Spanish Imperialism and the Political Imagination

Studies in European and Spanish-American
Social and Political Theory 1513–1830

Anthony Pagden

Yale University Press
New Haven and London · 1990

Designed by Isobel Willetts

Set in Linotron Bembo by Best-set Typesetter Ltd, Hong Kong
Printed in Great Britain by The St Edmundsbury Press

Library of Congress Cataloging-in-Publication Data

Pagden, Anthony.
    Spanish imperialism and the political imagination, 1513–1830/
Anthony Pagden.
      p. cm.
    Includes bibliographical references.
    ISBN 0-300-04676-6
    1. Spain – Foreign public opinion.   2. Spain – Colonies –
Administration – History.   3. Latin America – History – To 1830.
4. Naples (Kingdom) – History – Spanish rule, 1442–1707.   5. Milan
(Italy) – History – 1535–1859. I. Title.
DP75.P34   1990   89-22644
325′.346 – dc20   CIP

For Chantal

Contents

Acknowledgements   viii

Introduction   1

1. Dispossessing the Barbarian: Rights and Property in Spanish America   13

2. Instruments of Empire: Tommaso Campanella and the Universal Monarchy of Spain   37

3. *Fede Pubblica* and *Fede Privata*: Trust and Honour in Spanish Naples   65

4. From Noble Savages to Savage Nobles: The *Criollo* uses of the Amerindian Past   91

5. Old Constitutions and Ancient Indian Empires: Juan Pablo Viscardo and the Languages of Revolution in Spanish America   117

6. The End of Empire: Simón Bolívar and the Liberal Republic   133

Notes   154

Bibliography of Works Cited   172

Index   183

Acknowledgements

Some of the material used in the first chapter of this book originally appeared in Anthony Pagden ed., *The languages of political theory in early-modern Europe* (Cambridge University Press, Cambridge, 1987). Chapter 3 has benefited greatly from comments made by the audience of the political theory seminar of Columbia University and by Simon Schama and Judith Shklar at Harvard. A briefer, and more markedly sociological version was published in Diego Gambetta ed., *Trust. The making and breaking of co-operative relations* (Basil Blackwell, Oxford, 1988). What are now chapters 5 and 6 began life as a paper delivered to a seminar on 'Problemas del liberalismo' at the Instituto de Estudios Avanzados in Caracas in the summer of 1988. I would like to thank the Director of the Instituto, Luís Castro, not only for all that he has taught me about the mind of Simón Bolívar, but also for having invited me to Caracas where, in the land Columbus understandably mistook for the Earthly Paradise, I rediscovered something of my own past and finally understood what I was trying to say. Geoffrey Hawthorn and Bianca Fontana read parts of the final manuscript and did what they could to clarify my thoughts and order my syntax. As always the substance of the book owes much to conversations with them, and with John Dunn, Judith Shklar, Peter Russell, John Elliott, and Istvan Hont at different times and in widely different places. The final manuscript was revised with painstaking care and, since I changed my mind more than once, considerable forbearance, by Isobel Willetts. I was also fortunate in having John Nicoll, encouraging, patient, and ironical, as my editor. Finally I would like to thank the British Academy and King's College, Cambridge for the generosity that enabled me to make a number of visits to libraries in Spain and Italy.

Cambridge – Caracas
June 1988 – June 1989

Introduction

i

On the ceiling of the throne room in the Royal Palace in Madrid the figure of Spain, young, female, remote, mildly contemptuous, and with one breast inappropriately exposed, gazes out along a room filled with images of imperial grandeur and religious piety. To the right of her are the pillars of Hercules, to the left, the hooded figure of the Church cradling the cross with one arm, holding the chalice aloft with the other. Beneath her is the royal standard, billowing over vanquished Moors, while ranged along the cornice of the room are Africans and Americans, Columbus and his ships, images of the Virtues and, at the far end of the room, the final overthrow of Ignorance and Envy. Giambattista Tiepolo's *The Triumph of Spain* is a celebration, filled, as the artist said himself, with 'grandiose ideas', of the monarchy of Charles III, apostrophied on the ceiling as 'Carole Magnanimum', who raises monuments that Time cannot destroy.[1] But, like the empire it celebrates, the painting is scattered over a vast surface and impossible to view fully from any single point. It is also the image of an illusion. In reality the youthful, half-naked figure on its throne of putti was already moribund. For Tiepolo's great picture was completed in 1764, more than a century after Spain had gone into irrevocable decline. Her empire, stripped of all its European dominions, had been reduced to the American 'kingdoms', and (as we shall see in chapter 4) even these were already distinct cultures with ambitions to economic, if not yet political, autonomy. The King of Spain could no longer claim the attention of Fame (poised overhead in homage) nor be of much immediate concern to either Apollo, who stands beside the throne, or to Hercules. And it is an unintended irony that the nation which, by the mid-eighteenth century, had come to represent for so many Europeans the apotheosis of wilful, institutionally enforced Ignorance, should now so often be heard protesting that its decline had been brought about by Envy.

Like the Roman, the Spanish Empire became, as much for those who came under its aegis as for those who did not, the image of a particular kind of polity. For nearly two centuries, despite the decline that began in the 1590s, the Spanish Monarchy was the largest single political entity in Europe. Even after the division of the Habsburg lands by Charles V in 1556 and the effective loss of the northern Netherlands in 1609, it still controlled, until the War of Succession, more than two-thirds of Italy and the whole of Central and South America. Its size and its power, together with the fact that, with the accession of Charles V, it acquired a distinct ideological identity, made it, with the exception of Venice, the most frequently studied political community in Europe.

The image of the Habsburg Monarchy, like that of the Roman Empire, changed, of course, according to the political preferences of the viewer. It changed, also, and sometimes radically, over time. For southern Europeans and for its American subjects – and it is with they that this book is concerned – it began in the early sixteenth century very much as Tiepolo, in the late eighteenth, had depicted it: the self-assured champion (and the exporter) of Christian cultural values, the secular arm of the papacy, and the sole guardian of political stability within Europe. It ended in the early nineteenth century, with the Peninsula itself occupied by foreign troops, the European possessions long since gone, and the Americas in revolt; as the paradigm of an archaic tyranny, a political analogue of that oriental despotate whose expansionist ambitions it had once fought so hard to keep in check.

The image of the Spanish Empire changed, however, not because the Empire itself changed, but very largely because it failed to. Despite the accession of a new dynasty in 1700 and the Bourbon reforms some seventy years later, which brought to what still remained of the Empire much of the administrative structure of Louis XIV's France, Spanish political objectives and Spanish ideological concerns remained remarkably cohesive over the three-hundred-year period covered by this book. There were, of course, changes and it may well be the case that the traditional account of the trajectory of Spanish history, from greatness in the sixteenth century to decline in the seventeenth, to final stagnation in the eighteenth and nineteenth centuries, is in need of revision. But viewed from one perspective, the only truly significant transformation was not in what the Empire was, but in what it came to represent. In the early seventeenth century that Monarchy had seemed to many, as it did to the Piedmontese Giovanni Botero, to 'surpass every empire that has ever been', not merely in its size and the distances it covered, but in its capacity to bring peace, stability, and prosperity to its peoples.[2] By 1812, as the Liberal Constitution of Cadiz made clear, the history of Spain from the accession of Charles V to the Napoleonic invasion could be written only as one sustained attempt to concentrate power in the hands of a single man, and thereby to destroy the ancient rights and privileges of the Spanish people.

ii

There never was, of course, a 'Spanish Empire'. Although contemporaries sometimes referred to the territories over which first the Habsburgs and then the Bourbons ruled as an empire, and although in many respects the administration of those territories was an imperial one, they were always, in theory and generally in legal practice, a confederation of principalities held together in the person of a single king. Naples remained a kingdom ruled by a viceroy, the king's *alter ego*, and Milan never ceased to be a duchy with the current Spanish sovereign as its duke. The Americas, as the *criollos*, the American-born Spaniards, were later forcibly to remind their king, were never colonies, but kingdoms, and – and in this they were unique – an integral part of the crown of Castile.

After the division by Charles V of the Habsburg lands, the Spanish Monarchy became, in effect, a conglomerate of six semi-discrete parts, each subject to a different Council of State. There was Castile itself, Aragon, Italy, the Netherlands, Portugal (between 1580 and 1640), and the Americas. This book, however, is almost wholly concerned with only two of these, Italy and the Americas. The reasons for this are twofold.

Although the political relationship between Castile and Aragon was, at least until the 1640s, no different in many significant respects from that between Castile and Italy, the Kingdom of Aragon was perceived by non-Spanish theorists, and indeed by many Spanish theorists, as a component part of what already by the early sixteenth century was spoken of as 'Spain', its former independence reduced, in Spinoza's words, to 'the specious names of empty forms of liberty'.[3] There is an Aragonese, and a specifically Catalan, political literature, but it is only ever incidentally concerned with the problems of empire. Portugal's association with Castile was too brief for there to have been any substantial, or interesting, consideration of its role, and the role of its own empire, within the Monarchy. This was not, of course, the case in the Netherlands. Moralists such as Furió Ceriol, Fox Morcillo, and Justus Lipsius, among others, wrote extensively about the nature of political association. The Revolt of the Netherlands also became, and remained until well into the eighteenth century, a powerful reminder that it was possible for a subject people to defeat a tyrannous ruler. And, because the Netherlands became a republic, its success was taken by many to be the triumph of democracy, a demonstration of what the 'people' might achieve if they were sufficiently organized and sufficiently determined. As the Neapolitan rebels told the viceroy in 1647, 'We shall do as the Flemings did' (*faremo come le fiandre*). It was not a message he could possibly have failed to understand.

But for all its importance, the Revolt of the Netherlands produced very little political reflection on the nature of the Spanish Empire. There is, of course, a large body of very distinguished, very subtle theorizing – by Grotius, Spinoza, and the De la Court brothers among others[4] – after the creation of the Dutch republic, but very little, if any, of this pays more than a cursory glance at Spain itself which, for obvious reasons, it dismissed as an archaic leviathan destined by the historical process to inevitable extinction. Most of what was said about Spain during the Eighty-Years War was, inevitably, harnessed to the war effort. Spanish atrocities in general, and the sack of Antwerp in 1576 in particular, led to the creation, at Flemish and English hands, of the so-called Black Legend. The Spanish image in Protestant Europe (and, it must be said, in many areas of Catholic Europe as well) as proud, cruel, and overbearing was in large part based on Dutch, and later English, propaganda. But like most propaganda, very little of this material, interesting though it is in other ways, is theoretically very compelling.

My second reason for concentrating on Italy and the Americas is this. Most historians of the Spanish Empire have confined their observations very largely to the Peninsula itself – to Castile, Aragon, and Portugal when it was ruled by a Castilian king – to the Americas and to the Netherlands. Spanish Italy – Naples, Sicily, Milan, Piombino, and the island of Sardinia – are generally passed over with barely a mention. There are obvious reasons for this, but most of them are anachronistic. To many contemporaries the Italian possessions, 'the garden of the Empire', as Charles V's chancellor Mercurino de Gattinara once called them,[5] seemed potentially the richest, certainly politically the most significant, of the Habsburg domains. Italy provided the Castilian crown not only with substantial revenues and, in Naples at least, an extensive source of patronage, it provided also a cultural incentive in the arts, in poetry, and in music. Spaniards may always have remained suspicious of Italians as over-subtle, irreverent, potentially subversive, and with a nasty reputation for political assassination; but the so-called 'Golden Age' of the late sixteenth and seventeenth centuries was in part the product of an extended political association with Italy. It is impossible to understand the political culture of the Spanish Monarchy, or the significance it had for southern Europe, without some understanding of the place within it of Italy, and in particular the southern Italian

4

states. For centuries, also, the Italians had been the most sensitive, most astute observers of the European political scene. It was the Italians, from Machiavelli in the sixteenth century to Doria, Genovesi, and Filangieri in the eighteenth, who provided the most extensive critique of the Spanish Monarchy and its objectives. It is not merely incidental, then, that the chapters in this book on Tommaso Campanella (chapter 2) and on the Neapolitan political and economic theorists of the eighteenth century, Paolo Mattia Doria and Antonio Genovesi (chapter 3), track, very precisely, the general shift in the image of the Spanish Monarchy from universal monarchy to oriental despotate.

iii

The first chapter deals with a largely unexamined aspect – rights of property – of the debates over the legitimacy of the Empire. These debates began in 1512, almost as soon as a Spanish monarch first attempted to take formal possession of American soil, and continued, in one mode or another, until the end of the eighteenth century and the effective end of the Empire itself. The extent and the intensity of the struggles over the rights of Spaniards in America are, perhaps, unequalled in the history of European colonization. These debates belonged, however, to a tradition of ritual legitimation that the Castilian crown had, since the later middle ages, regularly enacted when confronted by uncertain moral issues. The conclusions that the crown's advisors reached on these occasions were frequently ignored since, as the great Dominican theologian Francisco de Vitoria observed, kings were, of necessity, pragmatic beings compelled to 'think from hand to mouth'.[6] But the declarations issued by the theologians and jurists on crown policy formed an important part of the ideological armature of what has some claims to being the first European nation state. With the accession of Ferdinand and Isabella, that state had, effectively, secured the consensus of its own political nation. The troubles that followed the succession of Charles V posed little lasting threat to the authority of the crown, and with the defeat of the *comunero* revolt in 1521, the independent ambitions of the towns and the lesser nobility were effectively crushed. The only seventeenth-century revolt, the attempt in 1648 by the Duke of Hijár to make himself king of an independent Aragon with the help of Mazarin, was little more than, in John Elliott's words, 'a foolish adventure by a bankrupt grandee'.[7] Unlike France, and even England, Castile had, therefore, no further need to assert its own legitimacy against particular and factional interests. Its principal ideological concern became instead its self-appointed role as the guardian of universal Christendom. In order to safeguard that, it was crucial for the crown to be seen to act on all occasions in strict accordance with Christian ethico-political principles. The task of the theologians and jurists was to establish just what those principles were. This habit of seeking political legitimation ensured the existence of a lively and by no means uncritical inquiry into the behaviour of the state.

For most Spaniards, particularly after the abdication of Charles V in 1555 had finally severed Spanish links with the Holy Roman Empire, the Empire was largely a domestic affair. There were those, the 'humanists' of the reign of Charles V, Alfonso de Valdés, Juan Ginés de Sepúlveda, the historian Pedro de Mexía, whose ambitions for Spain closely resembled those of Campanella. But there remained a powerful, and no less popular, tradition of isolationism, in terms of which a king's first and sole duty was to his subjects. Any attempt to enhance his reputation by foreign wars which could bring his subjects no immediate or appreciable benefit was a violation of the contract by which he held his crown.

Throughout much of the sixteenth and seventeenth centuries many of Spain's most powerful theorists were unhappy with the Castilian crown's claims to sovereignty even in those lands where it was *de facto* ruler, and nearly all vigorously denied that any prince, even the Emperor, could exercise universal sovereignty (*dominium totius orbis*). But in Italy the possibility of a world empire – with the definition of 'world' left suitably imprecise – did not seem so absurd. The Italian states, in particular those in the south, were far more exposed to the dangers from which Spain offered, or seemed to offer, protection, than was Spain herself. For most Italians the concept of a universal empire had, also, for centuries been a familiar one. Dante's argument, in *De Monarchia* of 1313, that only a single universal ruler could bring an end to the faction struggles within Italy, had, not surprisingly, always had an appeal within the imperial courts.[8] The project of *De Monarchia* may, in the context of the early fourteenth century, have seemed an anachronistic ideal, but in the early sixteenth it looked like a distinct political possibility. Some regions of the political landscape had remained largely unaltered over the two hundred years that separated Dante from Gattinara. Faction squabbles still divided the Italian city states, and the relationship between the Emperor and the papacy was still uneasy – sometimes, in particular after the Sack of Rome by Charles V's mutinous armies in 1527, openly hostile. Now, however, the Empire under Charles V had become the most powerful single force in Europe, and there were two new threats to European peace: Protestantism and the Ottoman Empire.

6

In this Italo-Hispanic context, Tommaso Campanella's project for a universal—and by this he understood truly world-wide—Spanish Monarchy, discussed in chapter 2, was not intellectually so outlandish as it might at first seem. Where Campanella's universalism differed from that of Dante was in its scope, in its rejection of Dante's separation of imperial and papal powers (Campanella's monarchy was intended precisely to reunite the rule of the secular and the sacred), and in the methods that Campanella urged the Spanish crown to adopt. Those methods, with their emphasis on the role of science and religion, on eugenics and on bizarre modes of social engineering, may sometimes seem (as indeed they did to many of his contemporaries) to border on the insane. But beneath the messianic farrago there is a more orthodox, and more subtle, analysis of the role of cultural manipulation in political control, one that places Campanella far closer to the centre of a powerful tradition of Catholic political philosophy—that concerned with 'reason of state'—than has generally been recognized.

By the end of the seventeenth century, however, universalism of any kind, although it remained, as a political objective, of very considerable theoretical interest, was a spent force. It was, as Montesquieu said of it, 'morally impossible'[9] in a world where the only form of internationalism was founded on commerce and not, as were all empires, on force. When in 1698 Andrew Fletcher composed his curious little pamphlet, *Discorso delle cose di Spagna* on the probable outcome of the impending crisis over the Spanish succession, the best advice he could offer to anyone wishing to restore the universal hegemony of Spain was to seize command of the seas, of the trade routes to Africa and Asia. Only by turning its back on all it had once been—by introducing religious toleration, by adopting northern-European technologies, by surrendering large parts of its European territories, by privileging 'work and industry, those great inclinations which this nation has always held in hatred and contempt'—by, in effect, transforming an empire into a federation of trading nations, would Spain ever regain its greatness.[10]

Eighteenth-century political theorists, far from seeing a world monarchy as a protective agency, thought of it as a threat to individual liberty, for, as Montesquieu claimed, 'a Great Empire necessarily supposes a despotic authority in he who governs it'.[11] The history of Spain's imperial past now seemed to most Europeans to be little more than a saga of conquest, repression, and needless bloodshed, its political objectives not the defence of Christendom, but the preservation, at whatever cost to its subjects, of the territories it had acquired through chance or dynastic manipulation. 'In order to preserve America', observed Montesquieu, 'it did what even a despotism does not do: it destroyed the inhabitants'.[12] Even the Romans who had devastated the world to create the first universal monarchy were less barbaric than the Spaniards who had 'destroyed all to preserve all'.[13] Such accusations had, of course, been made before, most powerfully by Montaigne. But the legendary cruelties of the Spaniards had generally been attributed either to a defect in an intractable national character or, more widely, to the morally corrosive force of unrestrained human greed. Now, however, it was being claimed that the wasting of America had been the inescapable consequence of the kind of society Spain had become after the Austrian succession. It was a claim that was to be made with even greater force by the revolutionaries of the nineteenth century.

By the end of the seventeenth century it had also become apparent that the Spanish Monarchy had become impossibly overextended. It had grown too fast, was too heavily engaged on too many fronts at once. 'If [the Spaniards] had stayed to be strong within', observed Charles Davenant, 'before they exerted themselves too much abroad, they had probably established a dominion and power to which the greatest part of Europe must have submitted'. Instead they had 'aimed at sovereign sway without hands to hold it'[14] and, in consequence, had been compelled to rely for their political survival upon arbitrary and individual government.[15] And, as Montesquieu was the first to recognize, no society can practise tyranny abroad, and remain free at home. Inevitably, the habits of cruelty and repression, by which the Castilian crown had struggled to keep its foundering giant intact, had leaked back to the mother country.[16] By the middle of the eighteenth century, it had become clear, even to many Spaniards, that their empire had been the greatest curse the Spanish people had had to bear. It had brought them only long-term political enslavement and, by the 1730s, financial ruin, as all the resources of the state were squandered on retaining colonies that were now, in fact, independent – if not yet politically autonomous – communities. 'The Indies and Spain', observed Montesquieu in a passage frequently cited by the colonists, 'are two powers under the same master; but the Indies is the principal one, and Spain nothing but an accessory'.[17]

For the Italian political economists of the eighteenth century, Doria, Genovesi, Filangieri, the immediate realities of Spanish rule were already an historical memory. But they were certain that it was only by an analysis of Spanish despotism, and in particular of the means by which successive Spanish kings had attempted to coerce their Italian subjects – through, in Campanella's term, 'Hispanization', that they would reach an understanding of how southern Italy had been reduced to the economic and moral poverty in which it then found itself. The simple answer was that Spanish rule, by destroying political and individual liberty had, like all forms of despotism, destroyed the community itself. Despotates were not societies but merely collectivities of the enslaved. The solution, as Doria and Genovesi saw it, was, therefore, to reinstate by whatever means possible those political virtues that constituted the 'well-ordered republic'. For Doria and Genovesi this meant the re-creation of a society based not, as Castilian society was, upon honour, but, as the classical republics had been, and the modern states of Europe now were, upon trust. True political communities were not organized for protection; they were instead based upon co-operation between the members of the society for their mutual benefit. This claim was grounded upon two assumptions. One was the historical belief that Naples under its previous Aragonese and Angevin rulers, although a monarchy, had been a virtuous and 'well-ordered' society. Economic and political regeneration might, therefore, be achieved by reconstructing the political dispositions of a previous social order. The second was the conviction that commerce, and the commercial society, had created a world in which the kind of protection previous generations had looked to Spain to provide was no longer required. Commerce, as eighteenth-century political economists never tired of repeating, 'made men gentle' and ultimately would make war obsolete because, as the Abbé Raynal, the author of the fiercest contemporary condemnation of Spanish colonialism, the *Histoire philosophique et politique des deux Indes*, phrased it, 'a war among commercial nations is a fire that burns all of them'. In eighteenth-century Europe, Spain appeared to be the antithesis of the enlightened, commercial society. Its rulers were hopelessly wedded to antique notions of military grandeur and the honour-code; its Church which, as Montesquieu noted, might have provided some restraint on its rulers, had become an 'arbitrary power' in its own right;[18] its people were, in consequence, ignorant, backward, and desperately poor. Liberty, political liberty, the freedom (on some accounts the obligation) of each man to participate fully in the political process was what characterized modern Europe, since only free societies could be properly commercial ones. The republics of the ancient world, and certain medieval monarchies, in which ancient 'liberties' had been successfully defended – Aragonese Italy being one of these – had been properly free; so, too, were the states of Holland, England, and, after 1776, the United States. The period of stagnation, in which Spain was now irretrievably stuck, was the years of monarchical absolutism, the years that, in the rest of Europe, had come to an end with the death of Louis XIV. In Raynal's nicely self-referential characterization of the history of human progress,

9

Spain was still in the age of 'historian-orators', while modern Europe could be made intelligible only by those 'commercial philosophers' of which he was one.[19]

By the middle of the eighteenth century, not only the English, the French, and the Italians but also the Spanish crown's own American subjects had been persuaded of the force of these arguments. Their association with Spain was, however, far more complex than those of any of the Empire's other subjects. The native-born Spaniards, the *criollos* as they came to be called,[20] thought of themselves as Spanish in everything except a certain degree of cultural self-awareness until the very end of the eighteenth century. And when cultural self-awareness began to edge towards political self-assertion they, unlike the Italians, had no obvious non-Hispanic history to which they could make appeal. They had, therefore, as I describe in the fourth chapter, to invent one. What has come to be called '*criollo* patriotism' was founded upon an ambition to appropriate the past of the ancient Indian empires, first the Aztec and then the Inca, for the glorification of a white American-born élite. It was based on a widely accepted contemporary claim that cultural identity was as much determined by place of birth as by parentage and education. Since, however, the *criollos* also claimed the conquistadores as their 'founding fathers', and wished to avoid any suggestion of a racial contact with the Indian and half-caste (mestizo) masses, the project was poised forever on the edge of absurdity. In the first instance, its objective was limited to a relatively harmless wish to clear the Amerindian of the contemporary European accusations of indolence, stupidity, and sexual inertia, and to encourage an interest in the history and the archaeology of what one Mexican *criollo* described as 'these antiquities of ours'. Those *criollos* – the seventeenth-century polymath Carlos de Sigüenza y Góngora and the eighteenth-century Jesuit historian Francisco Clavigero – who sought to do to the Amerindians what the Romans had done to the Greeks generally refrained from placing any explicit political emphasis on their image of the wise and noble Indian. Above all they wished to insulate the ancient 'Aztec' or 'Inca' – both terms are intentionally misleading[21] – from any direct association with their modern, far from noble, though perhaps still distinctly 'savage', descendants. But cultural inquiries, in particular if they involve the rehabilitation of hitherto despised and oppressed masses, cannot hope to remain politically neutral for very long. In no sense was *criollo* antiquarianism directly responsible for the largely indigenous revolts of Tupac Amarú in Peru in 1780 and of Hidalgo and Morelos in Mexico in 1810: but it provided the language in which many of the rebel demands were couched, and it sustained the image, which was to haunt the Independence movements, and haunts Mexican political discourse to this day, of a fully autonomous Indian community.

For the radicals, however, for the Mexican Servando Teresa de Mier and the exiled Peruvian Jesuit Juan Pablo Viscardo (chapter 5), the plight of the *modern* Indian, from whom the *criollo* indigenists had gone to such lengths to shield the ancient, seemed to be directly analogous to the plight of the white élite. Both groups had been tyrannized by the same master, and if both could be persuaded to make a common cause of their opposition to Spain, then, finally, Spanish America might become the one, multi-racial, multi-cultural society that the great sixteenth-century Peruvian historian Garcilaso de la Vega had hoped for.

The ideology of the Insurgency was not, however, grounded wholly in Indian revivalism. It was also rooted in more traditional European revolutionary claims, the claim, in this instance, that since all legitimate monarchies are founded upon contract and established by ancient constitutions, the rule of the Spanish Monarchy, which disregarded both contract and constitution, was nothing short of despotic. The Spanish Monarchy's progressive denial of liberty to its subjects both in the Peninsula and in the Americas had, in Viscardo's view, transformed free, prosperous, and happy communities into nations of miserable, impoverished serfs. The merger of these claims with the nostalgic reverence for ancient Indians was not a difficult one. It had become fashionable in Europe, particularly in Italy where most of the exiled Americans, Viscardo and Clavigero among them, had made their homes, to describe the Inca and Aztec states as American analogues of the republics of Athens and Rome, paradigms of ancient liberty and political virtue. It required, therefore, only a limited degree of fantasy to conceive, as did the Venezuelan revolutionary general Francisco de Miranda, the idea of an independent America constituted as a new Inca Empire, 'improved' so as to include most of the institutional structures of a constitutional monarchy.

Like the Italian political economists, like Montesquieu, like, indeed, the framers of the Liberal Constitution of Cadiz of 1812, Viscardo and Miranda – if not Mier – could easily accept that a new virtuous *respublica* might be constituted under a monarchy, provided that the monarch abided by a constitution and a body of laws, observed the division of powers, and respected his subjects' liberties. It was also believed by many, Viscardo among them, that Spanish Americans had for so long been under the rule of kings that it would be impossible for them to conceive of any other kind of society. Although the North-American example might appear, as it did to Mier, to be 'a banner...to lead us to the gates of happiness',[22] the

11

aftermath of the French Revolution, and the uprising in Saint-Dominique in 1795, which had proclaimed 'the law of the French, the republic, the freedom of slaves', had made most of the *criollo* élite wary of republicanism even in its more moderate form. As Miranda himself observed in 1798,

> I confess that much though I desire the independence and liberty of the New World, I fear anarchy and revolution even more. God forbid that other countries suffer the same fate as Saint-Dominique...better they should remain another century under the barbarous and senseless oppression of Spain.[23]

But it soon became evident that the creation of new monarchies, even at the expense of importing old European princes,[24] was doomed to failure. As the greatest of the liberators and the liberation movements' only compelling theorist Simón Bolívar observed, monarchies depended for their legitimacy upon ancient traditions and for their support upon ancient nobilities, neither of which were available in America.[25] Bolívar, whose political ideas are the subject of the final chapter in this book, was certainly right, as the fate of the would-be monarchs of America – Augustín de Iturbide in 1822 and Maximilian in 1867 – was to demonstrate all too starkly. Only a state based upon the willing, and educated, participation of its citizens, only, that is, a state held together by a body of shared convictions could ever be built out of the ruins of an empire that had never attempted to provide its subjects with the smallest degree of political experience. Bolívar, however, had other equally chimerical ambitions of his own. On the banks of the Orinoco he had hoped to create – what the revolution in France had so spectacularly failed to do – a virtuous ancient republic. Bolívar's vision was flawed and, ultimately, incoherent because by rejecting the entire baggage of ancient constitutionalism and the illusion of revivified Indian empires, he was also compelled to reject any sense of continuity between the Iberian and Amerindian past and the projected republican future. His America demanded a far higher degree of commitment to the possibility of a new mode of political association than could ever be expected from the multiplicity of cultural groups of which it was, in reality, composed. It required precisely what the Spaniards had denied it: a civil society, a self-enforcing dedication to the shared cultural and political beliefs of the community. But because those few communities that did exist possessed, in effect, no beliefs to share, all Bolívar could offer was the idea of a government, and of a government held together wholly by a passionate belief in the power of abstractions. That, as he himself recognized, was the final legacy of the largest empire Europe had ever known.

1
Dispossessing the Barbarian:
Rights and Property in Spanish America

Spain acquired its American possessions almost by chance. Columbus's intentions, despite the grandiloquent titles he had secured from the crown, were, at least to begin with, relatively modest. Had he in fact discovered a western passage to 'Cathay' all he could have hoped to have done was to seize whatever off-shore islands he could, and establish a series of trading stations (*feitorias*), and factories, as the Portuguese had done in India. The Castilian crown, by virtue of the papal donation, might have claimed sovereignty over China and the Malay Peninsula as the Portuguese kings had done in Africa, India, and Persia, but it would never have been in a position to exercise it.

But America was not Cathay and its inhabitants had none of the technology of any of the Asian peoples. This made colonization a practical reality. The men who sailed first to the Antilles and then to the mainland in the years after 1494, unlike the immigrants from Portugal, came in pursuit of easy riches, in gold or land. For the most part they imagined themselves, whatever the reality of their social origins, as gentlemen (*hidalgos*), living, as the lesser aristocracy had done for centuries in Europe, from the labour of others and the profits to be had from war.

Technologically the colonization of the Americas was a relatively simple matter. Even Cortés in Mexico and Pizarro in Peru, though they faced large armies and opposition from highly organized political communities, had little difficulty in establishing Spanish rule and, ultimately, the semblance of Spanish communities. But the very simplicity of their collective enterprise, and the almost bewildering rapidity with which it advanced, posed for the Castilian crown serious problems of legitimation. From these early beginnings until Independence, the crown remained, as the liberal pamphleteer and champion of Simón Bolívar, Dufour De Pradt noted in 1817, overwhelmingly concerned with the need to defend its claims to

13

sovereignty (imperium) and property rights (dominium)[1] in America before an increasingly hostile world. Before 1539, the crown's principal claim to both of these had rested on the Bulls of Donation made by Alexander VI in 1493.[2] These had granted to Ferdinand and Isabella sovereignty over all the lands they might discover in the Atlantic not previously occupied by a Christian prince. But the power to make such donations was grounded in the papal assumption of temporal authority over both Christians and pagans, and although Ferdinand was perfectly willing, tacitly at least, to accept this assumption, his successors faced with less biddable popes than Alexander VI were uneasy about the implications such far-reaching claims might have in other political arenas closer to home. Papal 'plenitude of power', since it clearly had no basis in natural law, was also a concept that both the jurists and the theologians were reluctant to accept. Once, however, the Bulls had been sheared of their Caesaro-papal claims they imposed upon the Castilian crown only a duty, the duty to evangelize; but they could not confer upon it a corresponding right, and without such a right it was by no means clear that the Spaniards could legitimately establish settlements in the Antilles, much less seize the lands and effectively the persons of their inhabitants.

The first attempt to confront these problems in any detail occurred in 1504 when a committee (a junta) of 'civil lawyers, theologians, and canon lawyers' was called by Ferdinand to provide some moral and legal guidance on the matter. We have no record of what these men said. We know only that in the end they decided, not perhaps surprisingly, that 'the Indians should be given [to the Spaniards] and that this was in agreement with human and divine law'. The ruling, although it clearly implied the existence of prior property rights of the Castilian crown, something that the Bulls of Donation equally clearly did not, aroused no controversy and seems, for a while at least, to have settled the conscience of the king. In 1511, however, on the Sunday before Christmas, in what has now come to be regarded as a momentous event in the history of Spanish America, Antonio de Montesinos, a Dominican on the island of Hispaniola, launched a furious attack from his pulpit against the 'cruel and horrible servitude' to which the Spanish colonists had reduced the native populations, and promised them that if they did not mend their ways, they would be 'no more saved than the Moors or the Turks'. Montesinos's sermon was directed against the conduct of the colonists. Like most of his successors in the struggle to ameliorate the lot of the Amerindians, he did not challenge the crown's claims either to sovereignty or to property rights in the island. But his outcry was regarded, both in Hispaniola and in Spain itself, as an assault upon precisely 'the lordship and the rents [the king] has in these parts'.[3] For what Montesinos had inadvertently brought into question was the crown's *rights* (its *jura*) in America and above all its rights to what, in the language of Thomist jurisprudence, was called dominium. Montesinos's protest led to the convocation of another junta which met in Burgos the same year. To reinforce his claims Ferdinand, following a time-honoured procedure in matters of conscience, also appealed to two jurists, the civilian Juan López de Palacios Rubios (who had already produced a spirited defence of Ferdinand's 'Holy War' in 1512 against the Kingdom of Navarre) and the canonist Matías de Paz, for their rulings on the matter. Both of these men, and, so far as one can tell from the fragmentary surviving evidence, the members of the Burgos junta, agreed that the Spanish crown did indeed have rights to both sovereignty and dominium in America.[4]

What emerges from a reading of the treatises of both Palacios Rubios and Paz is the overwhelming preoccupation of the crown and its advisors not with the question of sovereignty, although this, too, was by no means uncontentious, but with property rights. What the crown wished to be told by its advisors was not whether it might *rule* the Indians – for no one, not even Bartolomé de Las Casas, the 'Apostle to the Indians' and the most radical defender of their interests, denied that – but whether it might legitimately benefit from the fruits of their labour and from the profits to be had from their land, and, more crucially, from what lay beneath their land.

The most compelling, at least to contemporary audiences, of the arguments employed by Palacios Rubios and Matías de Paz were very largely based upon the Roman legal claim that the peoples the Spaniards had conquered had never been able to constitute legitimate civil societies. For the Roman jurists, civil society was, by definition, a society based upon property, and property relations were what constituted the basis for all exchanges between truly civil men. It might, therefore, be argued that if, in fact, a society possessed no such relationships, and hence could not be described as a civil community, its individual members could make no claims to rights of ownership when confronted by invaders attempting to seize their lands. Their lands were not *their* lands but merely open spaces which they, quite fortuitously, happened to inhabit.[5]

These claims, when made about the technologically simple communities of the Antilles, did not seem implausible. But after the invasion of Mexico in 1519 and of Peru in 1531, they came to look decidedly less persuasive. Although the Aztec and Inca empires were, in many respects, neolithic ones, they were to European observers recognizable political communities capable of both ex-

15

ploiting and controlling the lands they occupied. Such societies could clearly not be deprived of their rights on the grounds that their members were still living in a state of nature. From the 1530s, therefore, the debate over the legitimacy of the Conquest took on a new urgency and a new complexity; and it became, in both the law and the theology faculties of the universities, a regular subject for disputation. The most famous, most powerful, attempt to provide a solution to the problem was made in a lecture entitled *De Indis*, delivered in 1539 by the Dominican Francisco de Vitoria, Prime Professor of Theology at the University of Salamanca.

Vitoria and his pupils, and the pupils of his pupils down to the generation of the Jesuits Luís de Molina (1535–1600) and Francisco Suárez (1548–1617) have come to be called 'The School of Salamanca', although the current Italian term 'seconda scolastica' is perhaps a better description of them. Though their views and the range of their interests – which ran all the way from theology to physics – were diverse they shared a common project: the elaboration of a rationalistic moral philosophy based upon an Aristotelian and Thomist interpretation of the law of nature. Central to that project was an understanding of what we refer to loosely as 'property', but which, in the language of natural jurisprudence, was called *dominium rerum*. The term dominium is dense and the meanings it was made to bear changed very considerably in the period between the middle of the sixteenth and the end of the seventeenth century. In the historical account of the origins of human society to which the Spanish scholastics subscribed, primitive man had voluntarily renounced his natural freedom in exchange for the security and the possibility of moral understanding that only civil society could provide. But he retained certain natural and hence inalienable rights, of which dominium was the most fundamental. At the most abstract level, dominium described the relationship that held together the three parts of the triad into which the Roman jurist Gaius had divided the natural world: persons, things, and actions.[6] In terms of specific human rights it described the *ius* that every individual enjoys in anything that pertains directly to him or (although women enjoy only restricted dominia) her. During the seventeenth century, the application of the term dominium was successfully limited by the Protestant jurists Hugo Grotius and then Samuel Puffendorf, to private property.[7] But for the Spanish scholastics men could be said to have dominium over not only their private property, their goods (*bona*), but also over their actions, their liberty, and even – with certain important qualifications – their own bodies.

For the theologians dominia were, above all, natural whether they were exercised in social practice or not. The Roman legal arguments which had been employed by Palacios Rubios were therefore rejected by the scholastics as deficient, no matter what the facts of the matter may have been, since they relied upon the claim that rights were exclusive to civil society. For even those who lived in the state of nature – provided, of course, that they *were* men and not merely humanoid – enjoyed the same natural rights as those who lived in civil communities. The conquest of America could be made legitimate only by demonstrating that the native populations had forfeited these by their own actions. And this, as we shall see, had to be done without endangering the claim that all rights were the products of God's laws, not of God's grace.

The definition of the term dominium had itself been the subject of a prolonged debate for which, in the end, Grotius's reductive solution was the only satisfactory one. Most of the Spanish schoolmen, however, until important changes were introduced by Suárez and Molina in the seventeenth century, operated with the definition provided by Domingo de Soto in his *De iustitia et iure* of 1556. 'Dominium', he said, 'is a faculty and a right [*facultas et ius*] that [a man] has over anything, to use it for his own benefit by any means that are permitted by law'. But since the Thomists upheld the distinction in Roman law between dominium – which constituted a right – and mere possession – which did not – Soto added that 'dominium is to be distinguished from possession, use, or usufruct...for dominium is not the ability simply to use something and take its produce, but to alienate it, give it away, sell it, or neglect it'.[8] As Richard Tuck has pointed out, the phrase 'by any means that are permitted by law' presented considerable difficulties because with that qualification it was hard to see how Soto's account of usufruct differed from *dominium utile*, a limited right that, while it belongs to the user, is nevertheless distinct from *dominium directum*, which is absolute and can thus be exercised only by a superior lord. Although a similar distinction between *dominium utile* and *dominium directum* had been made by both Accursius and Aquinas it was generally denied by the Spanish Thomists.[9] Soto's implicit acceptance of limited dominium had, however, important consequences for the arguments over the rights of the Amerindians, because it was introduced precisely to deal with the problem of the rights of children before the age of reason; for children clearly do have dominium even if they cannot be allowed to exercise it; they might, that is, be said to possess *dominium utile* although their parents or guardians retained *dominium directum* – a condition in which, as we shall see, the Indians might also be said to be.

17

ii

From all that he had heard, said Vitoria in his lecture of 1539, it was clear that before the arrival of the Spaniards, the Indians had been 'in public, private, and pacific possession of their things'.[10] There were, therefore, only four possible grounds for denying that they did not, at the time of the Conquest, also enjoy dominium over them: because they were sinners, or because they were infidels, or because they were *insensati*, or idiots (*amentes*). Only the first three of these had any direct bearing on the case of the Indians, since the mad are a special case whose rights can be considered only under the positive law, which clearly cannot apply to the Indians who, before the arrival of the Spaniards, were subject to their own laws.

The first claim – that the Indians had forfeited their natural rights by reason of their sins – invoked an old heresy associated with Wycliff and Huss which had now been revived by 'the modern heretics' – Luther and Calvin – that 'no one can have civil dominium if he is in a state of mortal sin'.[11] It was central to Vitoria's whole project to refute the claim of these 'modern heretics' that the authority of a prince depended not upon God's laws but upon God's grace, and the subsequent argument that if any prince fell from grace he might legitimately be deposed by his subjects or by another more godly ruler. The Thomists' attack on the arguments that the crown's apologists had hitherto used to legitimate the occupation of America and those used, as we shall see, by such men as the most strident champion of Spanish imperialism, Juan Ginés de Sepúlveda, and a number of canon lawyers, came ultimately back to this. For, in the end, Vitoria and his successors were far less concerned with the particulars of the American case than they were with the opportunities it provided for a refutation of Lutheran and later Calvinist theories of sovereignty.[12]

The accepted refutation of Wycliff's thesis provided by the Gersonian nominalists Pierre d'Ailly and Jean Almain depended – in Vitoria's somewhat schematized account of it – on the case of a sinner on the edge of starvation. If such a man does not have *dominium rerum* he cannot even possess the bread he needs to eat in order to stay alive. He is thus faced with an impossible moral choice: in order not to die voluntarily, which would be to commit one kind of mortal sin, he is compelled to commit another, theft. Since it is clearly impossible that God should have placed any of his creatures in such a position it follows that dominium must be independent of grace.[13]

This account of dominium implied, however, a theory of unlimited rights that, in effect, denied the Thomist's claim that *in extremis* all the necessities of life reverted to their common state, that every man may take what he truly *needs* from 'another man's plenty' without being guilty of theft.[14] It also obscured what, for Vitoria, was the main argument against Wycliff's thesis, namely that dominium derives from the fact that man is a rational being made in God's image, and that he cannot lose that characteristic of himself through sin. The sun, he said, quoting Matthew 5:45, shines on both the just and the unjust. And if this is the case then dominium is inalienable since, on Vitoria's own account, no act, however irrational it might seem, can be anything other than a temporary aberration. There may, of course, be certain acts that are so deviant as to suggest that their agents are not, in fact, men at all. As Locke was to argue, slavery was an option only for a man who had violated the law of nature and thus shown himself to be not a man but a beast.[15] But, in Vitoria's view at least, the Indians were not guilty of such acts. If, as he explained, neither their supposed cannibalism nor the practice of human sacrifice could deprive them of dominium then neither could their paganism.

This left Vitoria with the third of his claims. Truly irrational beings do not have dominium because this is a right (*ius*) and rights can be held only by those creatures who are capable of receiving injury. Since for Vitoria *ius* could be defined objectively only as 'that which is allowed under law', creatures who were incapable of receiving injury clearly could not be subject to laws and could not, therefore, be the object of rights.

At this point in the argument, the definition of dominium as natural to man by virtue of his rationality, which is what makes him an object of justice, raised for Vitoria what seemed to be a potential threat to any definition of dominium that made it a natural right independent of possession: namely the status of children. Children, claimed Vitoria, have dominium 'which is nothing other than a right to use something according to its proper use'[16] because, unlike say lions, they can be said to suffer injury; and in law their goods are held independently from those of their tutors. But as they cannot make contracts they possess these goods only as their inheritance.[17] The legal concept of inheritance can also, he implied, be transferred to a consideration of infantile psychology, for however irrational children may seem to be – and they are, he claimed in another lecture on the limits of human obligation, truly un-rational[18] – their reason is potential (just as their goods are potentially theirs), and since 'nature never fails in what is necessary' that potential cannot ever fail to become actual. As we shall see, this observation offered a powerful analogy with the condition of the Indian.

Having thus rejected all these categories as possible grounds for denying the Indians dominium before the arrival of the Spaniards,

19

Vitoria introduced what was to prove the most contentious claim of all. In 1510 the Scottish Dominican John Major had suggested that the Indians were the 'natural slaves' described by Aristotle in Books 1 and 3 of the *Politics*.[19] This had seemed to some to offer objective proof that they had never had any property rights even in their pre-contact state, for both by the terms of Aristotle's psychology and in law *servus* is the antithesis of *dominus*. Nor did the undeniable fact that the Indians had been legally 'free' in their own societies necessarily make them any the less slaves since, as Vitoria pointed out, a slave does not require a master in order to be a slave.[20] The theory of natural slavery is also predicated upon the claim that natural slaves (by contrast with civil slaves who are merely persons seized in a just war) are men who do not *possess* but only have a share in the faculty of deliberation and who, though they might be capable of understanding, are not capable of practical wisdom (*phronesis*). Since, therefore, such creatures lack free will they cannot have any subjective right to dominium either.

But, said Vitoria, even if the American Indians appeared to be 'very little different from brute animals who are incapable of ruling themselves', they did, in fact, have 'a certain rational order in their affairs'. They lived in cities, had a recognized form of marriage, magistrates, rulers, laws, industry, and commerce, 'all of which', as he observed, 'require the use of reason'.[21] This is a simplified version of Aristotle's requirements for civil life and it is clear that no people who fulfil them can be described as society-less and hence rights-less beings. At the very end of his lecture, however, Vitoria reconsidered this argument. Indian communities, he now claimed, possessed only the minimal requirements for social life. Indians had, for instance, no knowledge of the liberal arts, no proper agriculture, no true artisans. Theirs were societies in which no true *nobilitas*—in the Aristotelian and Thomist sense of the word—could exist and in which it would therefore be impossible to live a life of true *otium*.[22] But if the Indians do, in fact, live 'almost like beasts and wild animals' this is not because they belong by innate disposition to a state of semi-rationality, but because their 'poor and barbarous education' had rendered them incapable of fully rational behaviour. Since the cause of their cultural condition is to be found in the state of their education, then they may be not natural slaves but some kind of natural children and, like all children, heirs to a state of true reason. By the terms of Soto's definition of dominium they may be said to be in full possession of their rights without being able to exercise them. The Castilian crown might thus claim a right to hold the Indians, and their lands, in tutelage until they have reached the age of reason. The acceptance by any civil prince of such peoples 'into his care' might even, Vitoria concluded, be considered an act of charity.[23]

None of these arguments, of course, could provide the Castilian crown with dominium in America. In place of claims that made a direct appeal to either the natural or the civil law, Vitoria therefore substituted three based on the law of nations (the *ius gentium*). This was, by the definition given in the *Institutes* (1.2.1), 'that which is constituted by natural reason among men'. Just what this implied was a subject of much debate, but Vitoria took it, on this occasion, to be that which is 'of the natural law or derives from the natural law' and which consequently, like the natural law, cannot be modified in any way by human agency.[24]

Under the *ius gentium* the Spaniards possessed what he called the 'right of society and natural communication'.[25] Seas, shores, and harbours are necessary for man's survival as a civil being and they have, therefore, by the common accord of all men, been exempted from the original division of property. It had always, Vitoria claimed, been an objective right in law that no man could be denied access to any stretch of beach, no matter to whom it actually belonged, which is why Aeneas had rightly described the ancient kings of Latium as 'barbari' when they refused him anchorage. This right to travel (*ius perigrinandi*), therefore gave the Spaniards right of access to the Indies. There was also, under the heading of *communicatio*, an implied right to trade. As the Spaniards had come to America, or so Vitoria claimed, as ambassadors (*legati*) and traders, they had to be treated with respect, and be permitted to trade with all those who wished to trade with them. And since this was a right under the law of nations, it could (at least by the terms of Vitoria's present definition) be changed only by the consensus of the entire human community, not by the will of an individual ruler.[26] Vitoria also claimed that the *ius gentium* granted the Spaniards, together with all the other members of the human race, the right to preach their religion (*ius predicandi*) without interference – although it did not compel anyone to accept it; and that it permitted them to wage a just war against any tyrant 'in defence of the innocent'.

In the cases of the *ius perigrinandi* and the *ius predicandi* the Spaniards could enforce their rights if opposed, because any attempt to deprive a man of his natural rights constitutes an injury to him. The vindication of injuries is sufficient grounds for a just war, and ultimately it was only by means of such a war that the Spaniards could legitimate their presence in America.[27] By the terms of such a war the belligerent acquires the status of a judge with respect to his opponents and he may, therefore, appropriate their private property (their *bona* and usually only their movable goods) as he sees fit.[28] Similarly the victor acquires authority over the vanquished in order to defend himself from any future injuries, and prisoners taken in a just war may legitimately be enslaved. But in no other case may the

enemy be deprived of his *dominium rerum*. In circumstances, however, where the offence is very great–and this might apply to the
Indians–or where the enemy seems to be incapable of arriving at a
peaceful solution, it is possible to depose ruling princes to *tollere
principem* or *mutare principatum*.[29] The Spaniards might then be able to
send 'ministers' to protect their future interests and to depose
troublesome local rulers should the need arise.

Vitoria's third title, the 'defence of the innocent', is even more
limited in its application. The Spaniards may not, he insisted, make
war on the Indians because of their supposed crimes against nature,
since all nations are guilty of such crimes. If a prince has no right to
invade the territory of another in order to punish cases of 'simple
fornication'–since no nation on earth is free of that sin–no prince
can punish another for crimes such as cannibalism, sodomy, and
human sacrifice.[30] Cannibalism, sodomy, and human sacrifice are
evidently more serious crimes than fornication, but, for the Thomists, they were all crimes against nature and since such crimes are
offences against God not man, only God can punish them. To
suggest that any prince, however godly, even the Emperor himself,
could act as *flagellum dei* was to fall, once again, into the Lutheran
error of supposing that dominium is conferred by God's grace, not
God's law.

Vitoria had thus left the Castilian crown with a slender claim to
dominium iurisdictionis in America but no property rights whatsoever.
And, of course, such rights as the crown might be able to claim
under the *ius gentium* would only be valid if the Indians had indeed
'injured' the Spaniards. If, however, as seemed to be the case, 'these
barbarians have not given any reason for a just war, nor wish
voluntarily to accept Christian princes, the expeditions must cease'.
In the end all that remained was the starkly objective claim that since
the Spaniards were already there, any attempt to abandon the
colonies would result only in 'a great prejudice and detriment to the
interests of [our] princes, which would be intolerable.'[31]

iii

Over the next three decades all of Vitoria's pupils redescribed parts
of these arguments in their own lectures on the subject of dominium.
Perhaps the most important of these, partly because it is among the
most radical, at least as far as its implications are concerned, partly
because its author was later involved in the most widely publicized
debate on the subject, was delivered by the Dominican theologian
Melchor Cano in 1546. The Indians, Cano argued, may be said not
to possess dominium only if they can be shown to be irrational

beings. Since they clearly are not simpletons (*stulti*) the only possible argument is that they are 'slaves by nature'.[32] But this very theory is, he claimed, incoherent, not only because – as Vitoria himself had argued elsewhere – no man who merely had a share in the faculty of reason could properly be described as a man[33] – but because slavery could, by definition, only be a category in law. Aristotle's mistake had been to confuse a legal classification with a psychological disposition. Since the accepted definition of slavery given in Roman law (*Digest* 1.1.4) was 'someone who has been deprived of his liberty contrary to nature', there could evidently be no such creature as a *natural* slave. This confusion had, furthermore, been made in the interest of the parochial claim that Athenians were the wisest of all living creatures. And even if we understand Aristotle only to be stating the general principle that the wise should always rule the foolish, this, although it might indubitably be the case, cannot confer dominium, since dominium does not derive from wisdom any more than it does from grace. *Dominium iurisdictionis* derives from the will of the community and *dominium rerum*, of course, from the natural law.[34]

It may, of course, still be the case, as Vitoria had argued, that the Indians really are like children in need of education. But even if this were so, the Christians would not be entitled to 'take them into their care' if in order to do this they had to conquer them first, since any act whose purpose is to secure the utility of another is, as Vitoria had rightly suspected, a precept of charity, and no precept of charity can involve coercion. The position of the Castilian crown was thus, Cano concluded, analogous only to that of the beggar to whom alms may be due but who is not empowered to extract them.[35]

Cano also rejected Vitoria's other claims. The title 'right of society and natural communication' does not, he claimed, provide a right of entry to another's territory because, even if the *ius gentium* is of the natural law, it can only be so in the third degree and is consequently, like any code that relies upon an interpretation of the law, subject to abrogation and alteration. Like Vitoria himself on other occasions, Cano could not really accept the *ius gentium* as anything other than a positive law. For it was, he pointed out, clearly absurd to suggest that there could exist a law of nations that might forbid a prince from controlling the movement of foreigners over his lands. Such a law would prevent the King of Spain from denying entry to the French, which would be contrary to actual practice and in violation of the positive law of Castile. Furthermore, even if it were the case that merchants and travellers might claim the right of free access under the law of nations, the Spaniards had clearly not presented themselves to the Indians as such. They had gone to America as conquerors. 'We would not', he concluded drily, 'be prepared to describe Alexander the Great as a "traveller"'.[36]

This left only the *ius predicandi* and the right to defend the innocent. These Cano was prepared to accept, but he made it clear that they did not have the power to confer property rights upon any secular prince. The Castilian crown's rights in the Indies were, by the terms of Cano's argument, severely limited to political sovereignty. It clearly did not possess rights of *dominium rerum* in America any more than it did in Naples or Aragon. The Indians were, as Las Casas was to insist time and again, free subjects of the Castilian crown, and their property remained their own.

This injunction included not only their land and movable goods but, more polemically, what lay beneath it. As Domingo de Soto noted, even if the Indians themselves

> regard such treasures [i.e., their gold and silver deposits] as things abandoned, because the law of nations established a division between different regions, even if the inhabitants of that region hold such things in common, foreigners cannot take possession of them without the consent of those who live there. For neither can the French enter into Spain for the same purpose, nor can we enter France without the permission of the French.[37]

The Spaniards could, therefore, make no claim to either the lands of the Indians or their, barely exploited, mineral wealth. Only the question of the Spaniards' rights to Indian labour now remained unresolved. None of the Salamancan Thomists have much to say on this issue, partly because labour was not obviously property, and was certainly not a good (*bonum*) until Locke made it so; partly because labour could only be taken from the Indians by force – which was clearly illicit – or under the labour system (known as the *encomienda*) in which the Indians theoretically exchanged their labour for military protection and Christianization. The *encomienda* was legitimate, they generally agreed, when they mentioned it at all, provided that the Indians did indeed receive something in exchange for their labour and if they had – and the legal fiction maintained that they had – voluntarily entered into a contract with their *encomendero*.[38]

iv

By the middle of the century this modified version of Vitoria's argument was widely accepted by all the Thomists. They may not quite, as Dr Johnson supposed, have given it 'as their opinion that it was not lawful'[39] to deprive the Indians of their property, but they had come perilously close. As the Mexican insurgent Servando

Teresa de Mier in 1811 triumphantly, but not entirely inaccurately, summarized Soto's arguments, 'he could find for the King of Spain no legitimate title nor any right of dominion in the Indies, because religion cannot be one'.[40]

The changing tone of the legislation governing the crown's relationship with both the colonists and the Indians in the years after 1540, and the numerous, if ultimately ineffective attempts to curb the activities to prevent further atrocities, also suggest that the Salamanca theologians voiced their views to some effect in the influential circles where they moved.

There were, however, others with other views. Most of these, unlike Vitoria and his pupils, had first-hand knowledge of Indian societies and were deeply involved in the colonizing process. Their claims came not, therefore, from a larger concern with the implications of the American case for the status of dominium. They came from an identifiable political programme. Perhaps the most interesting of these programmes was provided in 1535 by the Franciscan bishop of Michoacán, Vasco de Quiroga, in a document, much read but never printed during his lifetime, entitled *Información en derecho*, and written in protest against the crown's proposal to lift the sanctions against slaving. Quiroga's argument is interesting partly at least because it comes from a man who was, during his lifetime and has been ever since, celebrated as a champion of the Indian cause. He is best known as the founder, at a place he named Santa Fé, of a number of 'village hospitals', communities where the Indians were protected from the attentions of their Spanish rulers and encouraged to live full Christian lives. Because of two passages in the *Información en derecho*, one a quotation from Lucian's *Saturnalia*, the other referring, indirectly, to More's *Utopia*,[41] and a close association with the archbishop of Mexico, Juan de Zumárraga, who owned a heavily annotated copy of *Utopia*, these 'village hospitals' have been interpreted as an attempt to translate More's work into a functioning communitarian project. Quiroga has been declared a humanist by most modern scholars, who have frequently assumed, by a process of semantic conflation, that he must therefore also, in some general sense, have been a 'humanitarian'.[42] But despite his opposition to slavery Quiroga, like most members of the Franciscan order, was, in fact, a fierce opponent of Las Casas and a consistent apologist for the *encomienda*.[43] He claimed, with some justification, that the *Información* had been written for the service of God and His Majesty *and* for 'the use of the conquerors and settlers', and in 1531 had written to the crown in support of Cortés's request to be allowed to extend the conquests, a letter in which he seems to argue that one of the many benefits that the Spaniards had brought to the Indians was a know-

ledge of warfare.[44] Despite his remarks about the primitive inno-
cence of the Indians, Quiroga's humanism was strictly legal and the
Información, although oddly structured for such, was, as its title made
plain, a legal treatise.

Quiroga, too, held that the Indians could not exercise *dominium
iurisdictionis* since that belongs only to those 'who at least know and
observe the natural law, do not worship many gods, and have a king
and an ordered and politic life'.[45] The Indians, he continued, live in
something very close to the state of nature, 'in tyranny of themselves
as barbarous and cruel persons, in ignorance of things and of the
good and politic life'. Their 'ignorance of things', their incapacity
to develop an understanding of the mechanisms of the natural world
(an understanding that was accessible only to civil men) made their
societies structurally weak and had allowed them to be easily over-
run – a point repeated by Sepúlveda.[46] Such communities as the
Indians did have – where, that is, they were manifestly not living in
the state of nature – did not constitute legitimate polities. For true
polities, said Quiroga citing Gerson, could consist only of the
classical mixed constitution comprised of monarchy, aristocracy,
and timocracy. Among such peoples as the Aztecs, however, there
were only tyrants worshipped, as Moctezuma had been, 'not as a
human being among free people but as a god among captive,
oppressed, and servile people'. Furthermore, succession within these
societies was elective which, he claimed – forgetting for a moment
that his own king had become emperor of the Romans by election –
was 'neither legitimate nor reasonable, but a tyranny'.[47] Casting his
eye over the other types of Amerindian political organization recognized by Europeans, he declared that those communities run by
war-lords (what he called *principalejos*) were mere oligarchies operating only for the private gain of their rulers, while the acephalous
villages (known as *cabezas*) displayed no collective interests in 'the
common good rather than that of the particular man'. None, in
short, was a true *respublica*.

If it was the case that, prior to the arrival of the Spaniards, no
Indian group had been capable of constituting a true civil community
(*civitas*), then, by the terms of the *Digest*, it was obviously the case
that no Indian leader could claim to exercise *dominium iurisdictionis*.
The lands of the Indian were legally unoccupied, the property of the
first civil men to take effective possession of them. Furthermore, he
added, it was proper, according to the *Digest* (43.16), that those
enslaved by tyranny, even by that tyranny constituted of nothing
more than the inevitable social 'disorder' (a word that has a prominent place in Quiroga's vocabulary) that plagues any imperfect political society, must be freed. It might even be claimed that to leave the

Indians 'badly ordered and barbarous in a savage and bestial life, and as untutored, scattered, sylvan, miserable, and insufficient as they are'[48] amounted to a violation of their natural rights as the men they indubitably were.

Those, however, who did not merely live out their lives in 'ignorance, bestiality, and corruption',[49] clearly did inhabit some Lucianic 'Golden Age'. But it was an age without property relations, without civil society. And for the Indians it was merely a beginning of a history which would one day bring them to the complex finished condition in which their Spanish masters lived. What was now required of those masters was, therefore, the imposition of a political system that would civilize them 'in such a way as they do not lose their primitive simplicity and transform it into our malice'.[50] This system might be, in some regards 'Utopian' (not least of all in its insistence that the idleness, 'into which they are reared and are accustomed',[51] was harmful to them), but it was a system intended to introduce the simple and uneducated into a way of life that would ultimately require them to become members of a full civil community.

Quiroga's argument, by insisting that political, and hence also property, rights could be held only by civil men in civil communities, that both Golden Age primitives of the kind described by Lucian, and tyrannous societies could not exercise dominium, translated the whole argument over rights into another language, with which when presented in this unmediated form the Thomists had little tolerance.

The best-known exponent of this language, however, was Juan Ginés de Sepúlveda, translator of Aristotle, a former pupil (or so he claimed) of Pomponazzi, one of the Emperor's chaplains, and his official historian. Sepúlveda's works were characteristically eclectic. He claims to have trained as a theologian and was certainly familiar with a wide range of theological and legal texts, both civilian and canonist. He was also, unsurprisingly for someone with such an education, a champion of the notion of a universal monarchy and he wrote two political dialogues entitled *Democrates primus* and *Democrates secundus* (or *alter*) in defence of what he took to be Charles V's universalist claims. The first of these was a standard exhortation to Charles to resume the offence against the Turks. The second was a strident defence of the crown's rights in America. It is important to remember the context in which this text was written, partly because it is one reason why the theologians – who had always opposed the crown's claims to universal sovereignty – were so hostile to Sepúlveda,[52] and also why other later writers such as Campanella were, as we shall see in the next chapter, so favourable.

Sepúlveda's argument in *Democrates secundus*, or rather that of his mouthpiece Democrates, is similar, to begin with at least, to Quiroga's. Since the Indians, says Democrates, had had no rulers and no laws in their pre-conquest state, they might legitimately be appropriated by the first civil man to reach their shores. For Sepúlveda (as in this case for Major) and for most Roman lawyers and their humanist commentators, all property relations are the product of civil society. They constitute, that is, objective not subjective rights.[53] To the Thomists who later examined his work, Sepúlveda seemed, by this claim, to have recast the whole issue of the legitimacy of the Conquest in the language of humanist jurisprudence. Worse still, in order to make good his claim that not merely the Taino and the Arawak of the Caribbean but also the Aztec and the Inca were pre-social men, Sepúlveda was committed to a far starker reading of Aristotle's theory of natural slavery than any previous author had been. The Indians, he claimed, were evidently not civil beings since they consistently violated the law of nature. To the objection of the other speaker in the dialogue (a mild-mannered German called Leopoldus who speaks throughout in the language of political Aristotelianism) that all men violate the law of nature and that in many societies such crimes are not even proscribed by civil law, Democrates replies that a man may perform certain unnatural acts *as an individual* and still retain his humanity. What he may not do is to set up 'laws and institutions' that are contrary to nature. Single individuals frequently, even in Christian societies, falter in their understanding of the law of nature. But if the consensus of the entire community, which is the only means of knowing the precepts of that law, is itself at fault, then it is clear that this cannot have been arrived at by a collectivity of rational beings. The 'crimes committed against human society' by such creatures therefore constituted, as the Canonists had always insisted, grounds for a just war in which the vanquished might be deprived of all their rights including their liberty, their *dominium corporis suis*.[54]

Sepúlveda was extremely proud of what he believed to be his discovery of the weakness in the Thomists' rejection of the argument that 'crimes against nature' constituted legitimate grounds for depriving a man of his natural rights. Leopoldo, however, objects that Mexican society, even if guilty of such crimes, had any number of other features characteristic of civil communities. Certainly, replies Democrates, for the Indians obviously possess some power of understanding; even natural slaves are men, not 'bears or monkeys'. But the communities they have created are not like those of 'truly civil beings'. For there are, he points out, many forms of natural association among animals that share some of the features of a true society but that are clearly not in any sense civil ones. A closer look at the Indian world would, he concludes, reveal that it was really not much better organized than a colony of bees or ants.[55]

Before the arrival of the Spaniards, the Indians had, Sepúlveda conceded, been lords in their own lands, they had enjoyed, that is, imperium under the terms of the law of nations which grants rights of occupancy to the first settler. But, he insisted, not only was imperium not dominium, but any claim made under the *ius gentium* may be abrogated by subsequent civil legislation since laws governing the relationship between nations were, as the humanists had maintained, positive not natural. The Castilian crown's claim to sovereignty in America, however, rests on the dictate of the natural law which grants dominium to all those who are civil beings over all those who are not.[56]

To Soto's argument (although Sepúlveda does not mention the Dominican by name) that even if the new civil regime created by the Spaniards could be shown to be legitimate, the Indians still retained use-rights over their lands and, more importantly, over their gold and silver, Democrates replies that God gave property to man for his use, and since use, unlike dominium, is limited, man may not *abuse* it. The Indians, however, have clearly abused their property, cannibalism and human sacrifice being the most grisly violations of those limited use-rights that men have over their own bodies. More importantly, they had used their gold and silver only for idolatrous ends. Like the Egyptians, then, they may be said to have forfeited whatever rights they had had over these metals because, in Augustine's words, 'they were sacrilegious and made ill-use of their gold'.[57] Furthermore since no Indian society had had a monetary economy, no Indian could be said to have exercised any rights over any precious metal. These were, therefore, still a common part of Adam's patrimony to which the Spaniards had a high moral claim by having traded metals which had been useless in the ancient Indian world, for such useful things as iron, European agricultural techniques, horses, donkeys, goats, pigs, sheep, and so on.[58] For Sepúlveda, as for such eighteenth-century natural law theorists as Wattell who, in the generation after Grotius and Puffendorf, rewrote the language of jusnaturalism in a more fully humanistic idiom (as indeed for Tocqueville), dominium could only exist if it were exercised. The cultivation of the land allotted by God to man is not, as Wattell claimed, merely useful: it is an obligation 'imposé à l'homme par la nature'.[59] Any people who failed to fulfil that obligation could have no claim against other more industrious nations who occupied and cultivated its lands. It followed, therefore, that the Christians might, in Democrates' words, take possession 'by private and public law' of all Indian goods. The Indians' historical relationship to their property may now, he concluded, be likened to that of a man who has been deprived of his goods by the court but granted the *ius utendi* until sentence has been formally promulgated by a judge. The arrival of the Spaniards, directed to America by divine providence, constituted that promulgation.[60]

Sepúlveda's argument, couched as it was in the language of a humanist jurisprudence that restricted all rights – and rights of property in particular – to the members of civil societies, met with fierce opposition from the Salamanca theologians. Their hostility to his work was, so Cano told Sepúlveda, based on the fact that his doctrines were unsound, that he was ignorant of what Vitoria had written on the subject, and that he seemed to know more about history and philosophy than he did about theology.[61] In part, as Sepúlveda himself recognized, this was the reaction of a professional intellectual coterie to interference from an outsider. But Cano's increasingly acrimonious correspondence with Sepúlveda makes it clear that the Thomists were concerned by two other issues. In the first place, Sepúlveda's objective (and conceptually somewhat confused) use of *ius* had allowed him to translate concepts from the positive into the natural law. In the second, his reliance on the Canonists' defence of the thesis that no man who had committed crimes against nature may possess dominium seemed, once again, to open the way ultimately to a Lutheran definition of sovereignty.

The most sustained attempt to meet Sepúlveda's arguments on these issues came in a series of lectures given at Salamanca between 1560 and 1563 by Juan de la Peña, a pupil of Soto and a close friend of Las Casas.[62] Peña began, as Cano and others had before him, by dismissing the theory of natural slavery. It was, he claimed, not only inapplicable, as Cano had argued, it was also incoherent. For if it were possible for there to exist whole races of partially rational men capable of performing some, but not all, of the actions of civil beings, this would seriously threaten the doctrine of the perfectibility of man and the unity of the whole species, both of which have been guaranteed by divine revelation. If natural slaves do exist they must be very rare beasts indeed, and they must *be* beasts. Peña was willing to concede the minor premise – that the wise should always rule the less wise; but the fact remains (*factum tenet*), he said, that in no actual society is this ever the case.[63]

If the Indians are rational men they have *dominium rerum* since 'the foundation of dominium is that man is a rational creature'[64] and no act they might perform can, *of itself*, deprive them of that right. The manifest errors of their society before the arrival of the Spaniards, like the errors of all non-Christian societies, were, Peña insisted, merely probable. They were, that is, the kind of errors into which any individual might fall if he were deprived of proper guidance, the kind of guidance that, in the end, only a Christian civil society can provide. But a man who is in error is still in full possession of all his natural rights. Sepúlveda's claim that only civil men could enjoy dominium is merely the legislative norm of a tyranny (the Roman Empire), and may ultimately prove to be as parochial as Aristotle's assumption that all those who are not Athenians are natural slaves.[65]

Sepúlveda's claim that the Indians had also forfeited their use-rights in the lands they occupied was similarly false. Use-rights were, Peña pointed out, not dominia and thus came under not the natural but the civil law. From this it clearly followed that whatever misuse the Indians may have made of their property could only be punished by those who enjoyed civil jurisdiction over them. Since, however, they had had dominium before the arrival of the Spaniards and were guilty of no offence 'in respect of another republic', they could not be punished under a new regime – even supposing that regime to be a legitimate one, which, in this case, was by no means certain – for crimes committed under another. If they were, in fact, unworthy (*indigni*) of dominia then it is up to *their* judges to deprive them of such rights and not the Spaniards, 'who have no authority over them'.[66] Far, therefore, from being, as Sepúlveda had suggested, under sentence of confiscation the Indians were now in the position of persons from whom a judge has taken far more than the law allows and, like all such persons, they were entitled to restitution.[67] And, Peña concluded, if that is the case then in order to press their claims for restitution the Indians are perfectly within *their* rights to make war on the Spaniards. The fact that they were pagans and the Spaniards Christians was irrelevant. However scandalous it might seem, Peña argued – as Suárez was to later with even greater force – pagans could fight just wars against Christians and be entitled to all the rights, including movable property, gained in war. The *iura* that governed the justice of war, like all *iura*, had no part in God's grace.

Like Cano before him, Peña was willing to accept that the Spaniards could make just war on the Indians, and thereby deprive them of their rights, in defence of innocent parties. This, at least, would provide a cause for just war among Christian princes. Henry VIII of England, whose *respublica* was, because of the offences he had caused its citizens, already in disarray, might legitimately be attacked in order to prevent further collapse.[68] Similarly it was legitimate for the Spaniards to prevent such tribes as the Caribs from eating each other by force. It was, however, by no means clear that the Mexicans – who, Peña claimed, did not eat their subjects – had sufficiently

31

offended a large enough number of their people to warrant European interference. The Aztec kings had been accused of only one major violation of the rights of their citizens: human sacrifice. But from what Peña had heard (and this must surely have been a piece of information given him by Las Casas), this was, in fact, only a ritualized mode of execution.

In the end it was impossible for Peña, faced as he was by the need to refute Sepúlveda, to find sufficient grounds in any of Vitoria's original titles for denying the American Indians their natural property rights. The only title that could escape careful scrutiny in the light of an increasingly detailed body of ethnographic information, was the *ius predicandi*, the right to preach. But as Vitoria himself had recognized, this only gave the Spaniards the right to be heard.

The obvious conclusion, and it had been obvious now for some time, was that, if the consequences of these arguments were going to be taken seriously, the Spaniards had to withdraw from America and return to the Indians all that they had taken from them. Although this was never considered as a real possibility because, as Vitoria had observed, it would be intolerable in practice, it was at one point widely believed in the colonies themselves that Charles V intended to 'abandon the Indies' to satisfy his conscience. The only possible argument that could preserve both Indian rights and the Spanish claim to, if not *dominium rerum*, at least *dominium iurisdictionis*, was the claim made by Las Casas in *De regia potestate* (1554) that 'the only title that Your Majesty has is this: that all, or the greater part of, the Indians wish voluntarily to be your vassals and hold it an honour to be so'. Vitoria himself had made much the same point in *De indis*.[69] Just as the French had elected Pipin, so the Indians might 'elect' Charles V, since every *respublica* 'may constitute its own dominium with the consensus of the majority'. But, unlike Las Casas, who seems always to have assumed that Moctezuma's 'donation' to Cortés constituted a legitimate political charter, Vitoria recognized that it would prove impossible in fact to discover what the consensus of the majority was.[70] Even if the Indians could plausibly be said to have chosen the Spaniards as their rulers this, of course, did not mean that they had thereby voluntarily forfeited their natural rights, for it is obviously in no man's power to do that; nor that they were any the less due for the restitution of their goods, and their liberties, even the liberty of self-government. For, by the terms of this formulation, the rights that the crown now had in the Indies were similar not to those it had over the people of Castile but to those it had in Milan. The Indian chieftains, like the dukes of Milan, ruled over polities that were, in all respects, 'perfect republics' and their subjects were consequently free men with full dominium under their own laws.

Philip II could no more parcel out the Amerindians to his Castilian subjects than he could give away the Milanese to the French.[71]

It followed from this, Las Casas wrote in 1555 to the archbishop of Toledo, Bartolomé de Carranza, who had been struggling with the Council of the Indies on his behalf, that the colonists must abandon the Indies leaving only 'the universal principate of the King of Castile'. A limited number of soldiers should remain to protect the missionaries, and once restitution had been made the crown might begin to trade for the precious metals it required.[72] Under this description America resembled less the Duchy of Milan than a Portuguese factory in India, an analogy that Vitoria himself had drawn at the very end of De indis, pointing out that there was no evidence to suggest that the crown of Portugal had acquired any less through licit trade than the Castilian crown had through illicit occupation.[73]

V

With the death in 1566 of Las Casas, who had done so much to keep it alive, the debate over the rights of the Indians lost much of its immediate force. The rapid decline of the Indian population itself and the collapse of the missionary ambition, which Las Casas had shared, to create a New Jerusalem in the New World, greatly reduced the urgency of the whole issue. The Castilian crown's own concerns with political legitimacy were now focused on the Netherlands and Italy where the issues—despite attempts by both Netherlanders and Neapolitans to turn Las Casas's arguments to their own advantage— were quite unlike those which had applied in America. When in 1631 the jurist Juan de Solórzano y Pereyra attempted to write what was, in effect, a history of the whole debate, the nature of the Vitorian project, the overarching concern to refute the Lutheran account of dominium, had become largely invisible. In its place had come a concern to preserve the force of the civil law and to strengthen the power of the crown. In Solórzano's view the entire debate had, from the moment Vitoria delivered his famous lecture, simply been couched in the wrong language. The Castilian crown's claims to dominium had derived, in the first instance, from Alexander VI's Bulls of Donation. But ever since Vitoria had cast doubt on these by denying the pope any degree of temporal power, the entire issue had been conducted in the vocabulary of natural rights. The point which had, therefore, escaped all the natural-law theorists was that even if the Bulls were invalid-and Solórzano seems inclined to accept that they were—neither Ferdinand nor Isabella was aware of this. As no less a person than Cardinal Bellarmine had pointed out, the Catholic monarchs had believed in good faith that the pope had conferred full dominium upon the crown, and the crown had, therefore, behaved in good conscience by acting as it did. In the terms of Roman jurisprudence, the civil law, sustained as it was by the will of the legislator and the moral authority of the state, was sufficiently compelling in itself to make further inquiries into its legitimacy unnecessary. It was an argument that even Vitoria had accepted, although only as a hypothesis. But in the more embattled political atmosphere of the early seventeenth century it had come to seem inescapable. As Antonio León Pinelo bluntly, if laboriously, put it in 1630,

> To Spaniards, vassals of the crown, it is sufficient to know that that is how the royal laws, made and promulgated by our Catholic monarchs, seen and consulted by ministers [of state] so pious, learned, and so zealous in their actions, as those who have always occupied, and occupy, the royal councils of this kingdom, are disposed; and thus it is neither just nor necessary to inquire into the justification for each law, but rather only to repeat them as sacred.[74]

Quod principi placuit legis habet vigorem. What both León Pinelo and, with greater theoretical nuance, Solórzano were now arguing, by recasting the whole debate in the language of Roman jurisprudence, was that if the crown had come into possession of the Indies by what it believed to be a legitimate right, then it could claim dominium by virtue of subsequent occupation. It was, as Solórzano pointed out, precisely this argument that had traditionally been used to legitimate the Roman conquests retrospectively. 'Even a tyranny', wrote Solórzano, and in this respect the Roman Empire was a tyranny, 'becomes in time a perfect and legitimate monarchy'.[75] Time, the Spaniards' historical presence, is then the sufficient condition of dominium, for it is the objective condition that confers legal rights; and, in the end, it is legal, not natural rights, that are under debate. A similar acceptance of a historical basis for rights was, as he pointed out, the only claim made by the other European maritime states to dominium over the seas closest to their shores. No one (except the wretched and heretical Grotius) denied the right of Alexander III to grant dominium over the Adriatic to Venice, or the right of the Genoese to the Ligurian Sea. Turn, he told his readers, to John Selden's *Mare clausum*, where you will find arguments that will do quite as well for Spanish claims to rights in the lands of America, as they do for the English king's claims to the North Sea and the north Atlantic.[76] Selden, of course, was writing in the language of 'modern' jusnaturalism, a language in which objective conditions played a far larger role than they had for the Spanish Thomists. But by the 1630s the entire discourse of neo-Thomist jusnaturalism was already beginning to look distinctly unwieldy and outmoded. As Solórzano concluded, the whole issue to which Vitoria and his pupils had addressed themselves was now only of 'antiquarian interest' and was raised, when at all, only by 'certain heretics out of envy of our nation'.[77]

And a subject of 'antiquarian interest' it very largely remained until the late eighteenth century when the Spanish overseas empire became, once again, a subject of international interest. 'What is the reason', wrote the Jesuit Juan Nuix (1743–83) in 1782, in apparently genuine bewilderment, 'for so much having been written in these past years against the Spanish occupation of America?' The principal authors of these attacks were the Scottish historian William Robertson and the Abbé Raynal. Nuix's misnamed 'impartial reflections' – which, as Servando Teresa de Mier acidly remarked, 'brings together all the absurdities of past writers with new inconsequentialities of his own'[78] – offer a picture of the Amerindians as far more primitive than even Robertson had depicted them. 'Not having entered into civil society', he wrote,

> nor having any other bonds other than those of the natural law [the Indians] did not form a common state [*estado común*], rather each one of those tribes composed a separate state, and thus the lands between them, which divide them one from another, not being necessary to those states (for they lacked any communication between them) were empty spaces for diverse foreign settlements which became [the property] of the first person to inhabit them.[79]

For Nuix it was 'that just title...which is *communication*' that granted the Spaniards the rights of initial occupation which they subsequently came to possess by means of settlement. As the Indians were not civil beings, their societies could not constitute 'states' and their members could thus only claim use-rights as individuals, and these 'do not extend beyond what is necessary and may be separated from actual use'. Similarly another exiled Jesuit, Cyriaco Muriel (1718–95), in a widely read treatise on the natural law which was heavily, and explicitly, dependent upon Puffendorf, argued that the Indians could not, before the Conquest, have exercised property rights because they 'were not settled in any one part' and because, although some of them might be said to have acquired rights through contracts, those contracts were 'very deficient and imperfect because they barely understand the natural law and the law of nations'.[80] Both arguments rely on the familiar humanistic claim that only fully civil beings can exercise rights; and neither makes any attempt to resuscitate the natural slave argument. But both Nuix and

Muriel had missed, or simply evaded, the point of their opponents' attack. For the struggle over the legitimacy of the Spanish Empire in America could now no longer be conducted wholly in terms of dominia. Now that the complex machinery of neo-Thomist natural law had been dismantled, the very possibility that the European nations exercised rights in America – or indeed in any other part of the world – had come, in Enlightenment Europe, to seem, as it did to the Neapolitan political economist Antonio Genovesi, 'the extravagances of centuries of ignorance'. 'Those rights', he continued, 'seem to me like those which the astronomers have acquired on the moon by the simple fact of having given their names to certain plains, valleys, and mountains of that world'.[81] Genovesi's attack, and that of men like Gaetano Filangieri, Montesquieu, and the Abbé Raynal, on the Spanish Empire, and on the complex political philosophy that had been employed to legitimate its existence, was overwhelmingly directed at the behaviour of the colonists, and at the effect that three centuries of colonization had had on the moral, political, and economic life of Europe. The image of Spain as a now decayed tyranny, hardly to be distinguished from the Ottoman Empire, had raised once again the spectre of conquistador brutality, and with it Vitoria's old question 'whether all this had been well done'. The only possible argument in favour of the Spanish Conquest was, as Raynal saw it, that the destruction of the Indian world had brought America, and Asia, into that world economy, and this might not only put an end to all international conflict but would, in the end, benefit the 'savage' peoples of the European empires as much as it had once benefited the Europeans themselves.[82] The issue now was commerce, and the extent to which 'all the peoples of the world' might be made one within a modern commercial society.

2

Instruments of Empire: Tommaso Campanella and the Universal Monarchy of Spain

i

Tommaso Campanella, 'that most politick friar',[1] is possibly the most bizarre of early-modern political theorists. 'A fantasist', the great eighteenth-century Neapolitan historian Pietro Giannone called him, 'of an unquiet and turbulent spirit [who] pretended to reform kingdoms and monarchies and draft laws and create new systems'.[2] These new systems were only in part political.[3] Although Campanella insisted that all human knowledge was of a whole, none of whose parts was intelligible without an understanding of all the others, most of his writings are more directly concerned with theology, astrology, and natural science than they are with politics. Like Giordano Bruno, with whom his name is often linked, he projected a new science, which was to be Platonist, since Plato was the pagan author whose ideas most closely prefigured those of the Church Fathers,[4] and heavily indebted to hermeticism and to the sensationalism of Bernardino Telesio (1509–88). His prime objective was the overthrow of contemporary Aristotelian science, Aristotelianism being, in his view, not only false as regarding its epistemology and its metaphysics, but also responsible for every schism, every heresy since the twelfth century. Although Campanella argued that Thomas Aquinas himself, despite being responsible for the diffusion of Aristotelianism in Christian Europe, 'was not a peripatetic',[5] such a direct attack upon the intellectual foundation of scholastic theology was not taken kindly by the Church. Campanella escaped the stake, unlike Bruno, but he spent much of his adult life in the prisons of the Inquisition. Like Bruno he was deeply concerned with the transformational potential of both magic and astrology. Like Bruno, too, he was regarded as a dangerous and unstable heretic by the schoolmen, and as little less than a madman by the sceptically minded architects of the seventeenth-century revolution in science. (After three hours with him, Mersenne noted wearily that 'I have learned that he can teach us nothing in the sciences' and Descartes refused to speak to him at all.[6]) His outspoken defence of Galileo – which has frequently been taken as evidence for his modernism – was largely inspired by the latter's anti-Aristotelianism and his atomism and because, as we shall see, the perfect harmonious Christian monarchy Campanella hoped to see established in Europe was to be founded upon scientific principles and inhabited by scientifically instructed citizens. The sun, whose light was 'simple and sincere. . .agile, living, and efficacious'[7] as a source of life and inspiration, also occupied a central place in his strongly metaphorical view of the natural world. It thus seemed obvious to him that it should be located at the very centre of the universe.

Campanella is best remembered today as the author of the *Città del sole* (The City of the Sun), a small utopian treatise which he began in 1602 and revised constantly until the end of his life. The image he offered there of a community of rationally educated beings ruled by a philosopher-king, where art is employed to instruct the citizens in their civic duties, is said to have been the inspiration behind Maxim Gorky's conception of 'socialist realism'. It certainly earned him, as a victim of ecclesiastical oppression, a role as one of the precursors of Italian independence from Austria, and – as one of the martyrs *avant la lettre* to a belief in the possibility of social engineering – a plaque in Red Square.

The *Città del sole* is a moral fable which, like both the *Republic* and *Utopia*, offers its readers a programme for what its author believed to be, irrespective of the contingencies of either time or place, simply 'the best state of the commonwealth'. But it is also the product of long reflection on the present condition of Europe, and underpinning even its most extravagant assertions is the persistent claim that the only hope for the future security of Christendom, and the only political system in which Campanella's hopes for a society that was both godly and scientifically rational might be realized, was a new universal monarchy. Although by the 1620s any such project had vanished as a real possibility, the concept, and for those – the English, the Venetians, the Dutch – who had no love for universalism, the fear of such a monarchy remained a dominant feature of much political speculation.[8] It is also the case that the sweeping nature of Campanella's suggestions often masks a far more familiar pragmatic approach to the politics of culture. This aspect of his work earned him the respect of Richelieu who sought his advice on Italian affairs, and to whom he dedicated in 1637 the final revision of his major work on magic, *De sensum rerum et magia*,[9] and the slightly bemused admiration of Hugo Grotius who wrote a detailed commentary on his most widely read work, the *Aforismi politici*. For although it was extreme in most of its claims, and unique in its

2.   Francesco Cozza, *Tommaso Campanella*, Palazzo Caetani di Sermoneta, Rome.

insistence on both the predictive value of astrology and the role of cultural understanding, knowledge, and love in the exercise of power, the main thrust of Campanella's thinking, as Richard Tuck has pointed out, belongs to a recognizable late-Renaissance tradition of political thought, although in a markedly theocratic version: the doctrine of 'reason of state'.[10]

ii

Campanella was born in Stilo in Calabria in 1568, the son of a poor shoemaker. In 1599, after a number of previous sentences by the Neapolitan inquisition for his support of Telesio, he was arrested for his part in the so-called *congiura di Catanzaro*, a plot by a small number of friars, disaffected lawyers, and artisans, whose objective – or so the inquisitors claimed – was to overthrow the Spanish viceroyalty with the assistance of the Turkish fleet, and to establish in its place a utopian ecclesiastical republic. 'He persuaded the friars of his convent', wrote Giannone, who had access to a record of Campanella's trial,

> that in the year 1600, according to the position of the stars, in which he was well versed, there had to take place a great revolution and a mutation of the state, especially in the kingdom [of Naples] and Calabria; and for that reason they must prepare themselves, and gather armed men, for, in that revolution, he had set his heart on transforming Calabria and the entire kingdom into an optimum republic by removing the tyranny of the King of Spain and his ministers, crying *liberty*. And because he was a great deceiver he frequently claimed in his preaching that he had been destined by God for such an undertaking, and that in the prophecies of St Brigit, The Abbot Gioachim [of Fiore], and even the Apocalypse itself, there were signs of this which, although they were obscure to everyone else, were obvious to him.[11]

Campanella's involvement in the failed uprising of 1599 is obscure but it, and the circumstances out of which it was born, seem to have coloured much of his subsequent political thinking. By the end of the sixteenth century, the Kingdom of Naples, or so it seemed to contemporaries, was in such a state of advanced political and economic decline, 'like a human stomach so filled with ulcers', as the eighteenth-century political economist Paolo Mattia Doria – whom we shall meet again in the next chapter – was later to observe, that the 'smallest disorder' was sufficient to start an 'alteration';[12] what Campanella himself constantly referred to as a 'mutation of the state'. The willingness of the Spanish crown to sell off its patrimony and titles of nobility to Genoese and Tuscan immigrants had led to violent social conflict, bankruptcy, and capital-flight. There had been uprisings in 1510 and 1547, and in 1585 a revolt, which had received considerable bourgeois support and was suppressed only after a full-scale military action.[13] Over-taxation and a rapacious barony had resulted in widespread disorder in the countryside where, until the reforms that followed the anti-Spanish revolt of 1647, the viceregal authority was at best precarious. Beyond the cities there was a near-permanent internal war.[14] Bandits, as the Venetian ambassadors frequently noted, seemed to be in control of large numbers of the towns. The famous bandit leader Marco Sciarra, whom Campanella singled out for condemnation as one of the followers of an 'unjust cause' (bandits were agents of disorder not political regeneration), was able to maintain an army – in the words of one contemporary, 'of fine young people, well-dressed and well-armed' – in the field for nearly seven years in the 1580s. Men like Sciarra could count on the support of the majority of the peasants and the tacit compliance of many of the nobility, much of whose wealth came from contraband and who frequently employed bandit armies in their own internecine wars. Throughout his life Campanella insisted that, after heresy, the uncontrolled power and wealth of the nobility was the single most disruptive force within any community. In the *De Monarchia hispanica* he recommended that the income of the Neapolitan barons be limited to three thousand ducats a year and that they be fully Hispanized, and thus rendered socially quiescent, by compelling them to 'imitate the habits, customs, and manners of Spain'.[15] This, he believed, would allow the crown to manipulate them, 'under the pretext of honour', by compelling them to spend more than they earned, a strategy that, as we shall see in the next chapter, Doria later claimed had been the main cause of the political and economic decline of southern Italy.

The clergy, too, was lax and corrupt and not infrequently openly protected the bandits. 'I find', wrote a scandalized papal nuncio in June 1592,

> a most licentious mode of living among nearly all the regular clergy, for, to the scandal and aggravation in this city, they go, alone and accompanied where they wish and at whatever hours they choose, wearing forbidden arms, not only into the houses of suspicious women, but also to public plays [*pubbliche commedie*], so that the viceroy and the royal ministers are now convinced that nothing notable befalls this city without their connivance.[16]

Some of these, known as 'savage diacons' (*diaconi selvaggi*), wandered the waterless hinterland of the city of Naples with wives and children in tow, making a precarious living out of petty crime. When one of them, Marcantonio Capito, was arrested by the viceregal troops, the clergy, incensed by this breach of ecclesiastical privilege and under the guidance of the bishop of Milito, armed themselves and, crying 'Viva il papa', sprung him from gaol.[17]

Then there was the ever-present menace of the Turk. For over a century the Turkish navy in the western Mediterranean had been a constant danger to the coastal regions of southern Italy. But by the 1590s the defences of the Kingdom of Naples had become so weak that in 1598 the Turkish fleet sacked the coast of Squillace and, almost unopposed, took on water at the Cape of Stilo.

The Turk, civil disorder, economic decay, and 'luxury' had, in Campanella's view, turned the mind of the people. 'The *vulgo*', that 'great and varied beast that does not know its own strengths',[18] which was 'always desirous of new things, in whose hands the irrational forces [of the community] are located', had by 1599 become 'disposed to mutation and in the streets every citizen [*villano*] could be heard complaining'.[19] And, therefore, Campanella is supposed to have claimed, 'after having discussed with several astrologers, and in particular with Giulio Cortese, a Neapolitan, and with Antonio Stigola, a great mathematician, and with Giovanni Paolo Vernaleaone who had been in Naples for three years, I understood from them that there must be a mutation of the state'.[20] 'Mutation' – the Italian, and the Latin, suggest radical and complete transformation – remained the key term in his political vocabulary. Not only do states suffer mutation, so also, as we shall see, do systems of knowledge and even religions. Throughout his life he remained committed to the view that not only had the stars decreed that there would be such a mutation but that, more immediately, the states of Europe had to undergo radical change if they were to fulfil the purposes for which God had created them: the happiness of their members and the protection of the faith. In 1599, he seems to have believed, together with many of his more nervous contemporaries, that the final 'mutation' would occur in the year 1600, the year, too, in which the end of the world would begin. One of the conspirators, Giovanni Battista di Pizzoni, declared at his trial that he had had lengthy discussions with Campanella on 'de statu optimae Reipublicae' (a reference to the original Latin title of *Utopia*[21]), 'and as I spoke to him of the laws of this, he said praise God that they should be enacted, but that they were the laws of Plato which have never been enacted, and I replied that that republic would have to be created before the end of the world in order to bring about the human desires for the Golden Age'. Later, however, Campanella seems to have lost his pessimism about the possibility of ever seeing 'the Utopian commonwealth adopted' and to have told Pizzoni that 'the end of the world was near and before that there had to be the most wonderful republic in the world and that the monks of St Domenico [the main Dominican house in Naples] had to prepare for it according to the apocalypse'. The corrupt, decaying Spanish Monarchy would make way first for an 'ecclesiastic republic' and finally for the monarchy of Christ on earth.

Campanella was arrested and accused of plotting against the state. That there was a conspiracy to overthrow the viceroyalty and to replace it by some kind of republic there can be little doubt. It is also clear that Campanella knew many of the conspirators, some of whom were Dominicans, personally and that their objectives were largely inspired by his Utopian millenarianism. He was, said one of them, 'the first man in the world, the true legislator and the true Messiah, who was to grant to all men their natural liberty';[22] 'the foremost man in all the sciences', as one of his accusers put it, 'which means that with his knowledge he inspired people to follow him in all he wished'.[23] Whether he was involved in the preparations for the uprising itself or ever 'went about seducing the people to stock up arms against the King, intending to make the province of Calabria into a republic'[24] is at best uncertain. He himself, of course, claimed that he knew nothing about the conspiracy and that his plan for the 'Calabrian Republic' was solely a defensive strategy should the Turks invade.[25] The authorities did not believe him, and in 1602 he was condemned to perpetual incarceration from which he did not emerge until 1632.[26] In 1635 he was able to flee to France where he was received by Louis XIII (if not by Descartes). But he had for long been certain that the eclipse due on 1 June 1639 would be fatal to him. He took all the required magical precautions but died nonetheless, and before time, on 21 May.[27]

iii

Campanella wrote most of his more substantial political works (and indeed most of his metaphysical and theological ones as well) while in prison: *De Monarchia hispanica* (On the Monarchy of Spain) (1600–1); the *Aforismi politici* (Political Aphorisms (1601); the *Città del sole* (1602); the *Monarchia messiae* (Monarchy of the Messiah) and the *Discorso della libertà del re Cattolico sul Mondo Nuovo* (Discourse of the Rights of the Catholic King Over the New World (1605); the *Antiveneti* (Aganist the Venetians (1606); and the *Discorso della libertà e della felice soggezione allo Stato ecclesiastico* (Discourse on the Liberty and Happy Subjection to the Ecclesiastical State (1627).[28] The pro-Spanish, pro-papal line taken in all of these has been seen by some historians as constituting a volte-face under the pressure of long years of imprisonment, many of them punctuated by torture; an attempt to prove, by the only means open to him, both his extreme orthodoxy and his potential usefulness to the Spanish regime. But Campanella's writings are, in fact, remarkably coherent. There is very little evidence in his earliest political tracts of the anti-Spanish 'republicanism' of which he was accused. He wrote a (now lost) 'Discourse on the Universal and Christian Monarchy' before he was imprisoned. The *Discorso sui Paesi Bassi* of 1594, which although it condemns the excesses of the Duke of Alva does so for reasons that he repeats, almost verbatim, in the philo-Hispanic *De Monarchia hispanica*, offers advice to Philip on how to suppress the Revolt of the Netherlands, while the other major work written before the *congiura*, the *Discorso ai principi d'Italia* (Discourse to the Princes of Italy) of 1594 is an attempt to persuade the independent Italian states to unite under the papacy, and is entirely consistent with his wider theocratic views. His only substantial change of mind was over the identification of God's intended agent of the new universal empire. Until his release from prison he seems to have remained convinced, for both practical and prophetic reasons, that it was Spain. After his flight into France, however, he wrote three works, all in 1635, the *Documenta ad gallorum nationem* (Documents for the Gallic Nation), the *Aforismi politici per le presente necessità di Francia* (Aphorism on the Present Necessity of France) and *Le monarchie delle nationi* (The Monarchies of the Nations of the World); and a Latin translation of the *Città del sole*, all of which tried to demonstrate both that the decline of Spain had been the inevitable outcome of internal, moral as well as political, weaknesses, and that his previous prophetic utterances concerning the inevitability of Spanish world rule contained in the *Monarchia* could be read, with a certain degree of adroitness, to apply to France.

iv

For Campanella – and in this respect he differed little from the Aristotelian neo-Thomists he so despised – there could be no significant division between epistemology, metaphysics, theology, and politics. Since all human knowledge had originated in a single divine intelligence, and operated according to a single divine plan, it must display a natural unity. A true understanding of man could not exist independently of an understanding of the God who had created him and of the world in which he lived. Philosophy, he told Galileo in 1614, without the 'true and assured system of the construction of the world', which the natural scientists could provide, must inevitably be void.[29] In common with many of his contemporaries Campanella also believed that he had placed the study of politics on a properly scientific basis.[30] The humanist attempt, however, to create an independent political science for which Machiavelli, the *politicorum Coryphaeus*, the 'scandal, ruin, scourge, and fire of this century', whom he missed few opportunities to vilify,[31] was responsible, was, Campanella claimed, both foolish and pernicious. Foolish because politics by itself could never be a form of knowledge, since it does not treat of final causes, pernicious because any such project inevitably attempted to detach politics from ethics and ethics from religion.[32] A true science of politics, therefore, could only be one that was grounded in some other branch of knowledge that did deal with final causes, and that was closely associated with ethics and theology. There is, of course, nothing very startling about these claims. What is startling, and what vitiated the entire enterprise in the eyes of most of his subsequent readers, was the fact that the science of final causes he chose was astrology and prophetic hermeneutics. Although Campanella held the traditional view that not all prophecies could be correctly interpreted, and that astrology governed the likely, rather than the necessary, outcome of events astrology and prophecy were, nonetheless, predictive, and so, therefore, would be any political science based upon them. Astrology and prophecy could be used not only to establish how the universal Spanish monarchy should be formed, and its destiny, they also offered what Campanella claimed to be the only persuasive argument for its legitimacy. The concern with astrology and prophecy also meant that the operations of time, the gradual revelation of the divine intention in human history, and of what he calls 'opportunity', were as crucial to his science as they were to Machiavelli's.[33]

All human actions are, he argued, governed by what he calls 'fate' (*fatus*). Simply stated, fate is God's will operating in time. It is composed of three elements: God Himself, or rather the design for His creation; prudence (*prudentia*), the moral qualities possessed by the agent; and opportunity (*opportunità*, sometimes *occasione*),[34] the instances for action offered by the design.

For Campanella, prudence was the prime political virtue. Although there is an order in all human life which has, to some degree, been predetermined, men have also been endowed by God with free will. By acting prudently, they can choose the best of the several possible outcomes that opportunity offers them. Those who deny the effective existence of free will, as do the Lutherans and Calvinists, who believe (or so Campanella imagined) that *all* future human actions have been determined by God, can only create tyrannies doomed to eventual extinction,[35] since they inevitably

45

become the victims of *fortuna*. Fortune, on which Machiavelli had laid such stress, was for Campanella an indeterminate area, 'the succession of things', which God seems to have left to chance. *Fortuna* is the region in which brute force is located. It is also simple luck. No sane man, he argued, could build a political theory around such a concept. *Fortuna* is merely what befalls me if I find something I desire but am not looking for. If, however, I find something that I *am* looking for then, since my will has been instrumental in the search, that is prudence. Prudence, then, 'is in accordance with God, that is, with primordial Wisdom' and is, 'attendant upon Prophecy and the Divine Sciences' (i.e., astrology). It also is a part of knowledge,[36] since it is the virtue of perceiving exactly what *is* possible according to the design and of acting upon it. Campanella was not, of course, alone in stressing the value of prudence over all other traditional political virtues. The term was already an important part of the vocabulary of the 'new humanists' of the 1580s and 90s, of Justus Lipsius and of the Italian and Spanish Tacitists.[37] It was also, of course, though Campanella seems never to have noticed this, a significant term in Machiavelli's own political lexicon.[38]

But the operations of prudence had to be clearly distinguished from the strategies of 'reason of state'. Again, like all of the new humanists, Campanella argued that 'reason of state' theory was 'a contrived name for tyranny' since, by insisting that all laws might be transgressed 'in order to preserve the state',[39] it became nothing more than the expression of the personal interest of the rulers, the political equivalent of atheism,[40] which, in Campanella's view, would finally drive the Church and the 'Western Empire' into the hands of the Turk.[41]

The qualities of prudence were also to be found only in certain kinds of men. Kings, Campanella argued, come in three types: the wolf, the mercenary, and the shepherd. The wolf is merely a tyrant who looks upon the people as existing 'for his own use'; the mercenary – Machiavelli's Prince – does not 'devour' as the wolf does, but merely 'steals what is useful to him', while offering his flock no real protection. The shepherd, however, the political counterpart to Christ himself,[42] lives only to serve the people; and it is the shepherd, the secular counterpart to the pope, who is the only truly prudential ruler. Since it is he who dictates custom to the people[43] he must be a man of true *virtù*, not the dissembler Machiavelli describes. He must follow the mean in all things, loving honour, for instance, for no man who does not will ever be a just one, but never, as the Spaniards so often do,[44] to the point where it becomes *superbia*. He must be capable of suppressing in himself all emotions, even pity, when these might lead him to make purely personal decisions: for 'he who does not subject his passions to reason will not be able to rule himself, and no man who cannot rule himself can hope to rule an empire'.[45] But as the true ruler's objective is to make himself loved, he must display love towards his subject, be liberal with them, hate only those things (namely, in Campanella's view, heretics) that they hate, and be generous towards those who have served him. This is particularly necessary for the Spaniards whose hitherto illiberal and ungenerous manner have made them 'hated by every nation'.[46] As he claimed later from exile in France, the decline of the Spanish Empire could in part be attributed to the failure of successive Spanish monarchs to reward those (like himself) who had written in their favour and even those, such as Gonzalo de Córdoba (known as 'The Great Captain'), Columbus, and Wallenstein, who had served them in other, more immediately obvious, ways.[47]

At the most pragmatic level, prudence constituted the respect for his subjects' interests and beliefs that every successful prince had to show, particularly if he ruled over a large number of culturally distinct states. The Spanish experiences in the Netherlands (and later in Naples) had demonstrated conclusively that to govern, as the Duke of Alva had attempted to do in the Netherlands, 'with severity and ceremony not considering the customs of the country', could only ever lead to civil war, and, like most of his contemporaries, Campanella was certain that no ruler could ultimately resist the combined hostility of the majority of his subjects.[48] But the prudent ruler must not only be virtuous, generous, self-restrained, and respectful of local custom, he must also, in Campanella's understanding of the term, be a man of *scientia*.

Once again there are strong similarities between Campanella's requirements for the good ruler and those of many of his contemporaries. The Piedmontese ex-Jesuit Giovanni Botero for instance – long passages from whose *Della ragion di stato* (On the Reason of State) of 1589 were incorporated into the printed edition of *De Monarchia hispanica* – urged all princes to make themselves as learned as possible. 'Alfonso V of Naples', he quoted with approval, 'used to say that an unlettered prince was a crowned ass'. Botero's prince, however, is only required to grasp the mundane arts of eloquence and political philosophy.[49] Campanella's prudent ruler has to learn to exercise more arcane skills: to read the signs that God has left in the stars, in the scriptures, and in the records of the past, so that he might predict the likely outcome of any of his activities and, more generally, determine what God's intended purpose for him and his state might be. In the *Città del sole*, where all of this is set out as a fable, the supreme ruler, Sol or 'The Metaphysician', is chosen for his task precisely because he

> knows the origins and the proofs of every art and science; the similarities and the differences that exist between things; Necessity, Fate, and the Harmony of the worlds; the Power, Wisdom, and divine love of all things; and the degrees of the being and correspondence between the things of the heavens, the earth, and of the seas; and studies hard in the prophets and the astrologers.[50]

Campanella's new predictive, prophetic *scientia regnandi*[51] was directed towards one objective: the creation in Europe of a universal monarchy capable of destroying heresy within and of resisting the Turks without. Whatever Campanella was, he was not, as his accusers and those who later made him into a champion of the oppressed had claimed, a popular republican. Like Botero, who had foreshadowed many of Campanella's less extreme views on universalism, he had looked about him and found that most states were, and always had been, monarchies. Monarchies were simply closer to God's design than republics since God operated in the world 'by one understanding [*sapere*], one power, and one will', and because all things, however diverse, share a 'prime mover.'[52] Even in America, Botero had noted, where the political contingencies of Europe did not apply and where such societies as did exist were barely civil ones, there had been only one republic, Tlaxcala. Monarchies, he concluded, 'by their excellence draw all things to them',[53] to the extent that even those societies that begin as republics often become in the end, as did Sparta, *de facto* monarchies.[54] Unlike Botero, however, who had warned against starting quarrels with powerful republics because the love of liberty is there so deeply rooted that 'to overcome it is difficult, and to extirpate it almost impossible';[55] Campanella held that there was no necessary correlation between republicanism and freedom or between monarchy and tyranny. It is the unity based on love and a shared understanding, on knowledge (*scientia*), that constitutes the true *respublica*; and this could be found as easily – perhaps indeed more easily if the state was as impious as Venice – under a monarchy as under a republic.[56] For some two hundred years, furthermore, the stars, or so Campanella claimed, had been hostile to the continued existence of true republics.[57]

Campanella's involvement in the *congiura di Catanzaro*, however limited it might have been, and his personal observations on the collapse of Christian unity under the pressure of political ambition, confessional conflict, and the ever-present menace of the Turk, had convinced him that Christendom now faced the prospect of an Islamic invasion. Seen from Naples, which as Campanella pointed out was the front-line state, the Turkish threat was no idle one.[58]

Having the right set of religious beliefs was no guarantee against enslavement. Europe, he insisted, could fall to the Turks just as the Roman Empire had fallen to the Goths, or Judaea passed into the hands of the Assyrians, 'because of their neglect of the laws and internal discord'.[59] The only possible salvation from a similar fate was to transform Europe into a single, united mega-state and such a state could clearly *only* be a monarchy. 'Diverse princes and republics', he observed, 'can never resist a united monarchy as may be seen with the Assyrians, the Persians, the Greeks, and the Romans'.[60] Similarly although the Turks were now far stronger than any single Christian nation, they would be far weaker than a united Christendom.[61] He was not alone in this view. The writers of a slightly earlier generation, in particular Botero – whose *Discorso dell'eccelenza della monarchia* (Discourse on the Excellence of Monarchy) of 1607 is a similar, if far more restrained argument in favour of universal monarchy – and the Neapolitan Giovanni Ammirato, had already come to much the same conclusion. Europe by the 1580s and 90s was seemingly in a state of perpetual civil war, from which, ultimately, only the Turk would benefit.[62] If Christendom was to be made safe and Catholicism regain its former hegemony over the Christian world, the princes of Europe had to abandon the pursuit of their individual interests to make way for a single world monarchy. The various unions of arms which had, throughout the sixteenth century, been proposed and on occasions fitfully achieved could, in the minds of both Botero and Campanella, have no lasting success. The princes of Christendom were too many and their interests too diverse.[63] But a universal monarchy ruled by a single prince might. 'I believe', wrote Botero, 'that the human race would live most happily if it were all brought under [*si riducesse*] a single prince'. Such a world where one might travel 'with the same language and the same money' would constitute a common *patria*. It would eliminate the risk, and hence also the crippling cost, of internal war and consequently, by comparison with any existing monarchy, be able to reduce drastically the fiscal burden on its subjects. Botero's universal Christian monarchy, like Campanella's, would be a safer, richer, and hence happier place.[64]

Campanella, however, differed in one crucial respect from Botero, Ammirato, and from such men as the imperial secretary Alfonso de Valdés and Charles V's chancellor Mercurino de Gattinara who had proposed similarly universalist schemes in the 1520s and 30s. For them the new universal empire was to have been a secular political order, an ally and protector of the papacy, but not its client; a revival, under other rulers, of the Ghibellinist vision of Dante's *De monarchia*.[65] For Campanella, by marked contrast, Ghibellinism was a heresy – in some accounts the root of *all* modern heresies – an ideology, first dreamed up by the Aristotelian commentators, that linked Marsilius of Padua to Luther, Calvin, and Machiavelli in one sustained attempt to create a wholly secular, world government.[66] Campanella's universal monarchy, by contrast, was to be a world ruled spiritually and, in a far larger degree than was then the case, territorially by the papacy. In the last instance, he argued, the ideal human community was a theocratic monarchy. 'There has never been on this earth', he wrote,

> a state [*respublica*] wholly without injustice, without sedition, without tyranny...Such a state can never be except under the perfect rule of Christ, and we pray that he comes to make the will of God on earth, as he does in heaven, at least proportionately...[Then] there will be in the world but one flock and one shepherd, and then we shall see the Golden Age sung by the poets and the optimum republic described by the philosophers, and the state of innocence of the patriarchs and the happiness of Jerusalem delivered out of the hands of heretics and infidels.[67]

The great empires of the past, he argued, had all been the creation of priest-kings. Alexander had claimed to be the son of a god, as indeed had the Roman emperors, and Cyrus (who played a special role in Campanella's prophetic history) had styled himself 'the commissar of God'.[68] Similarly in the *Città del sole*, 'The Metaphysician' is both supreme ruler and high priest.[69] Where there is 'an armed high priest no one can aspire to universal monarchy, for that which is superior above all things will not let it grow'.[70] An ecclesiastical empire would, therefore, be both more durable and happier than any secular one, 'for not even the father of a family can reach such perfection of government as the pope'.[71] In the last days, as the world comes to its close, the purely secular rulers (the *principi mondani*) will indeed all be displaced to make way for the sole reign of Christ's vicar.[72] But in the present world where secular powers were *de facto* stronger than any ecclesiastical one, the papacy was in no position to defend its interests against heretics and infidels unaided. It had, therefore, to be protected and sustained politically by a secular power. Charlemagne had fulfilled that role in the past: the Spaniards were to fulfil it in the future.[73] 'This monarchy of Spain', he wrote, 'which embraces all nations and encircles the world is that of the Messiah, and thus shows itself to be the heir of the universe'.[74] Spain was, therefore, irresistible. 'I say', he warned the Italian princes in 1607, 'that it is impossible to resist this monarchy, and all those who oppose it will fall, and in particular the republics will be discomforted, like those in the Low Countries, Switzerland, and Venice'.[75]

V

But why Spain? In part because the *Regnum italicum*, the natural candidate for any world empire, had already passed into political decline and history had shown that no empire can ever recover its former power (a claim he was later to direct against Spain itself);[76] in part for reasons of climate, custom, and personal psychology;[77] in part because of 'the religiosity that they [the Spaniards] had displayed in fighting the Moors', and the virtue that had allowed them to conquer the New World.[78] For Campanella, however, the final and most compelling answer to this question was not to be found in an examination of the kind conducted by the odious Machiavelli into present political contingencies, since Spain's role was not determined by the kind of society it was (much of the *De Monarchia hispanica* is, in fact, an attempt to persuade the Spanish monarchs to turn their kingdoms into a wholly different kind of society). The answer was, instead, to be found in the fulfilment of a prophecy, or rather of a series of prophecies. For the Spanish Empire, he wrote, 'more than all the others, is founded upon the occult providence of God and not on either prudence or human force'.[79] And the 'occult providence of God' could be known only through a proper reading of world history, human and sacred.

Campanella's view of history was inevitably, given the nature of his enterprise, both cyclical and linear: cyclical in that every phase of human history is believed to have an end that confirms, and sometimes reproduces, its beginning; linear because each cycle replicates, in some form, the one that preceded it. The world has seen a succession of empires, each of which, he claimed, had declined into tyranny and finally collapsed into barbarism; but its legacy, what he called its 'angel', had always passed to the next, and so on until the promised and always imminent end of the world.

In this general scheme the Spaniards were the descendants of the Carthaginians and, as such, heirs to the kingdom of Cyrus. From Cyrus they had inherited their dominium over the seas, as well as their well-known tendency towards *superbia*.[80] They had also, through him, become the successors of all the empires of the ancient world. The papacy, however, since the Old Testament foreshadows the New, is the heir to the most enduring empire of them all, the *Regnum hebraicum*,[81] the rule of God's chosen people, once Israel, now Rome. Before the end of the world arrives, and the wished-for *Monarchia Messiae* is achieved, Spain will bow before the papacy, thus bringing the ancient Babylonian Empire (which Campanella understood to have included successively both Persia and Greece) to its knees before the Church. The prophecy of Ezekiel will then have

51

been fulfilled. This fanciful piece of juggling with Biblical history was intended to serve specific Hispano-Italian ends. The Roman Empire was the natural successor to the Babylonian. But the collapse of pagan Rome had led to the division of the Empire into three, what Campanella calls, the left, the middle, and the right. The 'left-hand empire' – the Turks – had, at the time he was writing, devoured the middle (Byzantium) but, in the fulfilment of time, the 'right-hand empire' – the 'Germans' – would devour the left. By 'Germans' he seems to have meant the entire Christian world; and the Habsburgs, clearly *echt* Germans, by linking themselves with Spain, and through Spain to Cyrus and through Cyrus to Byzantium, had gone a long way towards uniting the various fragments of this confused picture. But Rome, though it may no longer itself be an imperial power, as the last great pre-Christian empire, remained the *fons et origo* of the modern world. It was *the* empire which all later world-states were destined endlessly to rebuild. Furthermore this unique status had been given a deeper eschatalogical purpose by the *translatio imperii* from the emperor to the papacy.[82] It was, therefore, in Campanella's view, the case that 'the house of Austria cannot arrive at a very great monarchy according to fate except under the auspices of the Italian empire, which is Roman [i.e., papal], which is of the right-hand'.[83] The task of this empire is to lead the Church out of its Babylonian captivity (to the Turks) which was 'the office of Cyrus'.

It was also the case that all religions were, in some sense, subject to the same historical laws as civil societies: ignorance is transformed into piety, piety passes into cynicism and indifference, cynicism into atheism. 'All religions and sects', wrote Campanella in the *Aforismi politici*,

> have their cycle, as do the monarchical and the popular republics... Thus when the sects come to atheism, the final evil of the people is born, and the end of the wrath of God; and they return to the good only with difficulty. When they come to deny divine providence or the immortality of the soul, they necessarily undergo reform or change [*mutamento*], because both the people and the princes lose the check [*freno*] of conscience, and the former become seditious and the latter tyrants.[84]

The final stage in this cycle brings with it divine intervention. Thus Christ had come to confound the Saducees, 'of the religion of Moses', when they had fallen into unbelief, and the Romans, apparently, had been sent to confound the Epicureans. The Spaniards had dragged the American Indians from their godlessness; and now the Japanese, who had gone so far as to abandon their belief in the immortality of the soul, would, so Campanella believed, find it hard to resist Spanish political domination (something which Grotius, however, thought unlikely).[85] Even Christianity itself was not exempt from this process. The Reformation marked the beginning of just such a slide into godlessness, and it was obvious, to Campanella at least, that God was now preparing to restore the world to righteousness through the new universal monarchy, the modern heir to Rome and the secular arm of the *Regnum hebraicum*.

If the King of Spain observes the rules of prudence – which the *De Monarchia hispanica* is intended to teach him – he will have little difficulty in restoring Christendom, in reuniting the three parts of the Roman Empire, in bringing that together with America and finally in subjugating Asia, for he will be fighting

> under the auspices of the German empire, which is Italy, which is Persia, which is Greece, which was of Cyrus, which was later Media and Babylon: and he will be aided by many angels and by the force of Cyrus and of [the archangel] Michael, and after that everything will be given over into the hands of the saints, making one community and one shepherd [*unum civile et unus pastor*].[86]

This argument, which appears in one form or another in nearly all Campanella's political writings, seemed (to its author) not only to offer proof of Spain's historical role; it also provided what he insisted was the prime, sometimes the sole, legitimation for its empire. Campanella's arguments for Spanish *dominium* in America, for instance, employ, on occasions, arguments that resemble those of Sepúlveda[87] (whom he clearly had not read), and of the Canonists, which he clearly had, but they cast both into a completely different idiom. Dominium in America had, he insisted, been conferred upon Ferdinand directly by the papacy – whose claims to *dominium totius orbis* were, for Campanella, unassailable – and by the Indians' violation of the natural law. (Later, in Paris, he would argue that the Spaniards themselves, because of the cruelty and arrogance they had displayed in America, would one day, like the Amerindians before them, become the prey of another state.[88]) 'That which Spain has acquired under the victorious auspices of Christ', he wrote in the *De Monarchia hispanica*, 'is hers. And I say this because in the conquest of the New World, the Indians who had transgressed the natural law opposed the King of Spain [who was fighting] under the auspices of the Christian religion, which is the defence of the natural law, and he thus justly possessed it, as Moses justly took possession of the Holy Land'.[89]

Those, like Vitoria and Soto,[90] peripatetics and 'pseudotheologi', who had denied (as we saw in the last chapter) that the Indians' violations of the natural law deprived them of their natural rights as men, and who had rejected the claims of both the papacy and the Empire to confer on the Spanish crown rights in America on the grounds that the New World lay outside the former territorial boundaries of both the Roman Empire and the Church, were, in Campanella's eyes, infected with Machiavellianism and came close to being heretics.[91] The papacy could, Campanella asserted, confer dominium by virtue of papal plenitude of power; the Emperor, because he was master of the whole world. But it was also the case that the discovery of America had fulfilled the prophecies of Psalm 2 (Ask of me and I shall make the nations/your heritage,/and the ends of the earth your possessions), by reuniting the 'Empire of Cyrus' under the rule of Christ, and had thus provided Spain with an irrefutable argument for conquest. Why otherwise should its discoverer have been named 'Christopher' the *Christus ferrens*?[92] The King of Spain, as the political heir of Cyrus, and the 'arm of the Messiah',[93] is the agent by which the world will, once again, be reunited.[94] Any quibbling over rights was a denial of God's design, a human impediment to His purpose, for which the likes of Covarrubias and Soto had already been consigned to the flames, though, Campanella added cautiously, 'I do not know whether Infernal or Purgatorial'.[95]

In Campanella's view dominium was conferred directly by God through his vicar on earth. Claims to political rights could be expressed not in the arid syllogisms of the Neo-Thomist theologians and jurists, but only in terms of prophetic readings of human and Biblical history. For this reason the Spanish crown should, he urged, abandon its allegiance to the theological treatise, the *opinio*, as a device for legitimating their rule, and commission instead histories – 'like the Book of Kings' – which alone could persuade the rest of the world of the futility of any resistance to what amounted to God's design for the future.[96]

vi

This was more than the half-demented vision of a man with no practical understanding of politics, whose world had too long been bounded by a prison cell. If you hold, as most of Campanella's contemporaries did, the belief not only that God has a design for the universe, but that He has left hints, clues, encoded suggestions, as to how that design was to be fulfilled, then Campanella's prophetic utterances were bizarre only in their range and complexity. Botero, although he never attempted to map out the future in such detail, clearly held not dissimilar beliefs in the divine inevitability of the last universal monarchy.[97] Like Campanella he also seems to have believed – though he nowhere explicitly states – that this was to be a further extension of the Habsburg Empire since that empire had been the only one in human history to successfully embrace such a vast area and 'such a great variety of peoples, divided by language, customs, religion, and by every other quality'.[98]

But as with all prophecies Campanella's were only inquiries into God's more general strategy. Spain would only be able to fulfil the role that God had clearly intended for her, if her kings complied with the dictates of prudence. If, however, they failed to do so, as Campanella later came to believe they had, then some other reading of the evidence might allow the passage of the future empire to another European monarch. Most of the *De Monarchia hispanica*, the part that prompted William Prynne, the author of the preface to the English translation of the work, to describe Campanella as a 'Second Machiavel',[99] consists of a detailed account as to how the Spaniards might acquire their prophetically ordained world empire, and having acquired it, retain it.

Empires, Campanella argued, subject as are all the parts of God's universe to triadic distinction, are founded upon three things: language, wealth, and the sword. These, in their turn, are instruments of *prudentia* and *fortuna*. 'Language', he wrote, 'is the instrument of religion, of prudence, that is, of the goods of the soul. The sword is the instrument of the body and of fortune, while wealth has only the status of a secondary instrument of the body'.[100] Of the three, by far the most important was language, something that, he claimed, the Spaniards 'understood by instinct'.[101] The practical prescriptive elements of Campanella's political science were very largely concerned with the operations of culture. He displays little interest in any of his writings in the institutional structure of the state, still less in economics. Wealth was, he seems to have believed, inessential to the world dominion he urged upon the Spanish Habsburgs. Caesar had done without it, and so had the Turks, the Tartars, and the Huns. Money, he claimed in the *De Monarchia hispanica*, 'serves only to maintain [an empire]'[102] and even then is not a necessary condition. Later in his life, it is true, he seems to have modified his views somewhat. The explanations for the failure of the Spanish Monarchy given in both the *Discorso politico . . . tra un venetiano, spagnolo e francese* (Political Discussion . . . Between a Venetian, a Spaniard, and a Frenchman, 1632) and the *Aforismi politici per le presente necessità di Francia* repeat at some length contemporary commonplaces about the role of capital-flight and over-taxation.[103] But, unlike Botero, for instance, he appears never to have accepted the increasingly important role that economics, however crudely conceived, was coming to play in contemporary political thinking. Neither does he have very much to say about the role of law beyond the repeated injunction that all laws must be simple, respect the customs of those for whom they are intended, and be in accordance with natural reason.[104] It is the normative aspect of political control that concerned him. Politics was primarily a matter of knowledge and of love, and in his relentless pursuit of a political vision that was overwhelmingly concerned with what ought to be, he paid scant attention to what could be. He was also, although this is often obscured by the language he uses and by his concern with the mechanics of astrology, writing within a recognizably humanistic Italian idiom in which the operations of custom, of mores, are central.

Finance and the purely institutional arrangements of states belong to that part of politics that he characterized as 'the sword'. But it is 'language', as he says time and again, that is the principle instrument of empire. Those who conquer by the sword alone, as had the Assyrians and the Turks, 'swiftly gain and swiftly lose'.[105] The true science of politics is primarily concerned with the exercise of power over the minds (*animi*) not the bodies of men. Those who acquire 'the empire over minds [are able] soon and little by little to found states'. Arms are, in any secular state, a necessary evil (only the papacy can be *wholly* pacific[106]), but they serve only to 'confirm what language grows or plants',[107] and what language 'plants' is not merely love and respect for the ruler, but an identification with his aims and ambitions. The true empire will in effect be a single community governed by the same unity and respect for the laws as all single states should be. To achieve this end, however, the King of Spain has to export more than a body of legislation. He has, to use a wholly anachronistic term, to 'acculturate' his subjects; he has, as Campanella put it, to Hispanize (*hispanizare*) them.[108]

But the would-be imperialist must also respect the customs, and above all the laws, of the peoples he seeks to control; for, as we have seen, respect for local custom is a part of prudence. The alteration of laws, the realignment of political and social loyalties, can be achieved only by the manipulation of the existing normative order. Any other strategy would require the introduction of 'novelty' and, as Paolo Mattia Doria was later to observe of the Spaniards' cultural politics in Naples, any attempt, in particular by a new ruler, to impose novelty will lead to opposition and to mistrust.[109] It was precisely their failure to understand the disruptive force of novelty, claimed Campanella in 1601, that had hitherto prevented the French from ever being able to create an empire outside France.[110] Similarly astuteness, that mode of false prudence 'some call reason of state', so strongly advocated by the Machiavellians, has little chance of success. For astuteness which, in Botero's formulation, 'takes nothing into account but interest',[111] operates by defrauding the people, and since the people can never be defrauded for very long, the merely astute ruler, like Cesare Borgia, 'teacher of the impious Machiavelli',[112] will eventually come to grief. 'The prudent man', wrote Campanella, 'looks to the customs of the country, the astute one, only to his own',[113] for prudence 'woos [the people]...in order to bind them', and only the prudent ruler, such as Numa, has any hope of being able to found an empire.[114]

Of the three, what Campanella termed, 'guardians' of the law – 'the honour of he who observes it'; 'the love of the good (*utile*) which comes to the observer'; and fear – the last is by far the weakest.[115] Any new law that the king passes should, in the first instance, conform not only to custom but also, since Campanella was an environmentalist, to the natural climatic disposition of the people. (Those of the north require temperate, those of the tropics, severe laws.)[116] Later, in 1635, he was to claim that it had been precisely their mistaken attempt to 'govern all the nations according to one manner and not according to the customs of the land and the heavens appropriate to each', that had been responsible for the Spaniards ultimate failure to seize the 'Monarchy of the World'.[117] Hispanization, however, which requires the cultural transformation of the community, will, in time, change the customs of the people so that the introduction of new laws will become imperceptible. For cultural behaviour – and this is true even of such things as music – 'if it changes [*si vien mutata*]...changes the customs of men's minds, and their minds change their bodies and their entire exterior fortune in which consists the state'.[118]

vii

The prime instrument of Hispanization was, of course, language. At the most basic level this meant the imposition of a common tongue in which, following the Roman example, all the laws of the monarchy should be drafted.[119] At a deeper if also more evasive level, language constituted the most effective (what Campanella calls 'convenient') means of cultural persuasion. This was not, of course, a novel idea. 'The victors', Botero had advised, 'would do well to introduce their own tongues into the countries they have conquered, as the Romans did extremely successfully'.[120] And the more general claim that those who control the means of persuasion control the means of power was a humanistic commonplace. When, in 1492, Antonio de Nebrija presented his Spanish grammar to Queen Isabella, she is said to have asked what use she, who spoke Spanish already, could have for such a work. To which he is said to have replied, 'Madam, language is the instrument of empire'. It was a phrase that, like so much else he wrote, he had taken from Lorenzo Valla. But it was not merely vacuous, an adroit exercise in special pleading. For the humanists the association between language and power had been given added force by the example of imperial Rome, and by the particular ways in which their own social and political landscapes were being transformed by the spread of the new Latin scholarship. Spaniards, who for centuries had struggled with an alien culture that was, in nearly all respects, more sophisticated than their own, were particularly sensitive to the coercive impact that the imposition of the conqueror's language, and his culture, inevitably has upon the conquered. 'We have seen', as one Castilian observed in 1580, 'the majesty of the Spanish language extended to the furthest provinces wherever the victorious flags of our armies have gone'.[121] The acquisition of another language, other speech habits, and another cultural vocabulary, led ineluctably, or so it was believed, to the acquisition of the cultural habits, the customs, and mores that give meaning to that language.

In the interests, then, of *realpolitik*, the citizens of the universal Spanish monarchy should be encouraged to speak Spanish. But for Campanella 'language' was more than mere speech. It was, more broadly, the means – the power (*potentia*) – by which the community came to acquire wisdom (*sapientia*). Societies, in Campanella's sketchy account of their origins, begin merely as instruments for protection.[122] But through the use of language, and with angelic guidance, they rapidly develop into sources of wisdom. Finally, under a godly prince, who fully recognizes that the end of all states is the knowledge of God, they are transformed into places of love (*amor*). In the perfect human community, which is the *Città del sole*, the supreme ruler is 'The Metaphysician'; but beneath him are three 'officials', charged with the social operations of power, wisdom, and love, the three primalities (*primalitates*) of human existence.[123] Any ruler who, like 'The Metaphysician', works through the power provided by knowledge will finally be able to lead his people to love; and ultimately it is love, not fear, as the impious Machiavelli had claimed,[124] that alone is capable of sustaining the state. Even those, like Caesar, whose empires had been based (at least in the first instance) on the sword, had triumphed because of the love that they had been able to inspire in their forces.[125]

Power, or 'the sword', is exclusively the domain of the secular ruler. But 'language' is the domain of religion and also of the religious. 'Religion', Campanella told the dissident Venetians,

is the soul of politics which lovingly unites the citizenry under one faith...and religion is, all in all, the body of the republic and in each part of it and in all; and there is no science or law, other than religion, which is the equal of the good will [*buona voglia*] that binds the souls, and in consequence the bodies and the common ends, in certain, safe, and voluntary health.[126]

Religious belief was the source of all knowledge and, as such, the only secure base on which to found a state. 'To bring the world to universal monarchy', Campanella declared in one of his later works, 'the work of religious eloquence is sufficient'.[127] But Campanella, in common with a number of late-sixteenth-century Catholic theorists, also wished to avail himself of the classical Roman, but now inescapably Machiavellian, notion of a 'civil' religion, a religion, that is, that would unite its believers not only as believers and benefactors of a shared body of knowledge, but also as members of a single civil community. 'So great is the power of religion in government', Botero had written, 'that the state cannot have secure foundations without it'.[128] In this respect, at least, it was perfectly possible for non-Christian religions to possess a measure of *political* virtue, since, Campanella claimed, any religion 'whether it is true or false always has virtue when it is believable [i.e., if it can be said to constitute a form of knowledge]...for it links the sword and language which are the instruments of empire'.[129]

Since the aspirant to a new empire must change, with the prudential use of cultural persuasion, the customs and beliefs of the peoples he wishes to rule, he must, in effect, generate a new community of knowledge. To achieve this end, he should, wherever possible, create a new religion, 'another better religion, without arms', to go with it.[130] This is what Muhammad had done and Romulus and Pythagoras. That, too, had been the good fortune of Charlemagne and the objective of both Henry VIII of England and Luther's patron Frederick of Saxony.[131] Such an option, however, was clearly not open to the King of Spain. For Campanella, like Botero and other Catholic 'reason of state' theorists – but unlike Machiavelli, for whom civility was *all* that was required of a religion – wished to argue that Christianity, far from having 'made the world feeble' and thus the easy prey of 'villainous men',[132] was, in fact, the most perfectly civil of all religions. Legitimate political power and right, as manifest in the only true religion, could never be in conflict with one another, anymore than could the pope and the true universal monarch.[133]

Since, according to Campanella, it is the priesthood that has control of 'language', it has always been the case – in Assyria, in Babylon, in Persia, in Rome – that no secure political power has been possible without its support. Similarly no modern monarchy can hope to rule its subjects without the co-operation of the Church, for 'he...who wishes to be lord of Christendom will do so only by declaring himself to be the protector of the Church',[134] or, in the non-Christian world, of some analogue of the Church. This is acutely the case with those rulers who aspire to universal monarchy, since that depends, more than any other state, on the power of 'language'. 'No Christian prince', said Campanella, 'has ever been able to aspire to universal monarchy without assistance from the tabernacles of Sem, that is, of the papacy'. The Spanish Monarchy must therefore cease its interminable squabbles with Rome and declare itself to be wholly dependent on the papacy 'as the heir of Cyrus'.[135] The Church and State would then become, in effect, one. In order to make this a reality, Campanella urged the princes of Italy to make the papacy their heir, and the King of Spain to surrender Naples and Milan to papal jurisdiction so that the *Regnum italicum* would once again be united under the spiritual and temporal dominium of the pope.[136] At a rather more pragmatic level he also advised the Spanish king to secure the election of a Spanish pope,[137] and to send his son to Rome to be educated.[138]

But Campanella was not only a Christian providentialist, he was also, in his own terms, a scientific rationalist. At its most bizarre, this took the form of a programme of eugenics, copied into the *Monarchia* almost verbatim from the *Città del sole*. The universal monarch, he argued, should choose his wife for her 'great body' and potential fecundity, rather than her lineage; he should make love to her only when the stars were right – and slowly (to increase the sperm count), after a good meal, and 'with the greatest love'. Since the periodic failure of Christian armies to defeat the Turk was probably due to a progressive 'weakening of the semen', the inevitable consequence of the fact that, in Europe at least, 'the people take more care over breeding horses than they do of themselves',[139] the Spanish king should follow the example of the sultan, and establish a janizary corps whose military success, in Campanella's view, had less to do with their training than with their genetic purity.[140]

Scientific rationalism could also, more plausibly, be applied to the organization of the state. Knowledge, as we have seen, leads unfalteringly to that love which is the only guarantor of political stability. Scientific inquiry, therefore, the reading – in the metaphor that Campanella, like Galileo, so often employed – of the 'book of nature',[141] was man's highest calling. For 'God Himself', he claimed in defiance of those who urged an unquestioning obedience to the Word, 'loves His things to be known'.[142] The universal monarchy had, therefore, to be a society of rationally educated men, for not only do philosophers make better ploughmen than illiterate peasants, but, more crucially, 'an educated people does not easily bear tyranny nor is it easily deceived by sophists and heretics as is an uneducated people'.[143]

The man who rules such a society must, insofar as is humanly possible, be more able and more gifted than his fellows, and he should create a nobility of intellect rather than of lineage. How this is to be achieved in seventeenth-century Europe Campanella does not say explicitly. In the *Città del sole*, however, 'The Metaphysician', together with his three ministers, 'Power', 'Wisdom' and 'Love', is elected from among a carefully bred élite, and remains in power only so long as no one better suited to the post arises. And in most of Campanella's political writings, together with an insistence on the need for an elected senate, there is more than the mere suggestion that, since the uncertainty of human genetics makes hereditary succession at best an imperfect means of ensuring that the wisest always rule, the forthcoming universal monarchy should be an elective one. There was some truth in Prynne's accusation that Campanella wished to 'change our hereditary kingdom into a commonwealth, or at best into an elective kingship'.[144]

But, no matter how he was selected, the universal monarch had to be able to govern in accordance with *scientia*. This did not necessarily require that he possess the intellectual qualities of 'The Metaphysician', since in the less than perfect world outside the *Città* the pursuit of an active scientific career might distract him from his true vocation, as it had done Alfonso the X of Spain, called 'The Wise', who though among other things a good astrologer, had not been a wholly successful ruler. If the monarch cannot himself supervise the scientific ordering of his kingdom, it is imperative that he should surround himself, as did Alexander,[145] with learned subjects (by whom Campanella largely understood the members of the religious orders), with scientists, and in particular, of course, with astrologers and philosophers, rather than with men remarkable only for their pedigrees.

Science, and in particular astrology, is not merely a means to the understanding of how to rule. It also offers direct access to power, for 'the true knowledge of the world is the half of its possession',[146] and is the means by which a ruler might make himself 'admirable' to his subjects. Furthermore, every ruler, claimed Campanella, who has 'created a new monarchy', has also 'changed [*mutato*] science [as he has, if he can, religion] to make himself agreeable to the people'. This is what Numa had done to the Assyrians, and what Alexander had done in adopting the teaching of Aristotle. 'And the Macedonians', claimed Campanella, with privileged insight into Greek intellectual history, 'abandoned the ancient doctrines and took up those of Aristotle which wholly contradicted them; and this pleased Philip, his father, who could see that such a novel doctrine was the basis for a new empire.'[147] Since the Spanish king cannot adopt a new religion, he has an even more pressing need than any of the rulers of the ancient world to create 'new sciences' with which to sustain his claims to cultural hegemony. For Campanella, not surprisingly, the creation of a new scientific order could be achieved by abandoning the traditional Aristotelian and Thomist programmes current in the universities of Spain and Italy, and replacing them with 'the Schools of the Platonists and the Stoics which are more in keeping with Christian teachings'.[148] Telesio, for the support of whose writings Campanella had originally been sentenced as a suspected heretic, was, he still claimed, 'excellent, being in accordance with the Holy Fathers'. The theologians of the Sorbonne, by contrast, who, together with the Spanish Dominicans, opposed the idea of papal plenitude of power, were all for the most part heretics, and should therefore be placed directly under papal control. The new universities should also teach Greek, Hebrew, and Arabic, thus offering their students access to all the major astrological and cosmographical literature of the ancient world.

Campanella's understanding of science, however, went far beyond the limits of the traditional university curricula. *Scientia* was not only theoretical wisdom, it was also the practical knowledge that would be used to enhance the power of the monarch. The new universal empire, for instance, required not merely a new theology; it needed also a new geography, one in which accounts of the founders of Spain's overseas empire, Columbus, Vespucci, Cortés, and Pizarro, would be substituted for classical geographical projections. Cosmographers, in particular the French and German ('in order to distract them from heresy'), should be sent to the New World 'to describe all the new stars which are beneath the Pole until the tropic of Capricorn.' The whole venture, the mapping of a new world empire which would embrace both hemispheres was, in Campanella's mind, to be a conscious emulation of the achievements of the Egyptians and the Greeks. 'For thus', he wrote, 'astrology is learned together with a knowledge of the heavens and combined with a veneration for illustrious men. And the whole world will look upon such an illustrious empire and wish to serve it'. In the final transformation the new *scientia* which unites the new universal monarchy will pass into a universal love, binding all Christians to their monarch under the spiritual aegis of the papacy.[149]

The *De Monarchia hispanica* was clearly not, as many of Campanella's Protestant readers (and not a few of his Catholic ones) took it to be, a 'Machiavellian' strategy for extending the power of the papacy and the Spanish Monarchy, so as to reduce the peoples of the world 'under the unsupportable *Tyranny* both in [matters] *Civil* and *Spiritual*' of Spain.[150] God's design clearly indicated (in Campanella's view, at least) that His agent in the final unification of the world was to be Spain. But the purpose of the universal monarchy was, he insisted, not merely protective. It was to make its citizens 'happy' (Campanella never lost sight of either *The Republic* or *Utopia*), happiness and the unity of the entire community through knowledge and love being the true end of all states.[151] It could never, therefore, be a matter of indifference what kind of society the future Spanish Empire turned out to be. As he later told Louis XIII,[152] no state can hope to survive under an unjust ruler, and the only possible source of justice is to be found in the true *respublica* were the king is the servant of his people and the laws he makes are not 'useful to the king', but 'useful' to the community.[153]

Such a vision of universal monarchy, combining as it did a claim for the re-establishment of that papal plenitude of power that the most authoritative Spanish political theorists from Vitoria to Suárez had successively discredited, with the image of an elective or semi-elective monarchy, and of a community where the rule of law is superior to the will of the prince (not to mention the seemingly lunatic discussions of eugenics), was hardly likely to find very much favour either in Spain or within the princely states of Italy, although Campanella himself seems to have found this hard to understand.[154] The papacy was perhaps even less eager to further claims that most of its supporters no longer imagined to be either practicable or politically desirable, even if they had been advanced in less strikingly unorthodox ways. Campanella's vision was hopelessly eclectic. It was also too late. The end of the Turkish War in 1606 did not dispose of the Turkish threat, but, in southern Europe at least, it greatly diminished it. The truce between Spain and the Netherlands in 1609 also demonstrated to most observers that Spanish power was on the wane, and with it any further illusion about the Spanish capacity to reunite Christendom.[155] But for most Italians under Spanish rule, both the ambition to world hegemony, and the strategies used to acquire it – the subversion of customs and beliefs, the Hispanization of subject peoples – remained central to their image of what that monarchy was. As we shall see in the next chapter, by the early part of the eighteenth century the cultural and social consequences of these strategies had come to be considered the prime source of all the ills that had beset Italy for most of the seventeenth.

3.   Paolo Mattia Doria. Frontispiece to Paolo Mattia Doria, *Difesa della metafisica degli antichi filosofi*, Venice, 1732 (photo: British Library).

3

Fede Pubblica *and* Fede Privata:
Trust and Honour in Spanish Naples

i

In July 1647 the people of the city of Naples, led by a young fish vendor named Tommaso Aniello, or 'Masaniello' as he was popularly called, rose in revolt against the Spanish viceregal administration. The initial causes of the uprising were familiar enough in the seventeenth century: rising food prices, rising taxes, a succession of poor harvests, and urban over-population as the peasants fled from a disordered countryside. 'In the hearts of the people subject to the Spanish Monarchy', observed Pietro Giannone a little over a century later, 'the government's credit had fallen at this time because of the weariness of such long adversity; and the name of the king, which in times of happiness and power had been almost adored, was vilified in this time of misery, and because of the grievances of the war was little less than abhorred'.[1] All that was required to trigger off a revolt on the morning of 7 July was a rumour that a tax was about to be imposed on fruit, now almost the only thing the poor could afford to eat, and the presence in the central market of a tax inspector suspiciously fingering a pile of melons. Anywhere else in Europe this might have been a typical uprising of the starving and the dispossessed, suppressed within a few days, followed by exemplary executions and a few desultory reforms. Naples had experienced just such an uprising in 1547 and again in 1585 and neither its people nor its rulers had forgotten them.

But 'the revolt of Masaniello' as it came to be called was wholly untypical. It led to the viceroy's expulsion from the city and the incarceration of the Spaniards into one sector of it. It led to an unprecedented alliance between the city and the countryside and between the 'people' (the *populo minuto*) and the non-noble urban oligarchs (called in Naples the *populo civile*[2]), and a large number of underpaid lawyers who provided the ideological substance of the revolt. Most remarkable of all, it led on 17 October 1647 to the creation of an independent republic. This, in the opinion of its ideological architect, Vincenzo D'Andrea, was the re-establishment of the

65

government Naples had once had, before the 'hundreds of years this afflicted and miserable kingdom has been under the dominion of foreign kings, so that what was the most favoured garden of Europe has...by so much calamity and oppression been made into the mockery of the whole world'.[3] Compelled, however, to seek French assistance the republican leaders offered supreme command of the armies of the republic, a post that was held to be analogous to that occupied by the Doge of Venice, to the Duc de Guise. Guise accepted it, although he made an improbable democrat, angry at being compelled to remove his hat before the *populus* on the steps of San Gennaro, and would, as he admitted in private, have much preferred to have been offered the crown of an independent kingdom, a crown to which, as Giannone later pointed out, he could, and did, make some claim through his descent from the Angevin kings of Naples.[4]

'The Most Serene Republic of this Kingdom of Naples', 'The Royal Republic of Naples', the 'The Most Serene Republican Monarchy of Naples' as it was variously named, was, as these titles suggest, both modelled on the constitution of Venice and a declaration of faith in the contemporary belief that a true *respublica* could be constituted under a monarchical form of government. It lasted only a few months. The city was repossessed by a Spanish fleet on 6 April 1648. But the political significance of its existence was enormous. It took the monarchies of Europe by storm. For here in what had been one of the richest, most sophisticated cities of Europe, the 'people' had created for themselves a new independent political community, a community, furthermore, that was republican, dedicated as its laws made plain to the pursuit of civic virtue and the prosperity of all its citizens.

For monarchists Masaniello became a clear warning, for long after the event, of what Campanella's 'vast and varied beast' could do when unchained. 'You are so many Masaniellos', Thomas Hutchinson, the last governor of Massachusetts, is said to have shouted at the American rebels as they attacked his house. But for those with republican sympathies he, and his revolution, became a demonstration of just how much an alliance of the entire citizenry could achieve against a tyrant. Little wonder, perhaps, that Spinoza, a citizen of the first republic to be created out of the collapsing Spanish Empire, should have had himself painted in Masaniello's cap and smock.[5] And when the second, and the last, independent republic of Naples was set up in 1799 its leaders, mindful of their inheritance, renamed a quarter of the city after him.[6]

1647 proved to be a turning point in the history of Spanish Naples. The restored viceroyalty was compelled to take a long and critical look at the policies of its predecessors. In an attempt to prevent any

comirato inc.

Antonio Genovesi

4.   Antonio Genovesi. Frontispiece to Antonio Genovesi, *Della diceosina*, 1780, Library of Congress, Washington.

further unrest, the traditional political institutions, and in particular the representative assemblies of the kingdom, were in part restored and reformed to give greater voice to both the *populo minuto* and the *populo civile*. In 1698 an academy, the Accademia Palatina del Medinaceli, was founded under the auspices of the viceroy, the Duke of Medinaceli, composed of 'men of letters, mathematicians, and cosmographers'.[7] Its declared purpose was to discuss and to promote the arts and the sciences. But it also acted as a quasi-official advisory board on political and, above all, economic matters. The academy brought together an older generation of intellectuals, many of whom had lived through the revolt of 1647, and the new, men such as Doria, Vico, and Giannone, who were to be the architects of the Neapolitan Enlightenment. From this group there emerged a revision of the history of the Habsburg domination of the kingdom, a history most forcibly represented in the last eight books of Pietro Giannone's great *Istoria civile del regno di Napoli* which sharply contrasted the civic freedom and prosperity Neapolitans were supposed to have enjoyed under the Aragonese kings, and even under Charles V, with the misery suffered at the hands of Philip II and his successors.[8] After the abdication of Charles V, said the political economist Antonio Genovesi (1713–79),

This country became a province of Spain. It was no longer governed by those who were familiar with the inhabitants, powers, customs, laws, and economy [of the kingdom] but by foreigners, nearly all of them transitory and with their hearts elsewhere. They were frequently not well versed in our affairs, nor always as diligent and wise as they should have been, nor could they share the pleasure of the spirit of patriotism so necessary for both ministers and sovereign. And this was the cause of new and greater evils that many centuries have hardly been able to cure. Spain, being exhausted by the expense of wars, began to sell off the goods of the royal patrimony. [Much of this was then bought by Tuscans and Genoese], nations skilled in the arts of commerce, astute, and therefore rich in cash. Thus it was that we became indebted to these foreigners for very large sums...Feuds and acts of private justice grew, and in consequence royal jurisdiction collapsed and with it those laws which are the sole sustenance of states.

Each day the spirit and the labour of the inhabitants grew weaker and ever more enslaved. Poverty and ignorance increased; and despair, together with the weakness of the laws, excited the insolence of many, and generated a general malevolence and ferocity. There thus appeared an enormous quantity of vagabonds and indolent persons, which are always the true pestilences on the body politic. This is the condition in which the kingdom found itself towards the middle of the last century.[9]

The questions that confronted Neapolitan intellectuals in the century after the collapse of Masaniello's revolt were why, and more puzzling how, had the Spaniards reduced a once flourishing free society to an impoverished tyranny and, more urgent still, how could the process, once understood, be reversed? The first person to offer a sustained and persuasive answer was Paolo Mattia Doria.

Doria was born in the year of Masaniello's revolt but lived long enough to discuss the reasons for the collapse of the Spanish Empire with Montesquieu. He wrote treatises on philosophy, politics, and economics; a highly influential tract on good government, *Della vita civile* (On the Civil Life) written in 1710, which seems to have left its mark on *De l'esprit des lois*; and a short treatise entitled *Massime del governo spagnuolo a Napoli* (Maxims of the Spanish Government in Naples), to which I shall return. Doria's intellectual formation was, like that of Vico and Giannone, Cartesian, Platonist, and strongly committed to a humanist tradition which, in political terms, sought to provide a morally directed alternative to Machiavelli. 'You' said Vico of *Della vita civile*, 'created a Prince without all the evil arts of government with which Cornelius Tacitus and Machiavelli endowed theirs'.[10] Doria's successors, and in particular Genovesi (who was the first man to hold a chair of commerce at the University of Naples, or indeed at any university anywhere), were largely committed to an explicitly Newtonian and Lockean account of moral and social behaviour.[11] But despite these very important differences in their metaphysics and in the psychological underpinnings to their work, there is a marked continuity of purpose between Doria's political economy and that of Genovesi and of men like the jurist Gaetano Filangieri (1753–88). As one modern historian has rightly observed, 'in the period between Doria and Genovesi the principal themes in the debate over Naples were established, themes that were to be employed, with only the smallest changes in vocabulary, even after 1860 when the city had ceased to be the capital of an independent kingdom'.[12] It is with what seems to me to be the most important of these themes, and the one that determines how all the others were perceived, that this chapter is concerned.

ii

Imagine, said Doria in the *Della vita civile*, 'a republic that is lacking in all those civil virtues which normally go to make up the inner order of the virtuous state'. In such a society there would be no love of *patria*, there would be contempt for religion; the people would have abandoned all concern for the community 'and for their own homes, so that the economy and all good customs would be neglected'; the officers of state, overcome by 'luxury, rapaciousness, and avarice would no longer perform their civic duties'. Although Doria did not say so unambiguously, this was clearly his image of Spanish Naples.[13] The question to which he addressed himself in the *Massime* was how this had come about.

His thesis was a simple one. The Spaniards, he pointed out, had never maintained a standing army of any size in southern Italy since 'they had it as an axiom...that it should be maintained by politics rather than by force'.[14] The strategy of the crown had been, unknowingly perhaps, to follow precisely the advice that Campanella from his Neapolitan cell had offered it, to Hispanize its foreign subjects, to persuade them to exchange their old cultural habits (their *ordini e costumi*) for those of their alien rulers. As we shall see, in the terms of Doria's vocabulary, this meant the replacement of a society based upon trust for one based upon honour. For Doria the distance between trust and honour was the distance between the virtuous society and the corrupt and corrupting absolute monarchy in which the laws served not the public good but the private needs of the prince;[15] it was the distance between the life of civic participation (Ciceronian *negotium*) and that of private indolence (*otium*); [16] ultimately it might also be the distance between liberty and tyranny.

'Trust' (*fede*) was central to the analytical vocabularies employed by both Doria and Genovesi. Trust, as Doria wrote in the *Della vita civile*, 'is the sole sustenance of states and leads to their stable maintenance'.[17] It was, as Genovesi who, like all Newtonians, was fond of physical analogies phrased it, 'to the civil body what the forces of cohesion and mutual attraction are to natural ones'.[18] Crucially it was 'the cord which binds and unites society', an echo of Locke's account of *fides* (which in this particular instance weighed as heavily with Genovesi as it did with Doria) as 'the bond of society' (*vinculum societatis*).[19] 'In effect', commented Genovesi, 'where there is no trust, be it in that part which constitutes the reciprocal confidence that one citizen places in another, be it in the certainty of contracts, be it in the strength of the laws or in the knowledge and integrity of the magistrates, it will be impossible to find the two foundations of civil society and of virtue: JUSTICE and HUMANITY'. Societies without trust are like those of savages (Genovesi had no nostalgic longings for the state of nature) 'with no civil society, no, or very little, commerce, no commodities, and no culture'.[20]

For both Genovesi and Doria, and more widely for all the Neapolitan political economists, the necessary conditions for the creation of the true civil society were virtue, sustained by religion, and trust, which Genovesi repeatedly calls 'reciprocal friendship', and 'reciprocal confidence'. 'A nation without trust [*buona fede*]', he wrote, 'is no more than the illusion of a body without cohesion [*vincolo*]. . . It is an error to believe that a state can last for long without virtue and reciprocal confidence'.[21] What Bernard Mandeville claimed to be the mere outcome of education was, in fact, nothing less than 'a consequence of the nature of the world and of man'.[22] In a trust-less society

> there cannot also be any humanity, because in the absence of reciprocal confidence between men, each will regard his neighbour as his enemy. And how could such a society, which because it is so little bound and held together that it will fly apart at the first blow, and is nothing other than a heap of sand, inspire in the hearts of individuals that friendship which is necessary for the pleasure of humanity?[23]

Even a society of thieves depends for its survival upon the presence of 'reciprocal confidence'.[24]

But the term, which I have chosen to translate here as 'trust', presents some semantic difficulties. English distinguishes clearly between an Anglo–Saxon concept and a Latin one; between, that is, 'trust' which is (or is assumed to be) largely, sometimes wholly, based on rational prediction, and the conception of 'faith' which is, ultimately, entirely non–rational. In Italian, however, and in Latin (and indeed in most other Romance languages) the two conceptions are frequently indistinct: a derivative of *fides* describes them both. For both Doria and Genovesi (if not consistently for Locke) *fides*, understood as 'trust', involved rational calculation and what John Dunn has nicely described as 'a measure of buffering between indispensable hopes and expectations'.[25] For Genovesi the main force behind the 'basis for justice' (*ius cuique tribue suum*) was what he called *pietas*.[26] *Pietas* fulfilled much the same role as Puffendorf's *socialitas*, Cumberland's *benevolentia* and, most crucially for Genovesi, Shaftesbury's 'moral sense';[27] but it edged the notion of a self-consciously rational humanity, with which all these terms operated, far closer to the older vocabularies of belief in an immutable and benign natural order. Religion, although as we shall see Genovesi thought of it in a far more rationalistic and utilitarian manner than most of his Italian or Spanish contemporaries, was as crucial for him as it was for Locke in ensuring the continuing stability of social relations. For Genovesi, as for Doria, it was not the Protestant jurists' notion of self-preservation that underpinned man's sociability[28] but a love of his own kind – 'the love of one's species'[29] – which is innate; that 'concern', as Genovesi phrased it, 'we feel when confronted by the sufferings of others and the wish to help them'.[30] In this account reason now translates out as a species of humanitarianism. 'Homo homini', he claimed turning Hobbes's famous adage on its head, 'natura amicus'.

Men, then, might be thought to possess a natural disposition to trust one another. His faith in his fellow – his 'reciprocal confidence' and 'reciprocal friendship' – leads each man to believe that he can predict how the other will behave. But as both Genovesi and Doria (despite their declared faith in the ultimate beneficence of human nature) knew, although it might be perfectly rational to hold such a belief – given the premise that some prior 'moral sense' does exist – no one can, in fact, ever be in possession of sufficient information to *know* that those in whom he has placed his trust will not, in fact, act in entirely unforeseen ways. In trusting their neighbours or their friends, all men, therefore, are at some level compelled to have *faith* in them. In the absence of certain knowledge – until the outcome of his expectations is known – every man must maintain a *belief*. Trust, like Pascal's view of faith, will, in the end, come to rely upon a wager. Those who are prepared to make that wager are alone capable of what Genovesi constantly refers to as 'humanity'. Those, like the 'savages' he so often cites, who are not, are not really men at all.

For Genovesi there also existed two distinct forms of trust, the private and the public: *fede privata* and *fede pubblica*, and three distinct modes: the ethical, the political, and the economical. 'Ethical trust' (*fede etica*) is 'an exchange of confidence between persons, between families, [and] between the [social] orders founded upon an opinion of the virtue and the piety of the contractees'.[31] It constitutes the private moral basis on which all forms of public exchange are made. Economic trust is 'the security that derives from the security of funds from which all loans are made'; and political trust is 'that which is born of the conventions and promises sustained by the civil law, by the laws of religion, and by public custom and norms'.[32] Taken together these last two are constitutive of *fede pubblica*, 'public trust', which is the true *vinculum societatis*. 'Nothing', wrote Genovesi, 'must be cultivated so zealously as public trust, for on that men rely, and it is that which generates confidence, which produces and sustains agreements between men, which is the base not only of commerce, but of all of civil society'.[33] *Fede pubblica* alone both sustains the state and constitutes its credibility with respect to other states. 'Private trust', on the other hand, is a purely familial affair limited in its application to the individual and his – Genovesi's view of society was strictly patriarchal – kinship group. But although the two may be distinct, the former cannot exist in a world where the latter does not. Men may be naturally endowed with a love for the members of their own species; but that love will always be directed first towards their own immediate kind. 'When the foundations of ethical trust', he wrote, 'waver in a nation, neither those of politics nor of economics can remain firm'. 'Thus', he told his lecture audience in 1758, 'one must cultivate private trust with every delicacy and diligence; for it is the foundation of civil society, of the arts, and of public opulence'.[34] The downfall of the republics of Rome and Athens can be traced to an initial collapse of private or ethical trust, from which they inexorably degenerated into tyranny.[35] Genovesi was, however, equally certain that a society where only private trust was available would be no society (no *societas*) at all, since such societies are composed only of small self-interested groups united only by kin. The flight from the public to the private, from the concerns of the community to 'private pleasure and interests', also constitutes a violation of 'ethical trust', and must finally lead to social disintegration.[36] It was this, Doria insisted, that had brought down the Roman republic and was the principal disease of modern Italy.[37] Genovesi's insistence on this distinction between public and private, between conditions within the kinship group and without, was, of course, both a topical eighteenth-century preoccupation and a characteristic concern of the authors – Hobbes, Locke, Newton, Shaftesbury – Genovesi had read. But his conclusion, on the ultimate need to sacrifice the private for the public, was an unusual one;[38] one which in its implicit rejection of individualist explanations, or explanations in terms of unintended consequences, was close, very close, to Doria's own more obviously humanistic account. But some such solution was, as we shall see later, central to the accounts provided first by Doria, and later by Genovesi and Filangieri, of the necessary conditions for stability and economic growth within any society.

If trust (*fede pubblica*) depends upon security of expectation, it follows that it will be able to flourish only in a society where man's innate 'love of the species' is given full expression. For both Genovesi and Doria it seemed clear – and this, too, marks them off from their northern contemporaries – that the only kind of society capable of achieving that end was the virtuous republic (the Ciceronian *bene ordinata respublica*), where all laws are directed towards the public good and the sovereign rules in the interest of his people.[39] For Doria and his successors, the Spanish Monarchy, which had seemed to Campanella to offer a prospect of peace and political stability and a secure frontier against the Turk, appeared to be merely a tyranny. Doria, of course, did not fear sectarian violence or the

Turk. And although, like Campanella, his principal interest was in the operation of custom in society, his concern was with the creation of a state that would be capable not of coercing its members through force, but of binding them together as citizens. Only citizenship could persuade men that it was in their own interests to place the claims of the community over those of the family, for only citizenship, as Weber later observed of both the ancient Greek *polis* and the medieval city, could effectively cancel out the power of the kinship group.[40] The *virtù* of Brutus, claimed Genovesi, lay not in self-sacrifice but in preferring, at that crucial moment when the two came into immediate and tragic conflict, the good of the community to those of even his most immediate family. 'In short', wrote Doria, 'the good citizen is both a good *pater familias* and a devoted [*religioso*] lover of his country and of his children; but he should never come to love these with that excessive love which is common to most men, but with a love which is always less than that he gives to religion and his country'.[41]

Doria was also concerned with the need to rebuild a society that would be economically powerful. In his view (and it was one he shared with Genovesi, Filangieri, the Milanese political economist Gianrinaldo Carli, and others) only the well-ordered republic could provide for its citizens both wealth *and* virtue. What Smith, and above all Mandeville, saw as antithetical, the Neapolitans and the Milanese saw as interdependent. Trust provided the necessary conditions for the creation of wealth, but trust, as the defining feature of citizenship, was also able to sustain a community which would prevent that wealth from becoming ethically or politically dangerous in the form which the Scots most feared: luxury. Since the notion of luxury was, argued Genovesi, dependent upon a concept of needs, it could only be a relative term. No man needed more than he required to survive. But that was to take a very weak view of human society. Like all human desires the wish to accumulate could be beneficial if practised in moderation. Luxury generated trade, and trade was both the occasion for, and a condition of trust. 'Luxury', he concluded, 'is an occasion for trust, and moderation the foundation of all virtue'.[42]

For all the Neapolitan political economists it seemed, therefore, obvious that their task was to restore trust to a society made disordered by a rapacious and irresponsible foreign government, aided by an equally rapacious and politically myopic nobility that had betrayed and undermined the political institutions of its ancestors. But before that could be achieved, it was first necessary to understand how a state that, under its Aragonese rulers, had once been a virtuous and well-ordered society had been reduced to the ruinous condition it was in 1647.

iii

Doria's *Massime del governo spagnuolo a Napoli*, written soon after the Austrian occupation of the kingdom, claimed to offer its new rulers a carefully considered account of the means by which the Spaniards had destroyed the old political culture – virtuous and, because virtuous, prosperous – which had sustained the Aragonese kingdom. It is the most searing indictment of the two hundred or so years of Spanish domination of southern Italy, and among the most subtle, and subtly persuasive, accounts of how that domination was maintained. It is also close in certain crucial respects to Campanella's prescriptions for the universal monarchy, once they have been stripped of their prophetic and astrological plating. Both were overwhelmingly concerned with the impact of culture upon political behaviour. Doria, however, provides what Campanella most markedly lacks: a causal account of how these strategies operate. He is also far more concerned than Campanella was with the role of economics, and he assumes, as Campanella obviously did not, that the ambitions of the Spanish Monarchy were restricted to 'maintaining their state' while placing the maximum fiscal load upon their subjects.

Doria begins with the commonplace observation that all princes who live at great distances from their states have to employ 'some malicious art' if they are to preserve them.[43] As the Spaniards had discovered to their cost in the Netherlands, simple coercion is not sufficient, if only because at such distances the resources of the state are not up to providing the policing required. The Spanish strategy in Naples was founded on two classical maxims: *divide et impera* and *depauperandum esse regionem*. In the terms of the first of these, the Spanish kings had preferred weak dependencies to strong ones which is why, Doria explained, they had deprived their subjects of 'virtue and wealth and introduced instead ignorance, villainy, disunion and unhappiness'.[44] In the terms of the second, whereby the Castilian crown – at least in Doria's view – was concerned only with securing from its subjects the revenue it required to fight its foreign wars, there existed a trade-off between *relative* poverty and political compliance. So long as sufficient numbers of the nobility were able, with Castilian assistance, to maintain a properly 'noble' life-style, they could be relied upon to provide, or to compel their subjects to provide, the financial support that the crown required. Excessive wealth, particularly when concentrated in the hands of the *populo civile*, might, as it had done on occasions in Milan, lead to the creation of a powerful political group eager to rise out of the tax-paying class. But, of course, as at least one viceroy recognized, the custom of beggaring the better part of the economy in such relatively short-term interests produced a downward spiral from which ultimately it might prove impossible to recover. For as Giulio Genoino, a man who was to play a major role in the revolt of 1647, pointed out in 1620, since the nobles could not escape the general decline of the economy, they became increasingly unable 'to maintain themselves with the necessary decorum, but feeling compelled to do so they are obliged to oppress their vassals, which greatly damages the public good'.[45]

In the interest then of reducing the well-being of the citizens of Naples to a politically and fiscally acceptable minimum, and their political virtue to zero, the crown had set out to destroy the pre-existent bonds of trust within the society. At one level, Doria claimed, this had been achieved by the means that the French kings had already found very useful in coping with their nobility. They had created in large numbers 'a new order of nobles', unrelated to the old and 'linked to the new prince by love and interest'.[46] These men the king could trust because they were, in the language of Richelieu, literally his *creatures*. Their presence and pretensions had also helped to generate hostility and unrest among the older Neapolitan aristocracy, and effectively kept their minds off politics.[47] The crown had then set out to replace the society's normative values, (their *ordini e costumi*) – precisely, of course, those values on which *fede pubblica* depended – with new Hispanic ones. They wished, said Doria, 'to abolish all those customs practised by past kings, so that they wished that dress, modes of conversation, severity of behaviour, rigorousness with women, deviousness, and matters of honour should all be conducted in the Spanish manner'.[48] For, as Genovesi was later to reflect, it was not their systems of government that held communities together, much less the body of the laws by which they were ruled – crucial though these clearly were – it was their *costumi*, what the French termed *moeurs*, and what we today would call their political culture.[49] As Montesquieu had himself observed, a ruler who wishes 'to change these manners and customs should not do so by changing the laws, for that will seem too tyrannical: he should rather change them by introducing other customs and other manners'.[50] Once their political culture had been radically undermined by what Doria called the 'mutation of customs',[51] a people's capacity to resist innovation, in the form of alien values and the imposition of alien interests, would effectively be destroyed. The laws that guaranteed the continuation of the *respublica* would collapse of their own accord. No state can afford to ignore the simple Aristotelian axiom that, as Doria put it, 'it is necessary to care for and defend the whole, for without the maintenance of the whole, the parts will of necessity be destroyed'.[52]

What in effect this translation of cultural values had achieved was the replacement of a virtuous society based upon the mutual trust of all its members, with an aristocratic tyranny based on suspicion and self-regard, 'arrogance and self-love'. It had, in other words, succeeded in replacing a society based on trust with one based on another equally slippery concept, honour.

The term 'honour' has a place in two, frequently antithetical, ethical vocabularies. In the sense that Doria used it when describing what he, and indeed most European contemporaries, regarded as the single defining characteristic of Spanish culture, it implied the existence of a self-love vested in, and consequently at risk through, the persons and objects – and most particularly the persons viewed *as* objects, i.e., the women – by which a man (for a woman's honour is merely the repository for the man's) is surrounded. This Genovesi called 'false honour'; and 'false honour', he said, 'works only for interests; and interests without *virtù* are a dissolute force'.[53]

Such honour is, in effect, a commodity, and a commodity which a man is compelled to uphold in the opinion of others, before what was called – and the legal analogy was highly significant – the 'court of reputation'. If he acts, or is accused of acting, dishonourably then he must revenge himself upon his accuser, even if this involves the destruction of some larger good, such as the public peace, or implicates innocent parties. For, as one contemporary commentator put it, 'no law of any kind, neither that of the *patria*, nor that of the prince, nor the concerns of duty or even of life itself, should come before honour'.[54] But a man may also risk dishonour even if he only *feels* himself to have been dishonoured.[55] The judge in the 'court of opinion' may, in the end, be only himself. A true man of honour, like so many of the protagonists – they cannot be called heroes – of the Spanish theatre of the seventeenth century, may, for instance, be content to have the wife who has dishonoured him murdered in private by a hired assassin. But whatever the conditions of the dishonour, supposed or real, public or hidden, the honour-code remains essentially a private affair, a family matter, and as such cannot ever find redress in law for, of course, laws bind the entire community and it is their very impersonality that guarantees their authority. The 'court of reputation', on the other hand, is anything but impersonal. 'The man of honour', said Bernard Mandeville, 'acts from principles which he is bound to believe superior to all laws'.[56] He is, in Charles Duclos's phrase, 'his own legislator'.[57] Such persons are markedly private individuals and are clearly unlikely to have much regard for the virtues of citizenship.

But there is that other kind of honour, to be found in Aristotle's account in the *Nichomachean Ethics*, of *timé* (1095[b]5). Here honour is conceived not as a commodity but as a social relationship. It is linked with virtue, rather than courage and status, and is pursued only by those of practical wisdom 'in order that they may be assured of their goodness'. In this account honour is clearly directed towards, not away from, the larger community; it is, indeed, identified with happiness and said to be 'the end of political life'. *Il vero onore* Genovesi called it, and (in an attempt to dissolve Montesquieu's distinction between republics, which are motivated by virtue; and monarchies, which are motivated by honour) he claimed that true honour is simply 'that love of the *patria* which must be the centre of any definition, including Montesquieu's own, of political virtue'.[58] *Il vero onore* is also, of course, a crucial component of trust – it is the sense in which the term is used in such phrases as 'honouring one's bond'. *Onore e virtù*, to quote Genovesi again, 'honour and virtue', in the absence of any effective coercive mechanism, can be the only guarantors of a debtor's reliability. But, as we shall see, no virtue is possible in a society of honour understood in the first sense (self-love) since such societies are simply aggregates of private individuals pursuing wholly private ends. (It is worth noting that since the political culture of Spain laid such stress on relations of honour, Spanish possesses two distinct terms where English, and Italian, possess only one. *Honra* is used to describe honour when it is perceived as a commodity, and *honor* to describe it as a social relationship.)

Every true community, every society, that is, bound together by trust, depends crucially upon a free circulation of information. For not only are trusting societies by their nature open societies, if only because (unlike societies of honour) they have no need for secrecy, but it is also, of course, the case that a man will trust his neighbour only if he knows enough about him to be certain that he will return his trust. He will trust the state only if he is sufficiently well-informed about its behaviour to be certain that it is acting in his interests. As the first move in their attempt to destroy the older society of trust, the Spaniards, therefore, reduced the amount of information available to the citizenry – which is why Genovesi insisted that the new, enlightened administrations that he served should hold a census after the Roman model whose findings 'should be placed in public archives and open to the gaze of all'. For, he went on, 'There must be no mystery about that which links the families between themselves, or the sovereign to the state; about that which affects the peace of a nation or about those things which are public calamities; or about that which forms the foundations of the motor of industry and public needs...'.[59] By denying their citizens access to such information, the Habsburgs had rapidly transformed Naples from an open society into a closed one. They had, claimed Doria, 'in keeping with the best rules of reason of state' (something obnoxious to the virtuous republic which can have no reason independent of the good of its members) made a secret out of the business of government so that it should be 'reserved to them alone'. They had turned the older representative assemblies of the kingdom, the *Università* and the *Seggi*, into instruments of the barony and, a complaint that was echoed throughout the entire Hispanic world, had reserved the more important government offices for its own, Castilian, subjects. Open discussion, the necessary condition of a society all of whose members had a share in the political life, was replaced by the *secret du roi* and with it the familiar and fatuous claim that kingship, and kingship alone, conferred the necessary wisdom to govern.

But secrecy, though, in Doria's view, the prime offence of the absolutist state, was not, of itself, sufficient to destroy civic virtue. The high levels of expectation, which the virtuous republic required of its citizens, relied not only upon the ability of every citizen to participate in the business of government; they relied, too, upon an education and a religion that would merge the spiritual – and as we would say ideological – concerns of the individual with those of the wider community. Religion and education, said Genovesi, are the two things that distinguish civil societies from savage ones. The virtuous society is clearly one in which, as Filangieri put it, 'the dominant passions of its members are always those which are most useful to the state and to its citizens'; but it is only through public education (for which he provided a detailed programme) that 'the legislator can find the most efficient means of making those passions widely felt'.[60] The Spaniards, Doria complained, by resisting the 'New Philosophy' (that is Cartesianism and Newtonianism) by obliging the University to go on teaching Aristotelian logic, 'because it never explained anything', had effectively denied the citizen access to the knowledge he needed to fulfil his role as a citizen. The same was true of religion. For Doria, Genovesi, and Filangieri, the last two of whom had read Rousseau on the subject, religion should be, as far as was possible without falling into heresy, a civil one; what Genovesi, so as to avoid the Machiavellian and atheistical implications of the phrase 'civil religion', called a 'useful' or 'rational' religion;[61] a religion, that is, which, in addition to being true, served also to enforce the purely secular values of the community.[62] Like Campanella before him, Doria saw religion as the only instrument through which cultural, and thence institutional and legal, change can be effected. 'Religion', he wrote, 'has such powers over the human mind that it is not possible to pass laws or change customs in a manner that the people will accept and execute them, unless they are presented as a command from God and a concomitant of religion'.[63] It is religion, *fides* as 'faith', that provides the ultimate sanction against preferring private interests over public ones. On this point both Doria who was, so far as I know, a good Catholic and Genovesi who, though frequently accused of impiety during his own lifetime, had once hoped to hold a chair in theology, would have been in broad agreement with Locke's claim that once you remove God from the picture, 'neither faith, nor agreement, nor oaths – the bonds [*vincula*] of human society – can be stable and sacred'.[64] But although faith in the certainty of divine retribution may indeed constitute the ultimate guarantee of trust, there is, in Genovesi's account of the 'rational religion', more than a mere suggestion that faith may be subsumed under trust and, within the sphere of interpersonal relations, the public good come to replace a private God. What is clear is that whatever religion the society embraces – even if it consists simply in believing in the virtues of that society – it must be comprehensible to all those who participate in it; and it must be available for participation. Lack of information destroys trust. So too, of course, does mystification. For this reason then, as Doria pointed out, the Spaniards had 'wished that everyone should follow the priest in the ritual without examining it'.[65] In Genovesi's sociology the priesthood belonged to 'the class of educators' who had been 'elected by God and the people'. When they ceased to be 'useful to human kind' they became, more than any other group, 'the most damaging part of the republic'.[66] The clergy under Spanish rule had abandoned their true role as the guardians of public virtue, and encouraged instead what Doria contemptuously referred to as the 'religion of the people', those elaborate public religious ceremonies, the obsessive veneration for San Gennaro and the Virgin of the Carmine, that had played such a prominent, and in Doria's view lamentable role in the revolt of 1647, and which were hardly 'rational' and certainly had not made religion civil. Instead they had made civil society religious and, as a consequence, had provided the Spaniards with yet another set of devices for distracting the people from the correct understanding of their civic responsibilities. 'I am persuaded', wrote Genovesi, 'that nothing makes the *populus* more vicious and unruly than the interested superstition and bigotry of the hypocrites'.[67]

The same was also true of those public festivals that the Romans had employed to instil a love of *patria* in the plebeians and that, as the Milanese political economist Gianrinaldo Carli observed, had always 'among free people and principally in republics' served to calm the people. Under the Spaniards they had either been banned ('for fear', claimed Carli, 'that the people might become dangerous in their joy'[68]), or corrupted into drunken brawls.

Spanish corruption of the Neapolitan *ordini e costumi* also extended downwards into the web of social relations which had once held the community harmoniously together. The barons, who were given ever increasing powers over their peasantry, neglected their proper political role. Content, as one viceroy had phrased it, 'to traffic in the blood of their subjects', they spent their time in absurd and worthless pursuits, until finally, complained Doria, 'there remained [in Naples] no other virtue (if they can be called virtues) than scrupulousness in duelling and skill in arms and horsemanship'.[69] The *populo civile* were occupied with illicit trade and extortionist practices, or fobbed off with university doctorates, and the *populo minuto* were kept busy with public festivals. In each case the traditional political role of the three orders was emptied of all meaning and each made the slave of the one above, the whole society being thus easily subjected to the tyranny of the Spanish crown. The status of nobility which should have entailed an obligation to the community, conferred only ignorance and *superbia*; the doctorate of law, which should have obliged its holder to maintain justice, became merely a license for endless and costly litigation; the public festivals which should, like the Roman games had done, have encouraged a love of valour and of *patria* in the plebeians, became mere diversions and occasions for licentiousness. As a consequence 'the superior looked upon his inferior with anger, as one who thought himself to have been cheated of the veneration he believed to be his due, the inferior looked upon his superior as one who only thought himself superior, and in this way there was neither union nor love between the various orders'.[70] Each man became concerned neither with virtue nor with the welfare of his fellow citizens, but only with his own private ends or with those of his immediate kin.

In this disordered world each individual addressed his fellows only in the ritualized languages proper to men of honour. True civil life, for Doria as for most eighteenth-century political theorists, depends crucially upon free communication. It is conversation that ensures that 'virtue has the force to disarm ferocity and civilize barbarism'. It is conversation that guarantees that whenever a barbarous nation conquers a civilized one, it is the barbarians who eventually become civilized.[71] Civilization demands that men must have the means to converse with each other, not only across the social divide which separates one order from another, but also across the natural divide which separates one sex from the other. It was a commonplace of much eighteenth-century social theory that the company of women had a civilizing effect upon men. The aristocratic codes of courage and honour were, necessarily, male ones. Gentility and humanity were female ones. A civilized society would in no way be an 'effeminate' one. Indeed, it was one of Doria's claims that it was precisely the Spanish adoration of women, and the elaborate courtesies which of necessity accompanied it, that were conducive to what he called 'galanterie'.[72] But it would be a society that had been made civil, made *doux*, in Montesquieu's famous term, as much through contact with women as through that other great occasion for human interaction, commerce.[73] For Doria, one of the starkest changes that had overtaken Neapolitan society under Spanish rule was the destruction of what he claimed to have been a relatively free and easy relationship between the sexes, a relationship that had not only exposed the passionate Neapolitan male to the civilizing presence of the gentle female, but that had also been, in the private domain, what civil relations were in the public: opportunities for trust and conversation, opportunities, however, that can easily be made to collapse into honour and secrecy.

Previously, claimed Doria, the Neapolitans had thought of their wives as their friends. Sexual love, what Genovesi called 'that mechanical passion', could, in Doria's view, never last for long between married couples, nor could it ever be the basis for the kind of personal relations conducive to the politically virtuous society. But marriage, because it is so firmly based upon *fede privata*, is a microcosm of the political order. In a true marriage friendship soon comes to replace sex, and the surest route to marital friendship – as to stability and virtue within the state – is, therefore, for neither party to have any secrets from each other, for secrecy generates mistrust, 'and mistrust generates suspicion and suspicion makes friendship impossible'.[74] In all despotic governments, Montesquieu had observed, 'the women are commonly confined and have no influence in society'.[75] So it was with the Spanish, who thought of love only in crudely sexual terms just as they thought of government in terms of secrecy, obfuscation, and mystery. They set their women apart, treating them with a reverence that verged on idolatry, but that also excluded respect so that, complained Doria, 'to foreigners a conversation with a woman seems more like worship at a shrine than a discussion'.[76] Like the Roman attitude towards the vestal virgins, the veneration of the Neapolitan women had the effect of destroying their former gaiety, 'the spirit and the soul of their conversation', and of depriving them of all human contact outside the limits of the family. The Spanish attitude towards women made them into objects bound not to the code of love – which is a civil virtue – but merely to the code of honour. By thus encouraging in the males a corresponding 'excess of gallantry', sexual concerns turned their attention away from civil life into purely private concerns. Gallantry gave rise to effeminacy and (for Doria had an abiding hatred of Mandeville[77]) effeminacy to luxury, 'which are two valuable tools in subduing the strongest of peoples'.[78] 'The dominant nation', he wrote, 'will therefore treat women with a respect that verges on veneration, something that does not a little to dull the spirit of the people'.[79] Occupied thus, with paying grotesque compliments to women, with duelling and with fighting their neighbours over imagined slights to their honour, the aristocracy of Naples, the political nation, had abandoned its role as the promoter of the public welfare.

Thus, concluded Doria, by compelling men to change their customs, by making it easy for them to abandon the hard but virtuous ways of their ancestors, for the easy, unthinking, and ultimately destructive ways of the Spaniards, a society based on trust had been replaced by one based on honour, a rich and just community by an impoverished and unjust one. For the people nothing existed beyond games and ritualized devotion, for the *populo civile* nothing beyond litigation and private gain, for the nobility only the interminable and profitless struggle for status.

iv

In Doria's account the Spaniards had done to the Neapolitans exactly, and by the same means, what, according to Herodotus, Croesus had advised Cyrus to do to the Lydians: 'Make them wear tunics under their cloaks and high boots, and tell them to teach their sons to play the zither and the harp, and to start shopkeeping. If you do that, my lord, you will soon see them turn into women instead of men, and there will not be any more danger of their rebelling against you.' As the economist Thomas Schelling has observed of this passage, such cultural strategies, although aimed at habits and motivations, would 'at the same time deny the development of expectations and the confidence'[80] that are the basis of trust in one's neighbour and, in the larger sense, trust in the society itself.

The impact of the erosion of the older values, this 'mutation of customs and orders', resulted, as the Spaniards had predicted it would, in the steady collapse of the legal system. For a society of honour is clearly not one that values or respects that impartial justice which is a necessary condition of trust.

In any well-ordered republic there must be equality before the law. Equity is the prime indicator of the society of 'virtue and humanity'. In a corrupt society, claimed Genovesi, equity becomes iniquity and 'the civil body is reduced to a leonine society'.[81] Only, Doria informed the president of the Magistrature of Commerce in 1740, when the city was once again living 'in the liberty of its constitution and the trust that is sustained by a rigorous and strong justice', could it have any hope of being restored to political health.[82] For no one will be prepared to trust another who enjoys a different legal status to himself. The positive laws of the community are also, Genovesi insisted, civil contracts, on which the economic well-being of the community depends, and are, of course, more heavily dependent upon trust than they are upon the possibility – always precarious – of their being enforced. In the absence of trust, he pointed out, 'there can be no certainty in contracts and hence no force to the laws', and a society in that condition had been effectively reduced 'to a state of semi-savagery'.[83] The Spaniards had succeeded in destroying the purchase that the laws had had on the community by subverting the customs that had sustained them; they had destroyed the *rule* of law by setting up separate courts for both the barony and the priesthood, and by allowing into the legal system entire categories of exemptions and exceptions so that no one could predict the outcome of a case or know which part of the law applied to him.

The increase in the number of doctorates in the civil law had debased the standing of the title and the social status of those who held them, while the large number of lawyers prepared to sell their services at a low cost had greatly increased the amount of litigation. This, too, since there were insufficient controls over the grounds on which a case had to be entered, increased the degree of uncertainty that surrounded all early-modern legal procedure, and further eroded trust in the judicial apparatus of the state. Only when the number of lawyers had been reduced, and when the Dutch custom of obliging the loser to pay costs had been introduced, claimed Doria, would the courts regain some of the trust that had previously been confided in them.[84]

V

This erosion of the necessary guarantors of the well-ordered community led inexorably to the collapse of what for every eighteenth-century political economist constituted the principal instance of trust within all societies: commerce. Economic transactions are clearly more heavily dependent on the agencies of trust than any other, and in every European language they share a common vocabulary: 'commerce', 'credit', 'honour', and 'trust' itself are all terms which have specific economic applications. The confidence that your partner will act predictably – that he can be trusted – as Filangieri pointed out, 'is the soul of commerce', and the credit which trust alone can generate must be regarded as a 'second species of money'. Fraud, forgery, and bankruptcy constitute the severest threats to the social and economic order.[85] 'A prince or a republic', Doria noted, 'that does not observe trust cannot maintain a lively and flourishing commerce, because no one will wish to trade with it, since no one will hold its promises worthy of confidence'.[86]

Philip II's purpose, in Doria's view, had been to beggar the kingdom in order to secure its political compliance. 'For commerce', he wrote, 'is an art which unites men in civil society so that they give to each other mutual assistance...in such a way that neither distance nor any other consideration can impede this mutual aid'. But trade can only flourish under two conditions, 'and these are liberty and security in contracts, and this can only occur when trust and justice rule'.[87] In order for these conditions to be met it was clearly necessary for the laws to ensure that all trading practices – what is generally understood here by contracts – should be stable. All the Neapolitan political economists, from Antonio Serra in the early seventeenth century to Gaetano Filangieri in the late eighteenth, had criticized the laxity of the laws governing the issue of false bonds, counterfeiting – a crime that even the viceroys were believed, correctly it seems, to have been guilty of[88] – the creation of monopolies, sudden changes in the rates of exchange and in rates of interest, and so on. Montesquieu, Genovesi recalled, had noted that under despotic governments money ceased to have any currency value at all, precisely because money is 'a sign which represents value', and under a despot 'it would be a prodigy did things there represent their sign. Tyranny and distrust [méfiance] make everyone bury their currency'.[89] Counterfeiting in particular was, Genovesi pointed out, punished with the utmost severity even among 'barbarous nations'. The Incas, the Egyptians, the Spartans, the Athenians, and the Persians had all prescribed the death penalty for such crimes, which, because they 'open a very great breach in public security', deserve what Genovesi interestingly refers to as 'either civil or natural death'.[90] In Naples, however, a man might be executed for theft, a crime whose consequences were hardly to be compared to the loss of life, but let off with a fine for an act which, in Doria's view, 'offends against public trust and thus against the entire republic'.[91] As a result that republic had become, he claimed, 'like a merchant without trust since the slowness of the justice which is handed out to litigants breaks the trust which exists between persons'.[92]

With the collapse of the necessary conditions for true commerce, trade became a question of mutual deception. Bonds and even money, since so much of it was false, were no longer freely accepted and the Neapolitans were reduced to the condition of the savages described by Genovesi who will give with the right hand only if they simultaneously receive with the left.[93] What both Doria and Genovesi were offering was a causal explanation for what had long been seen as the kingdom's greatest single ill, the predominance of 'idle money'.[94] Nearly two centuries earlier the famous bandit leader Marco Sciarra, who in the summer of 1590 had laid siege to the city of Rome and captured the sister of Sixtus V, had described himself, during his brief seven-year reign over the Neapolitan hinterland, in a language which combined the messianic with the bureaucratic, as 'Marcus Sciarra, the flail of God, and commissar sent by God against all those usurers who keep money idle'.[95]

vi

By thus destroying the Neapolitans' ability to trust each other, the Spaniards had effectively reduced the kingdom to a state of semi-impoverishment, unswerving – at least among the barony – in its allegiance to the crown which had provided and sustained its cultural ambitions; able, and certainly willing, to contribute to the Spanish imperial machine, but too divided against itself, too isolated in its pursuit of private ends, of 'interests without *virtù*', ever to be able to create a politically virtuous life. After the Spaniards had done with it, this the most prosperous, most cultured city in the Mediterranean had been so far reduced, Doria sadly observed, that 'the Indies are not those in America: the true Indies are here in the Kingdom of Naples'.[96]

The revolt of 1647 had come as a great shock to the Spanish crown, although almost all the barons had remained loyal. Its relative success had compelled the government to recognize that although its tactics might operate in the short run, in the long they could only result in a state which was, as Doria observed, 'like a stomach filled with ulcers', capable of splenetic irruption at the slightest provocation. After the suppression of the revolt, the viceregal government had been forced to introduce reforms. But, in Doria's view, 'those though mild in appearance were no less contrived and ruinous'[97] than the previous strategies had been. The Spanish Monarchy was effectively bankrupt. Whatever protective purpose it had once served had now long since vanished. The future of southern Italy, if it was to have a future, could be assured only by substituting the normative cultural principles which had sustained that monarchy, for those of the well-ordered *respublica*, where the laws were sovereign and in which 'honour' – in any sense stronger than simply respect – would give way to public virtue, and *fede privata* be once again subordinate to *fede pubblica*.

The maxims, as Doria put it, that he 'whose object is to found a new civilization [*civilità*] or whose aim is to preserve one that is already established or to restore one that is already corrupt and decayed' are simply those calculated to install trust as the dominant civil mode. To achieve this end religion must be respected, respectable, and conducive to civil life; the individual must always be prepared to privilege the *patria* over the interests of his own family and those of his family over his own immediate, purely personal concerns.[98]

As with most eighteenth-century republicans, it mattered little to either Doria or Genovesi what form the *respublica* took. Both men lived under monarchies, and both were careful to stress the enlightened nature, 'the gifts of mind and heart', as Genovesi put it, of the kings they served. Like Rousseau, Genovesi believed that true republics were more likely to succeed in sustaining *fede pubblica*, for, in a republic, public instruction is 'more severe', there is less danger of a decline into luxury and, as a result, the state is more 'creditable'[99] and 'trust is more rigorously upheld'. Republics also have, 'as their prime concern', what he called 'diffusive force' (*forza diffusiva*), the force that drives men to care for their fellow beings, the force that is the substance of trust.[100] But it was also the case that 'a monarchy governed according to public laws, which are nothing other than the reflection of the common sense and the needs of the people, and by incorruptible magistrates [*efori*], and assisted by a council of wise men which is the senate of the nobility', would, in effect, like England, *be* a republic.[101] Doria was more sceptical about the future of republican forms of government. In republics, he admitted, 'the laws...are supported by a more constant trust because the people and the multitude when they are gathered in counsel are more trustworthy than a single man'.[102] On the other hand, a corrupt republic, since it involves the citizens in the process of corruption, will be worse than a tyrannous monarchy.[103] And in Doria's own brief, Tacitean account of the history of civil society, all modes of government are susceptible to corruption; monarchies and oligarchies can collapse into tryannics, and republics, particularly democratic republics – 'as it seems we must today call Holland' – into mob rule.[104] Like Machiavelli before them, both Doria and Genovesi made a sharp distinction between 'good' and 'bad' despotism, like Machiavelli, also, they were certain that what he had called the 'città corrotta' could only be put to rights from above by the legitimately constituted rulers of the state.[105] For this reason, Masaniello's revolt had been an aberration – the 'crown of all evils' Genovesi called it. Since all states are founded upon a contract, a revolution – whatever its cause – must, of necessity, constitute a violation of that contract, and a violation of contract is a betrayal of trust.[106] Although tyrannicide was, for both Doria and Genovesi, clearly permissible, they could not imagine creating a new society out of social conflict. What

Naples required was not popular revolt, but an enlightened prince – of the kind that Doria, at least, professed to find in the Austrian administration and Genovesi in the Bourbon monarchy – to establish the well-ordered republic.

vii

Doria's and Genovesi's observations on the state of Naples were, of course, concerned with the pressing need to remedy present ills and they were couched in a characteristically eighteenth-century idiom, the discourse of political economy; but their claims may shed some light on a far larger and more enduring problem: the always obscure conditions of social and economic growth in early-modern Europe.

For both Doria and Genovesi trust was the basis for the well-ordered republic. It was, in short, why a man might behave towards members of society at large in ways comparable to those in which he treated the members of his own kinship group. It, at least, provides strong reasons why he should not – except in purely private concerns – privilege that group over any other. For Doria and Genovesi, and, more widely, for most Catholic political economists, the only community in which trust was dominant, indeed the only society in which it could operate at all, was the virtuous republic as exemplified by Rome and Athens, and, somewhat less convincingly, Aragonese Naples. The kind of humanistic ethics that Doria and Genovesi were attempting to revive, which set this idea of the 'well-ordered republic' at the centre of all social relations, employed a similar conceptual vocabulary to Calvinism, or – to put it another way – the social ethos of Calvinism, and can be seen as constituting a special case of what has come to be called 'classical republicanism'.[107] In both cases there was an insistence on the priority of the community over the hearth, of the need for all members of the community not only to trust each other, but also to extend that trust to what Weber calls the 'out-groups'; in both cases, too, there was an emphasis on some kind of ideological cohesion which was represented by a 'civil' religion. If we accept this view then many of the problems that historians have had with Weber's famous thesis on the links between Calvinism and the rise of capitalism disappear, since it might be argued that it was not a specifically Calvinist or Puritan work-ethic that encouraged economic take-off in the Protestant cities in the seventeenth century, nor Christianity itself in the medieval cities of north and central Italy, but the secular ethic of 'classical republicanism'.

But we still need to know just what it is about classical republicanism that makes it so peculiarly suited to capitalism or, to use the contemporary term, to the commercial society. Doria and Genovesi in their analyses of the workings of trust, claimed, as we have seen, that the crucial fact about the virtuous and well-ordered republic – what indeed made it both virtuous and well ordered – was that by insisting upon the public good over private interests, it enabled men from different kinship groups, and hence from different societies, to trust each other; that, in Weberian terms, it allowed the 'out-groups' to be treated in ways similar to the 'in-groups'; and that only under such conditions was it possible to operate a properly 'commercial society'. This would seem to reinforce an aspect of Weber's work which, although it is never made much of in *The Protestant Ethic and the Spirit of Capitalism*, plays a major role in his analysis of China, namely the claim that if China had never experienced the economic growth of the west, this in the end came down to the fact that in China 'the fetters of the kinship group were never shattered', and that it had been, as he said elsewhere, precisely 'The great achievement of the ethical religions, above all the ethical and asceticist sects of Protestantism...to shatter the fetters of the kin'.[108] If we substitute 'virtuous republic' for 'ethical religions', we have a claim that looks very much like that of Doria and Genovesi. For only in a society where trust as public, in contrast to private, faith is held to be central, indeed the dominant social principle, will the good of the family be made subordinate to the good of the community at large, and only then will a 'commercial society' be fully possible.

I do not, of course, intend to suggest that it is *only* within the well-ordered republic, or in some functional modern analogue, that capital-dependent economic prosperity is possible. The case of Japan and of South Korea, to give only two modern examples, evidently precludes any such conclusion. But it may have been the only available model at the end of the eighteenth century. And it may, therefore, be the case that the problem that Doria and Genovesi identified in the eighteenth century may be an answer to the question of why it was that southern Europe, which, since the beginning of the Roman world, had been the most prosperous part of the continent, not merely failed to achieve the spectacular economic development experienced by Holland and England during the seventeenth century, but went into a precipitous decline from which it is only just beginning to recover.

5. Carlos de Sigüenza y Góngora. Frontispiece to Leonard Irving, *Don Carlos Sigüenza y Góngora: A Mexican Savant of the Seventeenth Century*, Berkeley, California, 1929 (photo: British Library).

4

From Noble Savages to Savage Nobles: the Criollo Uses of the Amerindian past

i

In their attempts to explain the deleterious effect of Spanish rule upon the culture and the economy of Naples, Doria, Genovesi, and Filangieri had called repeatedly upon the image of a continuous, and politically virtuous, past. As they were not and, despite the offensive language of some of the viceroys, had no sense of being colonists, they had no difficulty in identifying an alternative culture to the Hispanic one that had been imposed upon them. The citizens of Spain's dependencies in America, however, had no culture and no history fully independent of what had once been for all of them their 'mother country'. But by the mid-eighteenth century few of those born in the Americas of Spanish origin were fully Spanish in anything other than their political allegiances. The Spanish-American dominions were not colonies – that term is never used to describe any of the Habsburg possessions – but discrete parts of the crown of Castile. As early as the 1560s they had come to be seen by their inhabitants as quasi-autonomous kingdoms,[1] part of what came to be called 'Greater Spain', *Magnae Hispaniae*, no different, whatever the realities of their legal status, from Aragon, Naples, or the Netherlands.[2]

Such kingdoms had to have a continuous, instructive, and politically legitimating past. And the only past to which the *criollos* could lay claim, the only past they clearly did not share with their mother country, was that of the very peoples their ancestors had conquered. Some cultural association between colonizer and colonized had by the mid-seventeenth century become inescapable, if only because both groups were bound by what Benedict Anderson has called 'the shared fatality of extra-Spanish birth'.[3] Any attempt, however, to transform this indeterminate sense of a shared locality into a common history, was faced with massive and obvious difficulties, conceptual as well as practical. The technological and religious divide that separated Spaniards from Indians made the only available clas-

91

sical analogy, the expropriation by Rome of Grecian science, Grecian art, and the Greek language – hinted at but never used – unworkable. The presence of the living Indians was very remote from any current image of Greeks and Romans, and their condition too miserable for anyone of 'white' descent to contemplate direct association with them. Such links as the *criollos* were able to make between themselves and the Indians could, therefore, be mediated only through time. The *criollos* might not constitute one race with the Indians; but they could make some claim to being the true heirs of their imperial past. Even this presented formidable difficulties, since it clearly depended upon a dubious interpretation of the role of the *conquista* and, more alarming still, because any attempt by the colonists to raise the image of a glorious 'Aztec' or 'Inca' past, no matter how thoroughly sanitized, might result in the rebellion of the subdued Indian and mestizo masses. The continuing presence of claimants to the Inca Empire – 'Tawantinsuyu' – and of autonomous Indian enclaves in the Andes, all of which culminated in the Tupac Amarú revolt of 1780–3, made indeed any such attempt on the part of most Peruvians unworkable, if not actually unthinkable, until, as we shall see in the following chapter, the first decades of the nineteenth century.

But in Mexico, where the ancient Indian past was far more remote, the *criollo* élite had, by the late seventeenth century, begun to experiment with ways in which to appropriate for itself an indigenous 'classical antiquity'. The first such experiment was the work of the Mexican scholar and cosmographer royal, Carlos de Sigüenza y Góngora (1645–1700), the 'Mexican Swan' as the poet Sor Juana Iñés de la Cruz called him,[4] and it took the form of an iconographic programme for a ninety-foot-high triumphal arch erected in September 1680, to welcome Tomás Antonio de la Cerdá y Aragon, Count of Paredes, Marqués de la Laguna, and the new viceroy of New Spain to Mexico City. The use of such arches, to mark the King's transition from one part of his realm to another, through ceremonial conquest and then surrender (by the presentation of the keys), was the traditional way in which visiting kings were welcomed to the cities over which they ruled; and the viceroy was, literally, the king's royal body in another place. Had the Marqués de la Laguna, however, had the time to stop and look at the images that decorated the sides of this particular arch, he might have been somewhat surprised. Most triumphal arches, loosely modelled on that of Constantine, depicted the great victories of the king they were erected to honour, or, failing that, of the heroes of antiquity. 'It has been the habitual custom of the ingenious *Americans*', Sigüenza y Góngora pointed out, 'to adorn, with mythological ideas from lying fables, most of the *triumphal arches* which they erect to welcome their princes'.[5] But this one depicted no mythological fables. It was decorated instead with the achievements of the twelve Aztec emperors.

Sigüenza y Góngora's arch was an opportunity to press home, in as direct a manner as was available to him, ('for', he observed, 'it seems that it is painting that persuades with the greatest efficiency'[6]) a striking if still confused political message. He was not the first person, in a society singularly devoid of any autonomous political language, to employ such a public monument as the vehicle for a political statement. In 1554 Francisco Cervantes de Salazar, professor of rhetoric at the newly created University of Mexico, had written a programme for a ceremonial catafalque for Charles V. This had combined a traditional classical iconography, which alluded to the heroic achievements of the dead Emperor, with scenes from the life of Cortés. One of these showed Cortés in the act of grounding his ships, symbolizing the distance that had thereafter separated New from Old Spain. But there was little that was otherwise original in Cervantes de Salazar's tomb. Sigüenza y Góngora's arch, on the other hand, was, and proclaimed itself to be, a radical departure from tradition. For it spoke, clearly to those who cared to listen, about the political status and cultural inheritance of what its creator called 'our *criollo* nation'.[7]

ii

Sigüenza y Góngora's works are extensive. Like most colonial writings of the seventeenth century, they are also ponderous and heavily freighted with a superfluous encyclopaedic learning. But clumsy and disparate though they now seem, each was part of an attempt to provide a comprehensive description of the achievements of the *criollo* nation.[8] They extolled its heroism, its piety, its learning, its letters, its architecture, and its science.[9] These, he declared, in a variety of idioms, were all the equal of those of Spain. As an exercise in provincial self-assurance, Sigüenza y Góngora's enterprise was both popular (he was rewarded for his efforts with the chairs of mathematics and astronomy at the University of Mexico, was made chief cosmographer of New Spain, examiner of artillery, and chief almoner to the archbishop) and unremarkable. Political claims to independent excellence were, however, far more contentious. Mexican *criollos*, like all colonists, could make only very restricted use of arguments from tradition or example, because the only traditions and examples available to them – or the only ones they had hitherto thought suitable – were European ones. They had, therefore, either to insist on their Europeanness or to confine themselves to arguments from abstract principle. Sigüenza y Góngora, however, was now prepared to argue that the 'Mexicans' could draw upon a truly 'national' political tradition whose sources were to be found not only in the 'heroic piety'[10] of the conquerors (the *criollo* élite's true, if now infinitely remote, ancestors) but more specifically in the civic achievements of the civilization they had overthrown. In the ancient Aztec past, he argued, the *criollo* community possessed its own classical antiquity, inferior in many respects, but no less fantastic, nor any less instructive in the examples it could provide than that of Greece and Rome.

The purpose of Sigüenza y Góngora's arch was, he declared, 'to provide his Excellency the Marqués de la Laguna with a theatre of political virtues to serve him as a mirror'.[11] It was, he acknowledged, a radical, possibly even scandalous move to attempt to instruct a new ruler through *exempla* chosen from the history of peoples who had been reduced to such a state of misery that the idea that they had a past at all, let alone an instructive one, might seem absurd. But although the Aztecs were certainly 'buried in distant darkness' because of their barbarity, they had nonetheless once possessed 'politic schools in their antiquity'.[12] It was the lesson of these schools that Sigüenza y Góngora wished to impress upon the viceroy. For, he explained, it was evident that as

> it was my purpose to provide examples for imitation, it would be to offend the *patria* to supplicate from foreign heroes from whom the Romans learned the practice of the virtues, and even more so when there is an abundance of precepts for political instruction among those peoples thought to be barbarians.[13]

Sigüenza y Góngora published an account and an explanation of his programme with the title *Theatro de virtudes políticas* (The Theatre of Political Virtues). It is neither a very coherent nor a very powerful piece of writing; but its message was clear enough. The ancient 'Mexican Empire' is one in whose civic values the Mexican *criollos* can share, because, in the first instance, they too had been born in the land of Mexico. Sigüenza y Góngora fully recognized, however, that although birth might confer rights of both property and citizenship it could never be a guarantee of cultural continuity between two peoples who were not only culturally very different, but one of whom was the conqueror, the other, the conquered. The apparent inaccessibility of any intellectually compelling, single identity available to both ancient Indian and modern *criollo*, involved Sigüenza y Góngora in what to modern readers must seem an impossibly arcane quest for a direct link, in the person of a legitimating ancestor, between the Old World and the New.

The quest itself belonged to a larger contemporary attempt to account for the origin of the Indian tribes in a way that would both establish them as true sons of Adam, and yield some causal explanation for their seemingly unnatural cultural behaviour.[14] This search for origins had engaged men as remote from any direct intellectual concern with America as Hugo Grotius,[15] and became a matter of pressing urgency in a society like the Mexican *criollo*, which was itself engaged in the practice of fabricating its own origins.

Sigüenza y Góngora's explanation for the origin of the 'Mexicans' depends upon a reading of the name 'Neptune'. Beneath the fabulous guise of a Roman marine deity, he claimed, lurked a biblical figure, Nephtuhim, son of Mizraim, son of Shem. This person had been the probable founder of Carthage, and, in Sigüenza y Góngora's view, was also the certain 'progenitor of this New World'.[16] There were additional linguistic reasons of a more explicitly cultural kind for linking the Amerindians with the descendants of the sons of Nephtuhim. According to the Jewish historian Josephus, 'Nephthemi praeter nomina nihil scimus', a phrase that, according to Sigüenza y Góngora, meant not 'that we know nothing of Nephtuhim besides his name', as might have been supposed, but that 'they [his descendants] had a name so confused that it survived only in signs; they could give no certainties [about their origins] but had their origins in confusions, for they could not name with exactitude the place of their birth'.[17] A nomadic people has, of course, no language, no name, no true speech since all forms of utterance, beyond the most simple, are the creation of civil, settled communities. 'Truly', he therefore concluded, the sons of Nephtuhim 'have shown themselves to be the sons of Neptune since, other than the names by which they have been given here, we know nothing of them...Their name was changed and they remained unknown'.[18]

Unsurprisingly this description fits no people so well as the Indians,

> in particular those of Mexico, a people torn from their villages, foreigners in their own lands, a people scattered by their need to defend their homeland and torn to pieces by their poverty. A people terrible in their suffering, and after which there have been none so patient in their misery; a people who always seek for a remedy to their undoing, and find themselves trampled upon by all; a people whose lands suffer from hardships and continual flooding.[19]

If the Indians had shared the cultural, physical, and linguistic fate of the sons of Nephtuhim-Neptune, then this made them the heirs of the histories, and the cultural values, of the Old World. There was, however, one further link between the biblical past and the Amerindian present.

'These Indians', wrote Sigüenza y Góngora,

> were a people who were waiting, [*gentem expectantem*], and that they waited in hope was certain, for they had a prophecy that he who was their true king would one day come to govern them, for those who presently ruled in the Empire were only his substitutes.[20]

This person, he concluded, could also be none other than Neptune. In making this claim Sigüenza y Góngora's purpose seems (for he makes less of it than might have been expected) to have been to exploit another popular myth: the – by this time – widely accepted story that Moctezuma had donated his empire to Cortés in the belief that he was the Toltec culture-hero Quetzalcoatl who was thought to have been driven out of Mexico at some point in the remote past, but who had promised that he would one day return to claim his people and his lands. If Quetzalcoatl was yet another name for Nephtuhim then it might be possible to argue that there was a sense in which the Spaniards had become, by the terms of Moctezuma's donation, the political heirs of the Aztec Empire's founding father.

This elaborate, at times highly unstable edifice of synecdoche, analogy, and allusion linked the Indians with the Old World of the Hebrews and the Romans (and even at a later point with the ancient Egyptians[21]). By so doing it offered the *criollos* an association with an indigenous classical antiquity, a continuity between their present and the Indian past which – and this, as we shall see, was crucial – bypassed the Indian present; and it reinforced the idea that Cortés himself had tried to establish: that the Spanish conquerors were the Indians' legitimate and natural rulers.

Having made this association between the origin myths, and hence the legitimating political narratives, of the Old World and the New, the way was now open for a programme in which figures from this 'Mexican' history might be used to depict civic and intellectual virtues in place of the traditional classical ones. 'In the Mexican emperors', declared Sigüenza y Góngora, 'who really lived in this most celebrated empire of *America*, I discovered without difficulty what others had sought in *fables*'.[22]

The *Theatro de virtudes políticas* consists for the most part in an elaborate exegesis of the possible contemporary significance of the lives of each of the emperors who decorated the arch. The actual messages that these conveyed were not very radical. The vehicle for the expression of the classical virtues may have been American Indians, but the virtues remained classical. 'Acampich' (Acamapichtli) the Aztec chieftain who led the Aztecs out of slavery appears in the guise of hope. But this is of little direct political significance. Sigüenza y Góngora did not regard himself as a member of a captive race, still less did he wish to see an independent Mexico. His writings, and the *Theatro* in particular, are, however, an articulation of the need of the society to which he belonged to represent to itself its relationship to the lands it occupied, to the peoples over whom it ruled, and to a 'mother country' that as a source of cultural and political inspiration was rapidly losing its importance.

Sigüenza y Góngora's use of Indian imagery belonged to the same project as his 'Indian museum', an attempt to preserve what little now remained of the writings, the artefacts, and the art of the Amerindian past. In this, he saw himself as a lone figure. What shame, he wrote in the *Theatro*, 'our *criollo* nation' ought to feel that such work was largely done by foreigners, men like Samuel Purchas who had 'collected as much as there was to know about these matters as the most devoted lover of our *patria*'.[23]

But Sigüenza y Góngora's project took no account of the huge cultural distance that now separated the living Indians from their mythologized ancestors. For him, as for most *criollos*, the problem, like the subjugated Indian masses themselves, remaind invisible. But neither it nor they could remain invisible forever. On 8 June 1692, Mexico City was in part destroyed by an Indian uprising in which Sigüenza y Góngora, if we are to believe his own grandiloquent account of the event, came close to losing his life.[24] Thereafter he abandoned the project without a word. Real Indians had intruded too far into the imaginary spaces where their ancestors might have helped to create, for the *criollos* alone, a new perception of what it meant to be a 'Mexican'.

iii

The uprising of 1692 put an end to any further attempt to draw cultural or political inspiration from the Aztec past until the second half of the eighteenth century. The successor to Sigüenza y Góngora's project – although he cites the *Theatro de virtudes políticas* only infrequently and then often to criticize its factual content[25] – was a Jesuit, Francisco Javier Clavigero, and even he, though a *criollo* with an extensive knowledge of Indians both past and present, was writing from exile in Bologna, 'more than two thousand three hundred leagues from his *patria*'.

Clavigero was born in 1731 in the town of Veracruz in Mexico, the son of a Spanish-born immigrant who became the mayor (*alcalde mayor*) of Jicayan in the province of Oaxaca. In 1748 he entered the

97

Society of Jesus and after completing his studies taught philosophy, first at the Colegio de San Ildefonso in Mexico City and later at the Jesuit College in Guadalajara. In 1767 Charles III ordered the expulsion of the Jesuits from the colonies and Clavigero was dispatched to Italy. He settled in Bologna, together with a number of his former colleagues and remained until his death in 1787.[26]

The Jesuits, more than any other order, had encouraged the *criollos* in their aspirations to an independent cultural identity. They had arrived in the Americas too late to reap many of the benefits of the initial evangelization programme, and although they later gained control of some of the more remote areas, most famously Paraguay, their main concern, at least by the mid-eighteenth century, was with the education of the white population of the colonies. They were highly respected and exercised a powerful, and not consistently orthodox, hold over the political imagination of the colonial élites. Among a lax lay clergy they were, as the Peruvian revolutionary (and ex-Jesuit) Juan Pablo Viscardo – whom we shall meet again in the next chapter – observed, 'the only ones of any use', whose expulsion, 'affected the whole of Spanish America more strongly than it was possible to imagine in Europe', and 'occasioned serious and long-lasting reflections which changed public opinion towards the Spanish government'.[27] The Jesuits were, of course, a missionary order and their objectives were, broadly speaking, founded upon two claims: that the 'mission' extended to the entire world – that there was little effective difference between Austrian and Calabrian peasants, Chinese mandarins, Filipinos, or American Indians, in that all could be brought to a knowledge of Christianity by rational persuasion; and that conversion could, indeed should, be achieved with the least possible damage to indigenous cultures where those constituted 'civil republics'. These assumptions made the Jesuits particularly sensitive to the notion of a cultural continuum between Indian and *criollo*, and to the ultimate possibility of a single cultural identity for their *patria*. For the American Jesuits in Italy – Clavigero himself, Francisco Javier Alegre, Andrés Cavo, and the Chilean natural historians, Juan Ignacio Molina and Felipe Goméz de Vidaurre[28] – the experience of exile further enhanced the sense that what they had been forced to leave, seemingly (and in fact) for ever, had been a self-identifying political community. For many of them, particularly when confronted with hostile foreigners, Spain was still their *nación*, a word that indicated a common racial inheritance; but their culture, their *patria* – a far more powerful term – was 'Mexican', or 'Peruvian', or 'Chilean'. And when the interests of the *patria* clashed directly with those of the *nación*, it was the Spaniards who became foreigners ('extranjeros').[29]

It was in an attempt to articulate and to defend this identity with

98

the land where he had been born and to which he hoped until his death to be allowed one day to return, that Clavigero wrote his *Storia antica del Messico* (The History of Ancient Mexico). He composed the first draft in Spanish,[30] but on the urging of 'some Italian men of letters' – most probably the circle around the Milanese political economist, Gianrinaldo Carli – and because he soon realized that no Spanish press would be allowed to print it – he undertook the 'new and laborious task of translating it into Tuscan'.[31] It was finally printed in Cesena in 1780–1, read appreciatively by Gibbon[32] and proved to be the most popular, certainly the most influential, history of Mexico since the appearance of José de Acosta's *Historia natural y moral de las Indias* in 1590.

Clavigero's *Storia antica*, unlike the works of so many of his fellow exiles, which largely retained the styles and explanatory concerns of an earlier generation, is a characteristically eighteenth-century product. His intellectual preferences were, it is true, far from being wholly 'enlightened'. He sometimes deplored the freedom of thought that 'this century of enlightenment' (*este siglo de luces*) had brought and the threat that it posed to the authority of the Church. Much of his account of historical causation is conventionally scholastic; so, too, are many of his cultural assumptions, and the intellectual world to which he belonged remained, despite his reading of Descartes and Montesquieu, the Aristotelian-Thomist one in which he had been schooled. But like many Jesuits, even in the narrow intellectual confines of a colonial society, Clavigero had, in his years as a professor of philosophy, read many of what he called the 'moderns'. The names of Descartes, Leibnitz, Gassendi, and Fontenelle all appear in his writings and, as we shall see, many of his more original ideas about the origins of culture are heavily indebted to *De l'esprit des lois*.

Above all, the *Storia antica*, unlike nearly every other previous account of ancient Mexico, employs a wholly secular explanation of causation in human affairs. Clavigero was, for instance, particularly unhappy with the widespread notion (for which Acosta had been a powerful advocate) that only Satanic intervention could satisfactorily explain the aberrations of Indian religious practices. However skilful and malign the Devil might be, he was not to the 'spirit of this age' a plausible historical agent. Explanations in terms of non-human agency (unless they had been attested to in Holy Writ) were, he declared, like the supposition that the original inhabitants of America might have been carried there by angels, 'not pleasing to the century in which we live'.[33] Men were rational beings possessed of free will, and any explanation of human actions had to be expressed in terms of purely human agency.

The supposed existence of diabolic intervention in America had, in fact, possessed considerable imaginative advantages. If the Devil was responsible for whatever deviant forms non-Christian beliefs and practices might take, then the chronicler had no need to trouble himself with explaining their origins.[34] He was free, as Acosta had been, to describe and to map their formal relationship with those found in other pre-Christian societies. But the belief in Satanic origins made the intended association between ancient Indian and modern *criollo* cultures a hazardous business. Clavigero's modernism, then, removed the whole project from the threat of that eschatological reductionism that, in his view, had vitiated the writings of so many previous historians of Amerindian society.

All histories, Clavigero claimed, even those that touched upon sacred subjects, had to be the fruit of a meticulous inquiry into origins. To demonstrate the sincerity of this part of his enterprise he prefaced his own work with a lengthy account of all the sources he claimed to have used. The reader was thus assured that this was, indeed, a piece of historical research in the best contemporary manner. And if it lacked the stylistic embellishment that most past histories of the subject had displayed, so much the better, for in reality such frills merely distracted from the historian's true task which was to tell the truth. 'And the truth', Clavigero declared, in keeping with the contemporary rejection of rhetoric, 'is all the more beautiful the more naked it is'.[35] Clavigero also claimed to have incorporated into his narrative a large body of original material on the Indian past which has subsequently been lost. There are, and were at the time, some doubts about this. He certainly knew Sigüenza y Góngora's work and implies that he had access to his now lost *Ciclografía mexicana*, an account of Mexican calendar wheels.[36] But the *Storia antica* contains no new information on the Indian world, and most of what information it does contain is, in fact, very largely based on the work of one sixteenth-century Franciscan, Juan de Torquemada, whose massive *Monarquía Indiana* (Indian Monarchy), composed sometime around 1615, brought together an evangelization of the Indians. Torquemada's style was as tortuous as Sigüenza y Góngora's, but it was, so its author claimed – and probably with some justification – based upon a wide survey of Indian records, many of them since lost.[37] It was this aspect that appealed to Clavigero. For despite the accusations of such hostile critics as Clavigero's contemporary, the historiographer royal, Juan Bautista Muñoz, that all the *Storia antica* offered was a 'methodical compendium'[38] of the *Monarquía Indiana*, the *Storia antica* merely used the facts provided by Torquemada as, in Clavigero's own metaphor, Virgil had used the history of Ennius, 'to search for precious stones among the dung'.[39] It strips Torquemada's work of all its providentialist trappings and, as we shall see, harnesses the Franciscan's data to a quite different mode of historical explanation.

The *Storia antica* aroused a great deal of hostility in Spain. Clavigero never once mentioned the possibility of a rebellion among the colonial élite to whom his work was addressed, and protested vigorously to his friend the (violently anti-revolutionary) Jesuit Lorenzo Hervás y Panduro[40] that he was not, as some had claimed, 'disaffected with my nation',[41] by which he meant the Spaniards. But the enterprise on which he – like Sigüenza y Góngora before him – was engaged, was explicitly to provide the *criollos*, the 'Mexicans' as he called them, with an interpretation of the ancient Indian past that would guarantee them, as the supposed heirs to that past, a measure of independence from the secular history of the Old World. The *Storia antica* was, its author declared, 'a history of Mexico written by a Mexican'. And not so much a simple narrative as 'an essay, an attempt, a presumptuous venture on the part of a citizen who, despite the difficulties that he suffers, has buried himself in this that he might be of use to his country'. Like Sigüenza y Góngora, Clavigero lamented both the state into which the *criollo* understanding of the Indian past had fallen, and the fact that it had fallen into the hands of foreigners, not all of whom, like Samuel Purchas, had put it to good use. What Clavigero set out to do was to reappropriate for the *criollo* élite what he referred to as 'the remains of the antiquities of our *patria*'[42] and out of that to create a classical antiquity which would serve the 'Mexicans' as the past of Greece and Rome had served the Europeans, as a culture to be shared with the ancient Mexicans with whom they were connected by place, not race.

In order for this claim to possess any compelling resonance, however, Clavigero had to provide a cultural association between the ancient Indian past and the *criollo* present that would exclude the possibility of a continuous tradition, for any such tradition would obviously have had to have included not only the *criollos*, but also the Peninsular-born Spaniards. His history had, that is, to exclude the entire period of viceregal rule.

The simplest means of achieving this end was silence. The narrative of the *Storia antica* thus ceases abruptly with the conquest. It makes no mention, as all previous histories of Mexico had done, either of the evangelization or of the consolidation of Spanish rule after 1521. The narrative structure employs a chronology that runs from the arrival in the Valley of Mexico of the Toltecs, the first settled Amerindian communities and the first that Clavigero and his readers could regard as civil societies, to the arrival of the last, the conquistadores. For the *criollo* élite, the last of these events, the Conquest, had by the middle of the eighteenth century come to represent a Golden Age, a period when the colonists had held absolute power, when Mexico had been less a colony than a quasi-independent tributary kingdom. The narrative of the events is taken from Bernal Díaz's *Historia verdadera* and from Cortés's *Cartas de relación*; but Clavigero makes one significant modification. According to Cortés Moctezuma had donated his empire to Charles V in the belief that he was the 'great lord' who, in the Indian account of the creation, was said to have been driven from Mexico by demons, swearing that one day he would return to reclaim his lands.[43] This little story, which subsequently became an integral part of the mythology of the Conquest, is almost certainly a clever fabrication of Cortés's own. In Clavigero's version of the donation, however, Moctezuma is made to identify the great lord with Quetzalcoatl, a deified priest-king of Maya origin.[44] Although the story of Quetzalcoatl as told by the sixteenth-century Franciscan ethnographer, Bernardino de Sahagún, does fit Cortés's narrative, neither Cortés himself, nor any of his contemporaries, ever identified this 'great lord', nor do they seem to have heard of any Aztec deity other than the tutelary Huitzilopochitl.[45] Clavigero knew this. He also knew, if we are to believe his claims to familiarity with Sigüenza y Góngora's 'museum', that the identification of Quetzalcoatl as the legendary founder of the Aztecs was in direct contradiction to the Indians' traditional accounts of their own pre-history. Why, then, did he choose to attribute such claims to Moctezuma? The answer lies in the powerful mestizo interpretation of the figure of Quetzalcoatl.[46] Since the late sixteenth century, this deity had been identified as St Thomas, the legendary Apostle of Malabar who, so it was believed, had travelled from India to America where he had died leaving behind him, in legend and in the foliated crosses to be found on some Maya buildings, a now garbled memory of his presence. The belief in St Thomas's American mission, which was shared by Sigüenza y Góngora among others, was also closely associated with the Virgin of Guadalupe who, in 1648, had made a miraculous appearance to an Indian, Juan Diego, and who had become a 'national' virgin and the focus of a cult that united Indians, mestizos, and *criollos*.[47] The link, however implausible, between Amerindian deity, primitive apostle, and an Indian vision provided a powerful imaginative tie between Aztec past and Spanish present. By making Quetzalcoatl the 'great lord' of Moctezuma's donation, Clavigero had provided the final link in the chain. Quetzalcoatl could now be seen not only as a symbol of mestizo and *criollo* religious distinctiveness, but also as the source of the *criollos'* claims to political legitimacy. And although Clavigero does not, as Juan Bautista Muñoz sarcastically noted, treat Cortés 'as a good *criollo* of New Spain [should], as a Father and well-doer',[48] the Conquest in the *Storia antica*, as in most previous *criollo* works (Sigüenza y Góngora's among them), is represented as a heroic achievement. Here, then, was one level at which that community might come to accept the ancestors of Moctezuma – if not his progeny – as a part of their cultural heritage.

In order, however, to make this association at all persuasive, Clavigero had to counter an immediate objection: if the Indians had once been the bearers of a noble (if primitive) culture, why were they now so abject, so obviously incapable of any cultural achievements whatsoever? The stark discrepancy between real Indians and any mythic ancestors the colonist might wish to credit them with, had, ultimately, as we have seen, put an end to Sigüenza y Góngora's project. It had also threatened the attempts by some members of the *criollo* élite to claim a more direct association with the ancient 'monarchy' of Mexico, the precariousness of which is evident in the *representación* made to the crown in 1771 by the town council (*ayuntamiento*) of Mexico City. This, the work of a lawyer named José González de Castañeda, claimed that among the members of the *ayuntamiento* there were 'many [Americans] who can trace their origins to the highest nobility in Spain. There are others, no less commendable by their origins, who carry in their veins the Royal Blood of America'. But, continued Castañeda, lest any claim to Indian *blood*, however regal, implied a link with living Indians, the Indian strain in those whose ancestors had mixed their blood with the 'royal families of the nation' was now so weak that they had all become, in effect, 'pure Spaniards'.[49]

Clavigero had to avoid such absurdities. He also had to contest the growing number of European claims that the early histories of ancient Mexico and Peru had been fantasies meant to glorify the shabby military operations of the conquistadores, and that the Amerindians had, in fact, never been very different from what they were now.

Clavigero's strategy was to turn the gulf between past and present to his own advantage. The Indians' present miserable condition was, he claimed, merely the consequence of the life they had been compelled to live since the Conquest. Would you ever believe, he asked his readers, from the condition of the modern Greeks, that such a people could have produced a Plato or a Pericles?[50] The analogy was not, in fact, Clavigero's own: the French traveller Charles de La Condamine, whose observations on Indian languages Clavigero attempted to refute (as we shall see), had made the same association with regard to the Peruvians. So, too, had Carli, who corresponded with Clavigero and whose *Lettere americane* of 1780 contained a sweeping condemnation of Spanish colonialism. 'After two hundred years of destruction and persecution and slavery, of flight and a change of religion, of government', he asked, 'what trace could remain of their ancient customs?'[51] A barbarous and superstitious people will destroy 'all trace of the ancient customs and change the nature [of a conquered people] through slavery and misery'. Such a fate had befallen the Romans under the Lombards. Would any traveller in the seventh or eighth centuries, Carli continued, be able to discover 'the spirit, the character, the customs, and the laws of the ancient Romans'.[52] It was, of course, an axiom of the political theory with which Clavigero, La Condamine, and Carli were all familiar, that slavery was intolerable within any kind of civil society for, as Montesquieu had argued, slavery deprives the slave of a 'motive for virtue' and leads the master, 'by having unlimited authority over his slaves', to accustom himself to 'the absence of all moral virtues, and he, therefore, becomes fierce, hasty, severe, choleric, voluptuous and cruel'.[53]

Clavigero's analogy between ancient Indians and ancient Greeks also contained an explicit political point, for if the Indians were an analogue for the Greeks, the Spaniards could only be the Turks, and the Turks, apart from being the Spaniards' traditional enemies, were also widely employed by critics of the *ancien régime* as a metaphor for royal absolutism. This was not lost on his readers. 'Clavigero', fumed the Abbé Ramon Diosdado Caballero,

> has launched an ugly attack against the Spanish nation. His obvious and clear intention is that as the Greeks of today, because of the oppression, misery, and contempt with which the Turks, their rulers, treat them, are not as they once were, so are the Mexican Indians given over today to the oppression, misery, and contempt of the Spaniards.[54]

To further emphasize the distance between the ancient and modern, Clavigero renamed the ancient Indian culture of central Mexico the 'Aztec', the name by which it has been generally, although incorrectly, known ever since, and referred, as many subsequent Mexican historians were to do, to the 'Aztec Empire' by its Nahuatl name, Anahuac.[55] The modern *criollo* could thus simply ignore the presence of the modern Indian as unrepresentative both in name and behaviour of anything that his culture had once been. There was, however, still another and potentially more damaging threat to the status of the 'classical' Indian past. In 1769 the Dutch natural philosopher Cornelius De Pauw had published a book entitled *Recherches philosophiques sur les américains*, part of a larger project – which included studies of the Egyptians and the Chinese – for a history of the human species. In common with earlier diffusionists – Acosta and

Lafitau in particular[56] – De Pauw claimed that as all life must have originated in the Old World, the inhabitants of America must be the descendants of a prolonged migration. Unlike either Acosta or Lafitau, both of whom had argued that this migration would have had the effect of arresting the development of human culture, De Pauw seems to have believed that it must have resulted in a process of biological reversal, exacerbated from De Pauw's viewpoint by the peculiar climatic conditions in the Americas. Far from being the natural child the scholastics had made of him, the Indian for De Pauw was a degenerate who, unlike the primitive barbarians of Europe who had soon seen the advantages for themselves in Roman civilization, was incapable of learning anything from his European conquerors.[57] De Pauw's thesis is, in part, indebted to the observations made in 1766 by the famous French naturalist Jean Buffon on the apparent size and frailty of certain American species,[58] and was taken up with more caution than De Pauw had displayed by the Scottish historian William Robertson in his *History of America* of 1777.[59] De Pauw's book went through several editions and was widely read in the Spanish colonies where it was greeted by a howl of protest. The task of refuting Buffon, De Pauw, and Robertson became a patriotic undertaking to which a large number of *criollos* – and at least one Spaniard, the encyclopaedist Benito Gerónimo Feijóo[60] – dedicated themselves, the most extensive example being Antonio de Alcedo y Bexerano's *Diccionario geográfico-histórico de América*, which was printed in Madrid between 1786 and 1789, and which incorporated material provided by Clavigero and Molina.

As his part of this project Clavigero equipped his history with nine lengthy dissertations, which he dedicated to Carli, to thank him 'in the name of the Americans' for having 'studied accurately the History of America, and for having had the courage to defend those despised Nations against so many renowned Europeans who had declared themselves to be their enemies and their persecutors'. The purpose of the dissertations was to 'dissuade the incautious reader from the errors that a great band of modern authors had incurred who, with insufficient knowledge, have written about the land, the animals, and the people of America',[61] and to provide a theoretical grounding for the narrative of the *Storia*.

iv

De Pauw's thesis rested upon the claim that man's intellectual disposition was, in part at least, a product of the physical environment in which he had been born. Underpinning this was a modified Montesquieuian version of the ancient theory of climates which had been employed many times before to establish some common identity between all those born in the Americas, be they of Indian or European racial origin. 'Those who are born in New Spain', Bernardino de Sahagún had written as early as the 1570s, 'are born very much like the Indians for in appearance they are Spaniards but in disposition they are not, and I believe that this is due to the climate and constellations of this land'.[62] The inevitable consequence of this was to read off the supposed behavioural characteristics of the (modern) Indians to the *criollos*. If the Indians were obsessive game players, potential drunkards, and bad Christians then so too were the *criollos*.[63] Similarly, De Pauw claimed that not only were such animals as pumas defective tigers but that no animal had ever been introduced from Europe into America without its undergoing '*une altération sensible*'.[64] The same was clearly true of the *criollos* who 'in the fourth or fifth generation display less intelligence [*génie*] and less capacity for the sciences than true Europeans'. (De Pauw regarded Feijóo's attempt to refute this on the grounds that *criollo* children got up earlier in the morning than Spanish children did, as a collection of 'monstrous paradoxes'. But then how could one take seriously the arguments of a man who wrote reams to prove the existence of 'mer-men endowed with immortal souls'?[65])

For the *criollos* the *Recherches philosophiques* was but a further chapter in what Castañeda in the *Representación* of 1771 had described as 'one of the greatest injustices the people of America has had to suffer': the supposition that the Indians, 'despite all the evidence', were irrational beings. 'With no less injustice', Castañeda had continued, 'they pretended that those of us who have been born of European parentage on this soil have barely sufficient reason to be men'.[66] Whether they wished it or not, the American-born Spaniards were steadily compelled to defend the Indian past if they were to preserve their own claims to be fully rational civil beings.

Clavigero's project was not to refute the substance of De Pauw's thesis, since his own attempts to create a single culture out of Aztecs and white Mexicans was also dependent upon the premise that all men are somehow the creatures of the land they inhabit. Some such claim was the only way in which Clavigero could exclude the Peninsular Spaniards from the privileged ancestry he wished to create for the *criollos*. What he set out to do was to prove that the conclusion that De Pauw ('the principal target of my shots'[67]), Buffon, and Robertson had drawn from their evidence for the inferiority of the Americans was false and, furthermore, that the kind of cross-cultural analyses on which much of it relied was historically inappropriate.

Clavigero begins with the controversy over the origin of the

Amerindian tribes. If the biblical account of the repeopling of the world after the Flood was to be preserved, they had to be the descendants of one of the sons of Noah. The theory, which Acosta was the first to suggest, and which most subsequent Jesuit commentators had come to accept, was that they had travelled overland from 'Tartary', when the New World was still linked to the Old by a northern land-bridge. The relative cultural and technical inferiority of the Indians to the Europeans could, therefore, be attributed to the long period of migration necessary to reach America.[68] Like Acosta, Clavigero accepted that the Indians had originally come overland from the Old World; but whereas Acosta had allowed for only a single prolonged migration across what is now called the Bering Straits, Clavigero argued that America must once have been joined to Asia. An earthquake, or earthquakes, had then separated the two continents, thus isolating – and this was crucial to Clavigero's argument – the Amerindians from the cultural and technical knowledge that had subsequently developed in Europe and Asia.[69]

The principal evidence for this claim comes from language. All previous attempts – including Sigüenza y Góngora's – to locate similarities between Indian and Old-World languages, to employ philology to establish genealogy, had been prompted by the quest for some precise Old-World source for the Amerindians. They had also operated on the assumption of a historical continuity between the languages of Europe and those of Asia and America.[70] Clavigero, however, who was eager to avoid the suggestion that the Indians might share anything in common with any Old-World culture, stressed not the apparent similarity between Old- and New-World noun forms, but the sheer diversity of the Amerindian languages.

Such diversity – when the inhabitants of single villages spoke mutually incomprehensible tongues – demonstrated, he claimed, that no single European or Asian race could possibly have been the progenitor of *all* the Indian tribes.[71] It was an argument that had been used before, by Grotius among others, but its attraction for Clavigero lay in the force it gave to his contention that there was no reason to suppose – as most Europeans persisted in doing – that all the American tribes must share a culture.

One of his most telling criticisms of the claims of De Pauw and Robertson – and of La Condamine to whom De Pauw was heavily indebted – was that they had based their generalizations very largely on the great anthology of travel accounts by Samuel Purchas which dealt almost exclusively with the tribes of North America. If, however, the Amerindians had originated in different parts of Asia there was no reason to suppose that, as regarded their racial origins, the Huron and the Algonquin had any more in common with the

107

Aztecs and the Incas than the Finns or the Danes did with the Italians and the Spanish.

Clavigero's theory of continental drift thus relieved him of the need to explain, or explain away, the more obvious 'barbarism' of the northern tribes and left him free to concentrate upon the peoples of 'Anahuac'. His intention, however, was not merely to demonstrate that while the Amerindians clearly belong to the same genetic stock as the other races of man, they could not possibly be the descendants of a single Old-World group. It was, more ambitiously, to prove that culturally they were entirely *sui generis* with no roots in their place of origin whatsoever. To achieve this he had to establish when the great migration from 'Tartary' had taken place.

Like most eighteenth-century 'conjectural histories', the *Storia antica* does not operate with a strict chronology, but with a perception of the relation between past events in terms of what J.G.A. Pocock has called 'moments of creation rather than moments of transmission'.[72] The past is seen, not as a series of events, constantly modifying one another, but as a chain of homogeneous incidents each of which is responsible for the creation of a period, or epoch, of its own. It is the creative breaks in the continuum that mark the passage of time. Clavigero, furthermore, was working with two chronologies expressed in such terms. The first was the traditional Graeco-Roman account of the evolution of culture – from berries to the hunting of animals and from there to agriculture and the domestication of animals; from wood to stone to iron; from the family to the band to the society. The second was the biblical account of human pre-history, from the Creation to the Fall, from the Flood to the Tower of Babel. Because these time-scales served different heuristic ends (and had their origins in different cultural matrices), at no point did they intersect. Furthermore, whereas one clearly applied to all mankind, biblical history after the Flood could only apply to the Old World. To make good his claims Clavigero had, therefore, to establish the time of the migration both in terms of the Indians' own cultural evolution and in terms of the stage in biblical history when they had vanished from the record. To show that the ancestors of the Aztecs had already left Europe before anything that could be called a civilization had come into being, Clavigero looked, not as previous historians such as Lafitau had done, at parallels between words or at similarities in patterns of ritual behaviour or belief,[73] but, taking the terms of his first chronology, at their material culture.[74] This idea too may have been suggested to him by Carli.[75] But whereas Carli noted the absence of money, writing, and commerce (all of which play a central role in Clavigero's later argument), Clavigero focused his attention on the means of production. The

Indians, he argued, had no horses or cattle. Surely had they left the Old World after the domestication of animals they would have taken some with them? They also did not use wax or oil for lamps, 'which on the one hand are of ancient usage both in Asia and Europe and which, on the other, are very useful not to say necessary, and which once learned are never forgotten'.[76] Since we cannot unlearn what we know, the original migrants to America could have arrived only while their societies were still at the hunter-gatherer stage.

The corresponding date for the migration on the biblical time-scale could be discovered by an examination of the Indians' own historical records. These, which were contained within the Mexican picture writings which Clavigero claimed to be able to read, were generally held by Europeans to be of little real historical value. They were believed to contain a record of no more than eight generations[77] and to be largely indistinguishable from myths, which in the eighteenth century were generally thought to be the garbled reminiscences of oral cultures. But, although myths might not provide precise histories of past events, they could, Clavigero argued, be relied upon to record a people's awareness of the 'moments of creation' they had experienced. Without much difficulty he managed to locate an Aztec version of the Flood and a number of stories that, so he believed, referred to the building of the Tower of Babel.[78] But he could find no reference to any subsequent event, nor could he discover (another of Carli's observations[79]) any knowledge among the Indians themselves of the various races of the Old World. From this evidence he concluded that the Amerindians had been among the peoples who had helped construct the Tower of Babel and who, after the 'confusion of tongues', had been scattered throughout the earth. This, of course, established them as a culture with no recorded Old-World history, and one whose languages could have no possible connection with any European or Asian language. He had thus established, to his own satisfaction, that the history of America was wholly separate from that of any other known race.

But Clavigero shared, with 'the band of modern writers', the belief that no matter how independent its history might be, Amerindian society had to be judged by the same general principles as all the other races of the world. One of the principal functions of the *Storia antica* was to demonstrate that the Aztecs possessed a civilization at least as far advanced in the evolutionary cycle as many of the peoples of the ancient world.

For Clavigero, as for most eighteenth-century Europeans, civilization was constituted by a number of very obvious things: knowledge of the arts and sciences, the use of a script and (and these were frequently related) of durable building materials, the willingness to abide by a code of laws, to be led by recognized leaders, and to organize social life according to a web of laws and customs in conformity with the minimalist precepts of the law of nature. All of these outward signs of civility and of the capacity for understanding implied, above all else, the ability to communicate. A society is a body of communicating beings; and, since knowledge is cumulative, progress has only been possible in worlds where each generation has been able to convey its own necessarily restricted understanding to the next. Similarly laws and customs – in particular in pagan societies which lack the benefit of divine revelation – depended for their legitimacy upon the moral consensus of the community.

It is, of course, primarily the power of coherent speech that divides men from beasts. A barbarian, who is at best barely a man and certainly does not live in a true community, is only, after all, he who having no true language jabbers away in 'barbar'. For this reason it had been argued by the later scholastics, most powerfully by Sánchez, by the grammarians of Port Royale and, in more complex terms, by Locke, that if language-use was what was distinctive about man, then there must exist a direct correlation between human cognitive faculties and linguistic forms. But language is also an invention, a cultural artefact, and, as such, provides a mirror of the social world of its users. From Bacon to Herder, the natural history of language was read as the natural history of both human cognition and of society.

One of the most frequently repeated criticisms of the Amerindian tribes was, therefore, the supposed deficiency of their languages. Some Europeans claimed that even the 'civilized' races used a speech that was so complicated, so monstrous to the ear, so weak in all the proper terms that men require to describe the world, that they could hardly be counted as languages at all, but were merely, in the words of one sixteenth-century observer, 'the illiterate voices of birds and brute animals'.[80] And even Leibnitz had wondered if the language of 'America . . . and the extremities and distant places of Asia and Africa' were not so very different from the European 'by the entire quality of speech, not to mention body, that one would say it is another race of animals'.[81] It was also a commonplace of eighteenth-century social theory that savages could not think in terms of abstractions, but reasoned only in metaphor and simile since these made a direct appeal to observable phenomena. Primitive man was a poet because he was incapable of induction. His languages possessed no general terms and no terms for categories, because what he saw about him did not conform to any general law. The creation of universals and abstractions was believed to mark a decisive stage in the history of man's cognitive powers, since it involved the recognition that the

natural world is an intelligible order governed by a body of immutable laws; that there exist qualities not immediately accessible to the
senses; and that the same transparency that was believed to characterize the relationship between a concrete noun and a palpable object
also characterized the relationship between abstract nouns and abstract qualities. 'The mind of man, while still in the savage state',
noted Robertson, recognizes only such objects

> as may be subservient to his use, or can gratify any of his appetites,
> attract his notice; he views the rest without curiosity or attention.
> Satisfied with considering them under that simple mode in which
> they appear to him, as separate and detached, he neither combines
> them so as to form general classes, nor contemplates their qualities
> apart from the subject in which they adhere... Thus he is unac-
> quainted with all the ideas which have been denominated *universal*,
> or *abstract*, or *of reflection*.[82]

As many travellers had recorded, Amerindians had innumerable
names for trees, but no single word that could translate the term
'tree'. Neither were they able adequately to measure and describe
time and space, the two intersecting dimensions in which man,
unlike the beasts who lived (consciously at least) in space only, made
his being. 'All the languages of America', wrote La Condamine,

> of which I have some understanding are very poor. Some are
> energetic and capable of elegance, most notably the ancient lan-
> guage of Peru; but they all lack words with which to express
> abstract and universal terms, a sure proof of the scant progress that
> the minds [*les esprits*] of these people have made.

'Time', 'duration', 'space', 'being', 'substance', 'material', 'body',
'virtue', 'justice', 'liberty', 'discourse', 'ingratitude', he continued,
were all terms unknown to them, and it was impossible to render in
any Amerindian language any metaphysical or moral concept 'without lengthy parenthesis'.[83] De Pauw made a similar and harsher
observation. Not only were the Indians unable to formulate metaphysical concepts in their own languages, but they could not count
above three – a distant echo of Aristotle's claims that the Thracians
could not count above four – because they had no conceptual understanding of any larger number; and, because of these defects, they
'had never learnt to speak a European language except poorly'.[84]

Clavigero's reply to De Pauw's critique was twofold. Like most of
his compatriots – like Molina, who complained that the Europeans
had 'written about America and its inhabitants as freely as if they
were writing about the moon'[85] – he noted with some bitterness the
poverty of the information employed by De Pauw, Robertson, and

Buffon, and of the liberties they had taken with it.[86] The claim that Nahuatl lacked any digit beyond three could simply be disposed of as false, and to prove it he listed Nahuatl names for numbers up to forty-eight million.[87] De Pauw's other accusation – that no Indian language possessed any abstract or universal terms – was, however, more serious and could not be dismissed on simple empirical grounds. Although Clavigero does provide an unconvincing lexicon of abstract nouns,[88] it is the case that neither Nahuatl nor any of the other major Amerindian languages, as the missionaries discovered to their cost, possess terms into which Graeco-Roman universals can readily be translated. As the Franciscan Antonio de Zúñiga wrote despairingly to Philip II in 1579, of the Indians of Peru, 'among them there is no language sufficient to explain the mysteries of our Holy Catholic Faith, because all lack the vocabulary'.[89]

De Pauw's critique, however, was not merely an observation on the Indians' intellectual inadequacies, but, far more interestingly and, from Clavigero's point of view more damagingly, an attempt to locate the development of language in the same history as the development of agriculture. The ability to perceive the existence of universals is commensurate with the ability to exploit the resources of nature: both depend upon the capacity, which is only ever latent in the child, to perceive the potential in what is presently actual. The Amerindians, barely articulate and still very largely reliant upon hunting and gathering, therefore, 'have not yet left their infancy'.[90] Clavigero's response to this claim constituted a refutation of De Pauw's major premise – and the premise upon which every such evaluation of Amerindian culture was based – that abstract thought is one of the necessary conditions of civility. Abstract and universal terms were not, Clavigero argued, a crucial component of every civil discourse. They were merely the preference, and hence the invention, of one culture and one language, Greek. The Roman moralists, in particular Cicero, had had, he claimed, great difficulty in finding suitable expressions to match the Greek ones. Nor had modern philosophers done much better, being compelled in their search for an adequate metaphysical vocabulary to resort 'to the barbarous language of the schools'.[91] The scholastics had devised their own language to solve the problem; but theirs was a barbarous jargon precisely because it relied heavily upon neologisms and transliterations taken from a single, and alien, ancient culture. As the Mexicans, unlike the Romans, had had no occasion to come into contact with that culture or to acquire its mental habits, they did not 'occupy themselves with the study of metaphysics', and hence had no need to construct vocabularies for that purpose. On this account, the urge to speculate is not a natural disposition which all civil communities acquire. It is merely the preference of one particular culture and its heirs. The origins of Aztec civilization were, as Clavigero had shown, *sui generis*. There was, therefore, every reason to suppose that it would be distinct also as regards its intellectual concerns. Language, argued Clavigero, was functional. It had therefore to be judged according to the role it was required to fulfil. Buffon's argument that Amerindian languages were 'barbarous' because they were lexically poor [92] (though that, of course, was a rather different point which Clavigero does not address) and impossible for any European to pronounce was merely circular. To an Indian, French would sound just as barbarous. [93]

In Clavigero's account the arts and the sciences, like language itself, are neither the outcome of an innate human disposition, as they were for Aristotle, nor the creations of first legislators as they were for Cicero. They are a response to necessity. By the 1780s this view had, of course, become a commonplace, but Clavigero's source, the source of so much that is original in the *Storia antica*, is Montesquieu.

The savage Americans, Montesquieu had noted, are indolent and have few arts and sciences because nature provides them with all that they require. European inventiveness derived from the needs that the harshness of their environment had generated. [94] If the Indians did not possess certain arts and sciences that were common in Europe, this was likely to be owing, not to the absence of some innate disposition, but to the fact that for reasons that were intrinsic to their own culture they had not felt the need to develop them. 'Invention and progress in the arts', Clavigero concluded, 'for the most part owe more to luck, necessity, and avarice than they do to ingenuity'. [95] A culture such as the Aztec that lacked, among other things, iron and plaster, that knew nothing of navigation and could not construct either an arch or a dome (although Clavigero does attempt, somewhat unconvincingly, to show that the Aztecs had built arches[96]) was not therefore one of the mentally defective. It was a culture that had simply never experienced the *need* for such things. The sciences, in particular, are the product of a distinctively European concern with property. For, as De Pauw's critic, the Benedictine Antoine Joseph Pernety, had pointed out, 'if the Americans are ignorant of geometry this is because they know nothing of 'thine' and 'mine' and thus have no need to place markers to establish the limits of their usurpations'. [97] Long and hazardous journeys overseas, claimed Clavigero, with an even keener political intent, were the consequence of 'avarice and ambition' rather than the need to know. Since the Aztecs had never been driven by the need 'to usurp the states legitimately possessed by other nations nor to transport from distant countries precious metals of which they had no need',[98] they had never troubled to invent the compass.

In Clavigero's account, the Indians had all the technological knowledge that their culture required. What they did not have, they did not have either because like iron, horses, or cattle it was not naturally available, or because they had no need for it. Such arts and sciences as navigation, plaster-making, or arch building were only responses to necessity or, like the Greek taste for metaphysical speculation, the concern of a particular culture.

The basic instruments of communication between men, which alone made any kind of social life possible, were, however, clearly neither local nor normative. The two most powerful of Buffon's and De Pauw's criticisms – that the Indians possessed no written script and no money – could not, therefore, be so easily dismissed as merely the product of cultural ethnocentrism.

The Indians, Buffon had claimed, had no understanding of science because they lacked 'the art of transmitting by enduring signs the fact of the present to posterity'.[99] For Buffon, and for most Europeans, the sciences were cumulative enterprises which could only be registered over time by some mode of notation. The oral transmission of information, though a recognized procedure, was, in a culture so wholly convinced of the primacy of the text, necessarily regarded as of only very restricted communicative value. Oral societies were merely bands and limited in their extent by the range of the human voice. With no adequate means of registering knowledge, they were also virtually history-less, each generation being condemned to reinvent what the previous one had achieved.

Clavigero also shared these general assumptions. Where he differed sharply with Buffon, De Pauw, and Robertson was in the claim that the Aztecs were in effect an oral society.[100] The mistake the Europeans had made was to assume that writing must take one of the two forms – alphabetical or hieroglyphic (a category which included Chinese) – in which it appeared in the Old World. As the surviving Mexican pictorial manuscripts bore no resemblance to either of these, Buffon had come to the conclusion that the Mexican glyphs were only stylized pictures. And if they were that, then they were also very poorly executed. The Indians, concluded De Pauw, were not only ignorant of a proper script, they were also incompetent draftsmen. As a mode of communication then, their picture books failed dismally by any criterion.[101]

But, replied Clavigero, Mexican picture writing is indeed a script, for it consists of signs, as does any other representational system. The point he is making here is the same as the one he had made about the lexical quality of Amerindian languages. A culture, such as the

Aztec which had had no contact with the Old World, could not be expected to develop any of the forms employed in the Old World. If the Europeans had taken the trouble – and had they had the necessary expertise – to study the Mexican glyphs they would have seen that some of these stylized drawings were being employed, 'as our astronomers and algebraists do', to depict clusters of phonemes (it is worth observing that, so far as this goes, Clavigero was probably right) and that they therefore qualified as a true sign system.[102]

This insistence on the precise, and unique, cultural context for every human activity also underlies Clavigero's refutation of De Pauw's claim that the Indians possessed no money.[103] The accusation was a crucial one since it, like the claim that the Indians possessed no script, was an attempt to demonstrate that they lacked the necessary ability for communication, the *consortium* on which true civility is based. Money is vital for trade, and trade, in the discourse of eighteenth-century political economy with which Clavigero, through Carli and his own reading of Montesquieu, was thoroughly conversant, was not merely a necessary component of any civil society, since every commercial society must, of necessity, be a property-owning one; it was also, for Montesquieu and his heirs, the prime means of ensuring that men are civil towards one another. 'It is almost a general rule', Montesquieu had written in a much-quoted passage, 'that wherever the ways of men are gentle there is commerce, wherever there is commerce the ways of men are gentle'.[104] The presence of money became then a tangible sign of civilization. If you were washed ashore on some deserted coast, said Clavigero, quoting Montesquieu again, and were to discover a coin in the sand, you would be in no doubt that you had reached some civilized land.[105]

A lack of money thus clearly indicated a lack of civility. With this general principle, Clavigero was perfectly willing to agree. But just as Buffon and De Pauw had failed to understand the nature of the Aztec script, so they had failed to understand the nature of their money. For money shared another feature in common with language: it too constituted a sign system. The Aztecs did not use the kind of coinage Europeans could readily identify as 'money', but this did not mean they did not possess a token of exchange. 'If by money', wrote Clavigero, 'we understand, as Montesquieu defines it, a sign representing value', then the Indians did possess a 'money'. This was the cacao bean, which seems to have been used by the Indians of central Mexico as a means of balancing a transaction and as an important item in gift exchanges. Not only, Clavigero went on, was the cacao bean an adequate sign, it was far better suited to this role than the oxen and sheep that the Romans had once used for this purpose; for a bean, unlike either an ox or a sheep, fulfilled another essential criterion of the signifier – that it should be durable.[106]

Once the Aztec world had been correctly understood, not by reference to some European or Asian culture with which it had had no contact, and whose patterns it could not be expected to replicate, but in terms of its own cultural norms, then it would be clear that the Amerindians had indeed possessed the principal instruments of true civilization. In Clavigero's reconstruction Aztec culture thus became a noble, if also, as the ancient Greeks and Romans had been, a frequently savage civilization. He made no effort to disguise what he saw as its real barbarity. He does not deny that the Aztecs were cannibals (although it is unlikely that they were) or that they sacrificed men to their gods, although he went to some lengths, as Bartolomé de Las Casas had done before him, to point out that nearly every race, including the Iberians, had done likewise.[107] But if the Aztecs were no more advanced than, say, the Phoenicians or the Celts, their world was also not so very far behind that of the Greeks and the Romans. Clavigero had thus demonstrated, as Sigüenza y Góngora had tried to before him, that the *criollo* population might look with pride upon 'these antiquities of ours', as a pre-history rich in political symbolism, which, because of its origins, owed nothing to any European culture, least of all to that of Spain.

The *Storia antica* was not intended to further political discontent in Mexico. Its purpose was simply, as Clavigero's preface had made clear, to enhance the *criollos'* sense of pride in their *patria*, and the targets of the dissertations had been French, Scotch, and Dutch, not Spanish. But Clavigero's claim that white Mexicans could afford to take pride in the Indian past, that this past was both wholly independent from that of Europe, and in certain respects, superior to the culture of the Greeks and Romans, inevitably widened the cultural gap between *criollo* and Spaniard. The *Storia antica*, as Juan Pablo Viscardo phrased it, 'will be a great help both for destroying the prejudices which still reign about the New World in general, and for making the most interesting part of it, which is certainly New Spain, better known'.[108] Clavigero may never have spoken of emancipation, but, as we shall see in the next chapter, the project on which he was engaged helped to make emancipation imaginable.

5

Old Constitutions and Ancient Indian Empires: Juan Pablo Viscardo and the Languages of Revolution in Spanish America

i

Clavigero's historical reconstructions were not, as he frequently stressed, offered as arguments for political emancipation from Spain. Like most of the Jesuit exiles in Italy his loyalties were often painfully divided. He was committed to the notion of the Spanish Empire as a federation of quasi-autonomous kingdoms with only one king; and whenever any part of that federation was threatened from outside, as it was, for instance, by English and French commercial practices, he, like his fellows, reverted to speaking of Spain as 'our nation'.[1] But his *patria* was Mexico, a culturally independent community, as he had laboured so hard to demonstrate. In the closing years of the eighteenth century it was still possible, in particular from a sufficient distance, to maintain this distinction between cultural and political independence. But for those of a younger generation, and closer to the political process, the distinction was far less obvious. When the Venezuelan revolutionary, Francisco de Miranda, acquired a copy of the *Storia* in 1789 he read it as a potentially revolutionary document, a call to an explicitly political self-awareness, if not exactly a call to arms.[2]

The most powerful, certainly the most widely diffused, attempt to employ the cultural autonomy Clavigero had advocated to sustain an argument for political emancipation was the work of another Jesuit exile, the Peruvian Juan Pablo Viscardo. Viscardo, who was born in Arequipa in 1748 and died in London in 1798, wrote a number of political tracts, most of them intended to persuade the British prime minister, William Pitt, to provide military and diplomatic support for the liberation of South America.[3] Two, however, were meant to reach wider audiences. One, *La Paix et le bonheur du siècle prochain* (The Peace and the Happiness of the Next Century) of 1797, which was largely concerned with the pacifying potential of commerce, and the role which an independent America would have to play in a new world economy, was never published. The other, the famous *Carta dirijida a los Españoles-Americanos* (Letter Addressed to the Spanish Americans) was written in 1792, and printed by Miranda in London in 1801, together with a French translation.

The *Carta* was the first unequivocal argument for full independence from Spain. It was an attempt, as popularist revolutionary ideologies tend to be, to legitimate armed insurrection by appeal to a meaningful past. The New World Viscardo argued, as Clavigero had done, was a separate cultural entity from the Old. 'The New World is our *patria*', he wrote, 'its history is our history and it is in the light of that history that we must examine our present situation'. America had been the creation of a group of men who had self-knowingly renounced 'the civil protection that was due to them' from their native land, and who had endured unimaginable suffering in order to create a new society. Their part in this enterprise had conferred upon them a right, not, Viscardo acknowledged, 'the most just', but nevertheless 'better than that by which the Goths of Spain had to seize the fruits of their valour and of their labour'.[4]

Like most eighteenth-century *criollos* Viscardo believed that the conquistadores had been party to a contract with the crown, by the terms of which they, like all feudal vassals, had been granted, in exchange for the military aid (*auxilium*) they had provided entirely at their own cost, noble status and the right to high executive office (*consilium*). The Castilian crown's supposed violation of this agreement became one of the central props of the revolutionaries' claims against the mother country.[5] Even Bolívar, for whom, as we shall see, neither the language used by Viscardo nor the political suppositions on which it drew had much direct appeal, referred to the contract (though significantly cast into quite another idiom) as 'our social contract'.[6] The most complete, certainly the most powerfully argued account of what he referred to as 'our Magna Charta' is, however, to be found in the writings of Servando Teresa de Mier (1763–1827), the first historian of the Mexican Insurgency, and the representative for Nueva Granada at the first Congreso Constituyente of Mexico in 1822. There had never, of course, been any formal agreement between the crown and its subjects. But as Mier, the Venezuelan revolutionary Manuel Palacio Fajardo,[7] and such highly influential foreign observers as Humboldt argued, its existence could be inferred from the fact that since 1524, the year in which the Council of the Indies was created, the Americas had constituted a kingdom, in Mier's words, 'united to Castile, but preserving its own law codes, representative assembly [*Cortes*], congress, and principle of sovereignty'.[8] By the terms of this covenant Spain and America were 'integral parts of the Monarchy, subject to the King, but equal among themselves and without dependence or subordination of the one to the other'.[9] The Americas were not colonies 'in the sense that word has for modern Europe',[10] as, for instance, the English possessions in North America had been, but separate kingdoms, independent crucially as regarded their economic affairs but 'dependent upon the Spanish crown only in so far as the Spaniards themselves are dependent'.[11] It was for this reason that, with the exception of Navarre (and he might have added Naples) which was also a fully independent kingdom within the 'Empire', the Americas had been ruled by viceroys, men who possessed all the functional attributes of the King himself, and who Mier described as 'the fullest denomination of the *alter ego*'.[12] Into this picture of an ancient constitutional agreement between the Spanish crown and its (racially) Spanish subjects, Mier attempted to insert a number of similar claims on behalf of the Indians, the mestizos, and even the Blacks. All of these, he argued, had by reason of their birth acquired (if they were free men, and Mier was in no doubt about the injustice of slavery) the same rights as the descendants of the white settlers. But the Indians, whose cultural identity he, like Clavigero, was eager to appropriate, were in a special position as the only true possessors of *natural* rights in the Americas. Ferdinand and Isabella, he claimed, leaning heavily on an ambiguously worded passage in Solórzano y Pereyra's *Política indiana* (see p. 33 above),[13] had established a separate contract with the Indians which had granted them full political autonomy, with respect to everything except the propagation of the Gospel.[14] Ever since the reign of Philip II, however, this contract, which Mier, by transferring the supposed political status of the Indians to the *criollos*, was able to describe as 'the charter of our rights', had been buried beneath 'the refuse...of despotism and Machiavellianism'.[15] It was now, he claimed, the task of the revolutionaries to assume the contractual rights and (Mier was an attentive reader of Filangieri) the consequent duties that a succession of tyrannical monarchs had denied both Indian and *criollo* alike.

Had Mier's 'charter' possessed any legal validity, then the 'Americans', like the subjects of the crowns of Aragon or Naples, would indeed have had 'a natural right to hold appointments of honour and profit'. But as the Americas, though subject (as were the Italian possessions and Aragon) to a separate royal council, were in the anomalous position of being a corporate part of the Kingdom of Castile, the 'Magna Charta' was little more than a convenient legal fiction.

For Viscardo, however, whose version of this same *thèse nobiliaire* owed more to 'that sublime genius'[16] Montesquieu than it did to the legalism of Solórzano, the exact juridical status of the Indies was largely irrelevant. Every government, he argued, no matter what its nature, or its historical origins, depends for its legitimacy upon the consent of the governed. Any other arrangement is tyranny. 'If the government is to be above the duties it owes to the nation', he asked, 'what difference is there between it [the nation] and a pack of animals?'[17] The early Spanish monarchs, he claimed with suitable historical vagueness, had observed these ill-defined 'duties' towards their subjects, but, by the sixteenth century, they had succeeded in undermining both the tradition of representation, and those institutions of the kingdom that had sustained it, so that 'not even the shadow of the ancient *Cortes* existed any longer'.[18] The just, contractual monarchy had thus transformed itself into a despotate in which government by consent was effectively replaced by the arbitrary will of the King and his ministers. Laws, which in the old monarchy had been made in the interest of the people, now reflected merely the will of the King, and 'any law that is opposed to the universal good of those for whom it is made, is an act of tyranny, and to demand that it be observed is to force [the people] into slavery'.[19] The Castilian monarchs had effectively destroyed 'the natural, civil, and religious rights of the Spaniards', and by so doing had forfeited their claims to their vassals' loyalty.

By denying their vassals both executive office and the ancient right to interpret the law, the Habsburgs had 'overstepped the limits of the ancient constitutions of Castile and Aragon'. The consequence of this violation of ancient rights had been the immediate and precipitous decline of Spain, which had demonstrated in stark economic terms that 'absolute power, which is always allied with arbitrary power, is the ruin of states'.[20] For, Viscardo claimed, it had been precisely that 'noble spirit of liberty', which only contractual societies are able to encourage, that had provided the 'energy that had made our ancestors carry out such great enterprises'. 'Under the funereal shadow of a double despotism [the civil and the religious]', he wrote in *La Paix et le bonheur du siècle prochain*,

> general prosperity, glory, and the ancient and magnificent national character [of Castile], was eclipsed to the point where it had left no trace behind it except in memory. The power and the brilliance of the Spanish Monarchy diminished in proportion to the debasement to which it had subjected the people who had sustained it...[Liberty] is the greatest resource of a nation; once that resource has been destroyed, all will crumble away.

It was this same liberty that, in Viscardo's own time, had given the English, the Dutch, and the North Americans their ascendancy, they, in his account, being the only European powers that had managed—both, significantly, by force—to preserve their ancient liberties. 'The true history of the lethargy of Spain', he concluded,

> since the discovery of the treasures of the New World, is nothing other than [the history of] its enslavement. Just as the modern history of England, Holland and, more recently and even more remarkably, that of the United States of America, is nothing other than that of the creative and vivifying power of Liberty.[21]

None of the subjects of the Castilian crown had suffered more, and more continuously, from the desecration of their ancient privileges than those Viscardo was now calling 'Spanish Americans'. The Castilian crown's perfidy had begun with Columbus, whose descendants had been deprived of the rights which the discoverer had, in this case quite literally, contracted with the crown; and it had continued in Viscardo's own day with the betrayal and gruesome execution of the rebel Inca, Tupac Amarú. 'For three centuries', he wrote in a phrase that was to be echoed by later Insurgents, 'our history can be expressed by four words: *ingratitude, injustice, servitude,* and *desolation*'.[22]

But, oppressed though they were, the Spanish Americans were now the sole bearers of the Iberian contractual tradition—all vestige of which had finally been eradicated in the mother country by the Napoleonic invasion. The time, claimed Viscardo, was now ripe to revive an old legacy of resistance. In 1520, the communes of the cities of Castile had risen against Charles V in response to the earliest Habsburg attempt to override local privilege. The *comuneros* had taken up arms in protest against Charles V's attempt to force the *Cortes* to provide extra revenue to help pay for his coronation as Holy Roman Emperor. But their grievances against the crown had been based on a long-standing resentment against Charles's foreign courtiers, persistent attempts to undermine the authority of the *Cortes*, and the not unjustified belief that the wealth of Castile was being used to sustain other Habsburg possessions. The revolt of the *comuneros*, although it had achieved little in the long run, nevertheless remained part of the mythology of resistance to royal absolutism. The *comuneros* had risen first, claimed Viscardo, 'for fear that the wealth of Spain would pass to another country, although one that belonged to the same crown'. 'What difference', he then asked, 'is there between that situation in which the Spaniards then momentarily found themselves and the one in which we have been for three centuries?' 'Deprived', he continued, 'of all the advantages of government, we have experienced only the most horrible disorders and greatest vices'.[23] Spanish rule was, as Clavigero had hinted, now largely indistinguishable from that of the hated Turk.

Whatever motives of 'persuasion, prudence, or irony' had compelled Montesquieu to declare that despotism could not exist under Christian rule, a reading of the *tableau du despotisme*, provided in *De l'esprit des lois*, would make it clear that in fact the 'Christian government in America' (in particular when applied to the Indians) met all the necessary conditions of an oriental despotate.[24]

Rebellion against such a government was clearly legitimate, and in 1781 a predominantly anti-fiscal uprising in Nueva Granada had revived the name *comuneros* together with many of the more radical demands of the sixteenth-century rebels.[25] It, too, had been defeated. But since, or so Viscardo informed the British government, 'one of the remarkable characteristics of this insurrection was the hatred [of the rebels] for the European Spaniards', for having obliged them 'to suffer the humiliations and the pains which they themselves had inflicted upon the poor Indian',[26] it had struck 'the first sparks of indignation'[27] which would finally put an end to Spanish sovereignty in America. Similarly Mier and even Bolívar, in search of legitimating analogues for their own revolutionary ambitions, referred to the *comunero* uprising of 1781 as the beginning of the struggle for independence.

Much of this sounds not unlike the claims of any early-modern – that is to say pre-revolutionary – European revolt. The crown has violated its historical and inviolable contract with its subjects by depriving them of their 'natural' rights. It is, therefore, the crown, or its agents, that are the destroyers of order. The rebels are not, in the sense the term came to be used after 1789, 'revolutionaries', since they are not asking for any radical change in the structure of the society to which they belong. They are merely seeking the restitution of the status quo; theirs is a 'revolution' in the earliest, most literal, sense of the term. There were also obvious similarities between Viscardo's arguments and those used by the men of 1776, and, like all the advocates of independence for Latin America, he was very conscious of the lessons to be learnt from the North-American experience, even if his persistent attempts to secure British military support prevented him from pressing them too far.

ii

But the context and the language of Viscardo's claims differed from those of previous European resistance theorists in two crucial respects. The first is obvious. America is another place. For the Castilian *comuneros*, despite the claims of the junta of Tordesillas to exercise sovereign power in Charles V's absence, independence had been unthinkable. But for the Spanish Americans, it was not merely thinkable it was inescapable. Viewed from a sufficient distance, it could plausibly be said, as one apologist claimed, that the earliest attempts to create independent kingdoms in America, those by the Pizarro brothers in Peru and by Hernán Cortés's son Martín in Mexico,[28] had demonstrated that 'the project of the independence of America...had been born with the Conquest'.[29] All colonies must eventually become independent, just as all children must eventually become adults. Over the space of nearly three hundred years, time and distance had now made the Spanish Americans 'conscious of being a different people'. 'Nature', wrote Viscardo,

> has separated us from Spain by immense seas. A son who found himself at a similar distance from his father would be, without any doubt, a madman if, in the conduct of his smallest interest, he always waited upon the decision of his father.[30]

Had the Spaniards had the political intelligence to emulate the ancient Greeks, each of whose colonies had been, he claimed in *La Paix et le bonheur du siècle prochain*, like 'a favoured child...but also an emancipated child over which [the metropolis] attempted to retain no authority, nor to exercise any direct jurisdiction...[then] a new Europe would have flourished in the western hemisphere'.[31] But they had not. Instead, for three hundred years, they had subjected America to 'the tyrannical tutelage of the so-called metropolis', until it had become 'nothing other than an immense prison for all its inhabitants, which only the agents of despotism are at liberty to enter or to leave'.[32] Culturally and politically, emancipation was now the only way for the *criollos* to fulfil what Viscardo described as the 'inescapable obligation to preserve the natural rights bequeathed to us by our forefathers', so that 'the theatre of their glory' should not be reduced to 'miserable slavery'.[33]

'Emancipation' was what Viscardo demanded, a word that suggested a release from both slavery and parental restraint. In most previous claims against the tyranny of the crown there had been, as in the *Representación* made to Charles III by Mexico City in 1771 (see p. 103), a distinct, if by now slightly overclouded image of the concept of *Magna Hispaniae*, a federation of quasi-autonomous states, all of whose citizens would enjoy equal rights with all the others. When Charles III attempted to introduce a system to allow *criollos* to hold office – which Viscardo contemptuously dismissed as 'the ridiculous system of *union* and *equality* with our masters and tyrants' – he was, in part at least, meeting the *criollos* on their own theoretical ground.[34] But for Viscardo, as for most *criollos*, that ground had dropped away. Three hundred years was too long to wait for 'union and equality'. Like Montesquieu, he distrusted large scattered states.

No government so remote as the Spanish could provide 'the advantages that every man has a right to expect from any society of which he is a member'.[35] Universalism could only ever be a mask for tyranny; for the inconsistent, usually incompetent rule of a distant monarch. The rulers of Rome and Castile, he argued, by claiming that the benefits of the New World belonged to them alone had destroyed where they might have built. Universalism was at an end. 'All must now', he demanded, 'be returned to whom it belongs, and America belongs to its inhabitants as much as Spain, Italy, and Portugal belong to theirs'.[36]

Men for Viscardo were, furthermore, citizens – a word that he uses constantly, but that had no place in the vocabulary of the earlier *criollo* idealogues. And citizens had claims upon the community that went beyond the right to simple protection, which is all the Spanish crown could offer – and then only uncertainly, its large navy having been more often used, as Viscardo noted with bitterness, to restrict American commerce than to shield the Americans from foreign invasion.

Together with the right to representation, and to equality before the law, citizens had the right to free trade. Echoing both Montesquieu and Raynal, Viscardo argued that commerce was now, for all 'the enlightened nations', to be regarded as 'the true measure of power',[37] and since commerce involved exchange, and exchange required communication, commerce, which in Montesquieu's famous phrase 'made men gentle', was also the sole guarantee of a future peace. For this reason it was crucial that the goods of the whole world should be both the property of those who produced them (otherwise they would possess nothing with which to trade) and accessible, through trade, to all. The occupation, such as that practised by Spain, by one nation of another's resources, effectively deprived that nation of its ability to enter the world market, and by extension its right to take its place among 'the enlightened nations of the world'. But the Spanish crown was not enlightened, and, even after the Bourbon succession, continued to conceive power merely in terms of its capacity to coerce its subjects and destroy those it took to be its enemies. Wealth, as 'the profound Smith' had noted,[38] was, in Spain, taken to be simply a question of the accumulation of precious metals, which as an economic belief had rather less to recommend it than the Tartar assumption that cattle were adequate 'instruments of commerce'. In its search for gold the Castilian crown, driven 'by a spirit of unbridled cupidity raised above all the other passions', had first excluded from the Americas not only all foreigners 'but even Spaniards from the kingdoms of Aragon and Navarre',[39] and had then imposed upon the colonies a Castilian monopoly that had prevented them from trading among themselves. This, which like all monopolies, deprived 'fellow citizens and brothers'[40] of their natural rights of communication, was among the most damaging of the instruments of despotism. Since monopolies, in Adam Smith's words, 'derange more or less the natural distribution of the stock of society' and, in colonies, clearly run counter to the interest of the colonists, they can only ever be maintained through Draconian legislation, of precisely the type that had determined the relationship between Spanish America and her 'mother country'.[41] The entire history of Spanish commercial policy in the Americas had, complained Viscardo, been that of 'a government that is contemptuous of its own true interests, which are those of its people, to the point where it is affronted by the prosperity of others as if it were a personal calamity'.[42]

The rights of all citizens could be summarized as 'Liberty, property, individual security'.[43] These were what Viscardo called 'the first element of social union which is the first cause of all government'. Instead of fostering such political virtues among its people, the Spaniards had, in the Americas, taken their destruction to be its 'direct objective'.[44] What Viscardo was claiming – and it is a claim to which Bolívar was to give even greater force – is that Spain had, in effect, prevented the *criollos* from ever creating a civil society, or from developing the kind of political culture that might be capable of sustaining such a society.

iii

The second difference that separates Viscardo and his fellow 'Spanish Americans' from any European rebel or, indeed, from the North-American rebels was the inescapable presence of large indigenous populations. As we have seen, by the end of the eighteenth century in the two most powerful viceroyalties, Mexico and Peru, the histories of the Aztec and Inca empires had become a source of pride and of a precarious cultural nationalism for the *criollo* population, as well as, when required, a mirror for their own political fate. For the champions of Spanish-American independence and, more generally, for Enlightenment Europeans, the Inca Empire – Tawantinsuyu, to give it its Indian name – had acquired by the mid-eighteenth century many of the virtues of the ancient republics. Unlike the Aztecs who, even in Clavigero's account, seemed little more than a heroic warrior nation with a number of distinctively un-civil customs, the Incas could easily be cast as the nearly living representatives of the civic values of republican Athens and Rome, 'true disciples of Plato and

Xenophon'. Their kings combined, as Francesco Algarotti, political economist and author of 'Newtonianism for Ladies', put it, 'the divinity of oriental monarchs with the popularity of the European'. Like Romulus and Lycurgus, the Inca rulers had – or so it was popularly supposed – created a nation by force of language, not arms, and founded an empire by exporting a civilization.[45] They had known, as Algarotti tellingly remarks, 'how to increase the number of [their people's] needs, in order to keep them subject'.[46] Natural wisdom, enthused the great French economist François Quesnay, had led them to create an agricultural system 'so in accordance with nature itself that it surpasses all the speculations of the philosophers', and a society that, like the physiocratic France of his imagination, had 'no idlers, paupers, thieves, beggars [for] the natural law had dictated the laws of the state, and it had been allowed to regulate the *rights* and *duties* of the sovereign and of his subjects'.[47]

For Viscardo, as for Clavigero, appropriation of the supposed social and political virtues of the glorious Indian past was made possible by the claim that the final destruction of the great Amerindian empires had been the work not of the conquistadores, whose ultimate ambition had been to create a single nation of Spaniards and Indians, but of the viceregal administration and of the *audiencia*, that 'Gothic tribunal presided over by European judges', as William Walton called it.[48] For just as the crown had consistently violated its contract with the settlers and their descendants, so too had it violated its contracts with the indigenes. 'That ferocious hypocrite' the viceroy Francisco de Toledo, argued Viscardo – skipping over most of the details of the Conquest – by treacherously executing the last Inca, Tupac Amarú in 1571, had violated the contract made between the first settlers of Peru and the Inca's subjects.[49] It was the agents of the Spanish crown, the hated *corregidores* in particular, who having first usurped the positions rightfully occupied by *criollos*, had then devised the 'horrors and the violence...for the desolation and the particular ruin of the unfortunate Indians and mestizos'.[50] But of their shared grievances the *criollos* and the Indians would, so Viscardo believed, be able to agree upon a shared political objective. 'Let us', he declared, 'rediscover America for all our brothers, the inhabitants of this earth, from which the most insane ingratitude, injustice, and avarice has exiled us. The reward will be no less for them than it will be for us'.[51]

This ambition to unite *criollo* and Indian political objectives was not so illusory as it might seem. Indians and mestizos were fully capable of exploiting the language of European contractualism for their own ends, and of locating their own political activities within the context of the wider Spanish world. Rebellions by Whites and rebellions by Indians frequently made similar demands couched in identical terms. The leaders of the 'Inca' revolt of 1750, for instance, said they had taken up arms 'for God and our honour...as other nations have done to restore their kingdoms, as Portugal did and the Kingdom of the Two Sicilies'.[52] Viscardo himself had begun his career as a political agitator by attempting to secure British aid for the revolt–'if', he said, 'one can call it that'[53]–of the self-proclaimed descendant of the last Inca, José Gabriel Tupac Amarú in 1781; a revolt that had promised to 'extinguish the *corregidores* in the public interest'[54] and to abolish all taxes and internal customs dues – promises that lay far closer to *criollo* economic interests than they did to Indian ones. Despite, therefore, the fact that its leader was an Indian, whose ambition might reasonably have been supposed to be the re-creation of Tawantinsuyu, the uprising had attracted wide-spread *criollo* support,[55] and when Tupac Amarú was executed in 1781 in the *plaza major* in Cuzco with a brutality that foreshadowed that of the royalist armies to follow, it marked for Viscardo, and for many like-minded Peruvian *criollos*, not the end, but the beginning of a joint *criollo*-Indian struggle against the crown. 'The great public events of the last twenty-five years', he told the British government, referring to Tupac Amarú's execution and to the French Revolution, 'have prepared the spirit of the Spanish Americans to distrust the councils of their government, and to familiarize themselves with ideas of independence'.[56] For some of the Indians themselves, however, the Tupac Amarú revolt had been part of a more enduring indigenous resistance movement which lived in expectation of the resuscitation of the last Inca, the 'Inkarri', and the end of white rule in the Andes. The conflation of such purely Indian objectives with those of other, principally white, insurgents, remained a feature of South-American populism from the revolts of the late nineteenth century through to the activities of the *Tupamaros* of the 1960s and possibly to the *Sendero luminoso* of today.[57]

For the revolutionaries of the early nineteenth century, however, the Indian masses were not merely the heirs of now-vanished vir-tuous *respublicae*, they were also potential allies in a struggle against what men like Viscardo had largely persuaded themselves was a common enemy. When what Mier described as 'the Machiavellian laws' of the Spanish, which had created a rigid social hierarchy out of the huge variety of racial mixtures – White, Indian, Black, mestizo, *pardo*, and the various combinations that made up the *castas* – were finally overthrown, all the American racial groups would unite to form a single nation.[58] The *comuneros* of Nueva Granada had enlisted Indians and *castas* into their armies and employed the image of the politically deprived, cruelly mistreated Indian as a metaphor for their own condition. 'The greatest cause for horror', insisted the piece of *comunero* doggerel known as 'Our Decree' (*nuestra cédula*),

> In all these deeds of tyranny
> Was to see how, filled with villainy,
> They treated the poor Indians with such rigour,
> That, under the guise of their protector,
> They destroyed them with cruel treachery.[59]

This, and the demands made by the rebels for the reduction in Indian tribute to four pesos per Indian per year because of their 'most deplorable and miserable condition',[60] demonstrated, in Viscardo's opinion, 'the real and solid concern for them' shared by all *criollos*. He argued that it was simply false to claim, as so many of the European opponents of Independence had done, that the fact of the racial divisions within all the Spanish-American colonies, whereby the 'Americans' 'do not form a single people but many united, or rather divided, peoples',[61] would lead to anarchy and civil war once the restraining presence of the monarchy was removed. Far from being mere collectivities with no common bond, the societies in America were 'more tightly bound by sociability than are many of the provinces in some of the monarchies of Europe'.[62] The Indians, he somewhat optimistically informed John Udney, the English consul in Livorno, now reserved all their loathing for the 'European Spaniards'. The *criollos*, he said, offering the glossiest picture possible,

> far from being abhorred were respected and even loved by many of the Indians who called them *Viracocha*, the name of their Inca god. Born among the Indians, suckled by their women, speaking their language, familiar with their customs, and born on the same soil for two and a half centuries, they have become almost the same race.[63]

After the Conquest, 'a new order of things, a new system of society began in the New World. The heirs to the rights, or at least to the pretensions of the conquistadores had neither the avarice nor the ferocity of their fathers'. Two hundred and sixty years had passed since the Conquest, something that foreign authors chose to forget, years that had made the *criollos* 'more docile before the voice of nature and of religion'. The greater part of them now had Indian mothers and many, therefore, Indian relatives 'who were distinguished in their own country, and with whom they [the *criollos*] had, since infancy, established ties of understanding and friendship'.[64]

Viscardo's indigenism was not entirely fantastic. Since the middle of the seventeenth century the *criollo* élite of the Andean highlands, close to where Viscardo had been born, had attempted to appropriate the Inca past as a means of expressing their cultural and, finally, political independence from Castile. In the eighteenth century, the marqueses de Valle Umbroso claimed to be descendants of the Incas, assumed the Quechua title *apu* ('lord'), wore Inca clothing, and spoke Quechua.[65] Nor was it entirely absurd, particulary from a remote place of exile, to believe that, with British assistance, these nativized *criollos* might now be in a position to revive the project first mooted in a widely diffused form by Garcilaso de la Vega, and repeated by Clavigero, of a single state composed of American-born Whites, mestizos, and Indians. In Viscardo's projection this state would be built upon the ruins of the old Indian empires by re-creating the political and social values of pre-Habsburg Spain, values that, with a certain amount of manipulation, could also be made compatible with those of the ancient Indian world.

Independence for Viscardo was to be an act of restoration, a restoration of the political values of Castile, a restoration of the culture of the ancient Indian world and, in many cases, a restoration of the Garcilassan project for a multi-racial community. But, since no restoration ever wholly duplicates the *status quo ante*, under-pinning these objectives was a recognizably more modern idiom: the language of citizenship and of 'ancient liberty', the claim, if only implicit, that the community is made and defended by its members, that even monarchies must be societies of citizens, not just of men. This aspect of Viscardo's thought seems, however, to have gone unnoticed by those who read him. The language of citizenship, and with it, of course, of the republicanism that Viscardo was eager to avoid, would be appropriated only some years later, as we shall see in the next chapter, by Simón Bolívar.

Viscardo's *Carta* provided a rough ideological charter for many of the subsequent Spanish-American revolutionary movements. The declared political objectives of the Mexican Insurgency of 1810, for instance, were, at least in its initial stages, based upon just such a fusion of restored ancient Iberian and ancient Indian political values. In 1813 in the village of Chilpancingo, the rebel leader José Maria Morelos told his followers (in a speech written for him by the *criollo* lawyer Carlos Maria Bustamante),

we are about to re-establish the Mexican Empire, improving its government. Spirits of Moctecuzoma, Cacamatzin, Cuahatomoit-ozin, Xicontecalt [he continued], 12 August 1521 [the day that Mexico City finally fell to Cortés] is now followed by 12 September 1813. On that day the chains of our serfdom were fastened in

Mexico; on this, in the happy village of Chilpancingo, they are broken forever.[66]

'Improving its government', however, would mean greatly restructuring it. For underneath whatever still remained of the recoverable Indian past – of Clavigero's Indian past – Bustamante, and those like him, were determined to discover a paradigm of ancient republican virtue, of the kind that Quesnay, Carli, and Algarotti had found in the Inca. For Bustamante, indeed, the link between Indian past and Spanish-American present became a specific longing for union. The Texcocans, who had always been seen as the most nearly European, the most truly virtuous of the Mexican tribes, were for him simply 'our fathers'. 'You', he told the republican government of Mexico in 1826, 'are the worthy successors in the government of he who was the adornment of the human race (Nezahualcoyotl, the quasi-legendary, fifteenth-century poet-king of Texcoco). Enter into his same virtues'.[67]

iv

In all of this, however, there was a distinct and wilful vagueness as to what form the new governments of America would take. All of the Insurgents used the language of republicanism, in that all envisaged government by consent of the majority and equality for all before the law. Most, Viscardo and Miranda in particular, recognized that independent America would be predominantly a commercial society, which by the late eighteenth century had come to be seen as a further characteristic of the *respublica*. Only Mier, perhaps, was explicitly and consistently committed to republicanism as a form of government. But even Mier, who once declared that 'there is no better academy for the people than a revolution';[68] who was convinced that a republican form of government, 'beneath which the rest of South and of North America is constituted', was the one best suited to the the nascent Mexican state;[69] and who was prepared to endorse even the Terror[70] as preferable to a return to absolute monarchy, rejected any notion of absolute popular sovereignty. Rousseau's 'General Will' – of which Bolívar was to make so much – was, he warned the Congreso Constituyente of Mexico, 'a sofism, a mere sofism'.[71] Augustín de Iturbide's brief reign as 'Emperor of Mexico' in the first months of 1822 had fully demonstrated that 'the people have always been the victims of turbulent demagogues'. Only the legislative will was of consequence and that should always be restricted to a small number of those who know how to exercise it.[72]

Most Spanish Americans, however, like Viscardo and Miranda,

favoured a moderate form of ancient constitutionalism to even the most restricted sovereignty of the legislative – let alone the general – will. Somewhat disingenuously, perhaps, Viscardo told Pitt that the peoples of South America all possessed an unbounded enthusiasm for monarchy. The British must send a prince to the Pacific, for only a prince could 'fulfil the heroic role of the liberator'. And once liberation had been gained, such a prince would be able to 'elevate on the most solid basis of a universal oath two great thrones on the two parts of America'.[73]

The most explicit proposal – in that it had both military backing and something resembling a written constitution – for a form of government that would harmonize Iberian and Indian political cultures was that of Francisco de Miranda, 'that Don Quixote', as Napoleon once called him,[74] to re-establish the Inca Empire, but now so restructured that it should resemble, as far as was possible, the British constitution. Miranda's *Projet de constitution pour les colonies hispano-américaines* is only a fragment, and a fragment, furthermore, whose purpose seems to have been to persuade William Pitt of the commercial and political advantages to be had from backing Spanish-American independence.[75] But it combines in one bizarre mixture all the diverse, culturally incompatible elements on which the inchoate aspirations of the *criollo* élite then rested. The government of the new empire of 'Spanish America' – which was to reach from the Mosquito coast to southern Argentina – was, like all modern European governments, to be mixed 'and similar to that of Great Britain'. 'It will be composed', Miranda assured Pitt, who seems to have feared that Miranda intended to establish a Jacobin republic in Venezuela, 'of an executive power represented by an Inca with the title of emperor. This will be hereditary'.[76] Beneath the new Inca – who was, though Miranda does not say so, to be *criollo* rather than Amerindian – there came an upper chamber composed of 'senators or *caciques* nominated by the Inca'. These would be appointed for life but they would not be hereditary positions for Miranda, like Bolívar, realized the impossibility of creating a new American aristocracy. Beneath the upper there was to be, as in England, a second chamber, entitled, appropriately, the 'Chamber of the *Comuneros*', modelled in part on the *cabildos* of Castile, in part on the House of Commons. Its members were to be chosen from among the citizens by election, and their term of office was to be limited to five years. Standing guard over the legislature (but apparently not over the executive) were two censors, also elected by 'the citizens', whose role was to supervise the 'customs of the senators', the morals of the young, and the wisdom of the legislators. There was also to be an aedile, whose function was to promote the

131

construction of public monuments and to organize public festivals 'in order to edify the mass of the people', and two quaestores to watch over the treasury.[77] Miranda's *Projet* combines what, in the context of any imaginable political reality, would have been a wholly inappropriate Indian monarch with a 'mixed constitution' which, while borrowing features of the British constitution, makes explicit reference to the ancient constitutions of Castile and Aragon. Supporting the whole shaky edifice were three institutions – the aedile, the censors, and the quaestores – endowed with near absolute powers and taken from the political arrangements of the Athenian and Roman republics. It was, as Bolívar was later to say of projects like it, a chimera, a beast with too many heads and no body. Miranda may have abandoned his sketch for a constitution because he, too, realized how little chance it had of seeming intelligible to those who were expected to help make it a reality. But it is, in many respects, a programmatic embodiment – if such a thing can be said to possess a body – of the languages used, in differing registers, by Viscardo, Mier, Miranda, by Hidalgo and Morelos, languages that, immediately compelling though they were, could not be made lastingly appealing to any of the main social groups that stood to gain by independence. As we shall see in the next chapter, the only language that could, if only for a limited period, be made to sustain an entire political programme could do so only at the cost of abandoning very nearly all of the historical structure on which first a distinct *criollo* political identity, and then the ideology of the Insurgency, had been grounded.

6

The End of Empire:
Simón Bolívar and the Liberal Republic

i

Miranda's military failure in July 1812 marked the effective end, at least for South America, of any further monarchical projects, and of any further attempts to use the Indian to whip the Spaniard. Simón Bolívar, *El Libertador*, the leader, political and intellectual, of the southern Independence movements, had begun his career as one of Miranda's generals. We do not know how far, at that time, he shared Miranda's fantasy of a new, partially republicanized, partially Anglicized, Inca state. But by the time he came to draft his first sustained political thesis in 1815 – the famous *Jamaica Letter* – he had already, under the influence of a miscellany of Enlightenment authors,[1] come to believe that any future independent Spanish-America state had to be a very different kind of political society to anything that then existed in Europe or had ever existed in America itself. The *Jamaica Letter*, which is addressed to an unknown English champion of Spanish-American Independence, is, significantly, unconcerned with the problem of how to legitimate the *criollo* rebellion. By 1815 the persistent obstinacy of the Spanish crown – in the face of what the *criollos*, and increasingly the other European states, regarded as reasonable demands for economic and political autonomy – had already established their cause as a just one. Nothing is so odious as rebellion, declared the liberal pamphleteer, the Abbé Dominique Dufour De Pradt, former archbishop of Mechlin and Napoleonic ambassador, 'but if America is rebellious we must declare this a rebellion against the nature that tells man not to suffer himself to be crushed and ruined'.[2] The ferocity of the royalist armies after 1815 had also banished any further thought of reconciliation. 'Success', Bolívar wrote in 1815,

> will crown our efforts, because the destiny of America has been established irrevocably. The cord that bound us to Spain has been severed. Opinion was its sole strength; because of it the parts of

that immense monarchy were joined. But what once united us now separates us. The hatred the Peninsula now inspires in us is greater than the seas that separate us from her. It would be easier to unite the two continents than to reconcile the spirits of these two lands.[3]

What Bolívar faced was the need not to legitimate rebellion, but to imagine the communities that could be created out of the inevitable collapse of the Spanish Empire.

As we have seen, the first revolutionary activities in Spanish America, those of Hidalgo and Morelos and those of Miranda, had been conducted in the name of ancient Iberian constitutions mapped onto a vision of restored and revised Indian empires. For Bolívar, however, there could be no instructive or useful Iberian or American past. Time, he claimed after a vision he had standing on the top of mount Chimborazo in 1823, contained the 'secrets of the heavens' and could reveal 'the image of the physical universe and of the Moral universe'.[4] But despite this omniscience, time, for Bolívar, was constituted by a history that was only ever remote, exemplary, a history that, in Luís Castro's words, was conceived as the 'impartial witness of men and of their actions'.[5] It was the history of humanity, primarily Roman and Greek, sometimes English and French, but hardly ever Spanish, never American. He told the Congress of Angostura in 1819, which was to draft the constitution for the ill-fated union of Gran Colombia, that 'history will serve us as a guide in this course' but then went on to sketch out the political history of the great *respublicae* of Europe: Athens, Sparta, Thebes, Rome, and England.[6] There was no other choice. From the republican, liberal perspective, which Bolívar had adopted, America had no usable history: it was separated both culturally and geographically from Europe and inhabited by peoples whose cultural inheritance had been obliterated by conquest. As he told his English correspondent in the *Jamaica Letter*–a passage he repeated four years later in the *Discurso de Angostura*–the Spanish Americans 'hardly preserve a vestige of what was in other times, and...on the other hand, are neither Indians nor Europeans, but a sort of middle species between the legitimate owners of this land and the Spanish usurpers'.[7] Caught between two cultures and separated from both by time, race, and now political aspiration, it was simply impossible, he concluded at Angostura, for the Spanish Americans, themselves so recently conceived, 'to decide with any certainty to which family of the human race we belong'.[8]

The ancient Castilian and Aragonese constitutions could no longer be made politically compelling, because Spanish America, frag-

6.   Pedro José Figueroa, *Simón Bolívar, Liberator and Father of the Nation,* 1819, Quinta de Bolívar, Colombia.

mented and culturally uncertain, was not Spain,[9] not even, any more, a part of *Magnae Hispaniae*, that legal fiction which had sustained the Empire for so long. To revive those constitutions meant also to revive the notion of monarchy which, Bolívar was certain, was now neither possible nor desirable. Monarchies, since they operated through coercion, patronage, and the manipulation of personal interests, required long periods of gestation if they were going to survive, something that Iturbide's short-lived Mexican Empire in 1822 had usefully demonstrated. None of the new Bourbon monarchies that Chateaubriand had suggested for South America could survive with the support of only an imagined aristocracy: 'miserable', in Bolívar's words, 'and covered in poverty and ignorance'.[10] A re-constituted monarchism, however liberal, was, as most of the ideologues of the Independence movement recognized, a cultural impossibility in societies whose integrity as communities very largely depended upon their separation from a monarchical regime.[11] As a later historian of the emancipation of Peru bluntly phrased it, Peru 'became free because its sons became men, and its men became republicans because the republic is the truth'.[12]

By the end of the eighteenth century monarchies had also come to be seen as the natural enemies of liberty. Although Bolívar made the now-familiar point that the virtuous and prosperous *respublica* could be created under a monarchy, it could only be the kind of monarchy that England was (and Spain after 1812 had hoped to become), and this required a far higher degree of political awareness from its citizens than the absolutist monarchies of Europe had ever been able to provide. 'Some people believe', wrote Bolívar to Fernando Peñalver in 1822, 'that it is very easy to put a crown on one's head and that everyone will then adore you. But I believe that the days of the monarchies are past, and that they will not return until the corruption of men finally comes to drown their love of liberty'.[13] As this last remark makes clear, the new American states could be constituted only as formal republics, because, in the political and moral void that had inevitably followed the collapse of Spanish rule, only a republic could provide the kind of society that might be resistant to what contemporaries termed corruption – the unrestrained pursuit of personal interests – and to which free men might, therefore, willingly give their allegiance. In republics it is the laws – not the will of the prince – that are sovereign. Without sovereign laws, said Bolívar, repeating what had become a Rousseauian commonplace, 'society is a confusion, an abyss, it is individual conflict between man and man, between one body and another'.[14] 'Give us', he cried to the members of the Convención de Ocaña with

characteristic excitement, 'inexorable laws!'[15] Such laws had always
to reflect not particular interests, as they did in monarchies, but the
'General Will' of the people.[16] They were the legislative expression
of that 'public opinion', which, as he told the Consejo de Estado at
Angostura in 1817, 'is the foremost of all powers'.[17] Bolívar was
adamant, throughout his life, that if only the gothic, tyrannical,
legislative inheritance of Spain could be undone, a 'true liberal
constitution'–which, as he told the Congreso Constituyente de
Bolivia in 1826, 'lies in the codes of the civil and criminal laws'[18]–
could be created in Spanish America.

There was also a sense in which republics were not just the only
truly free, but also the only truly modern society, which in the
language with which Bolívar was familiar meant the only societies in
which commerce was fully possible. It had, after all, been in defence
of their–as they saw them–'natural' rights to belong to a world-
wide commercial society that the merchant oligarchy of Caracas had
first declared their independence from Spain in 1811. Bolívar has
little to say about the virtues of the commercial society. His own
vision of the ideal republic was, like Rousseau's own, in many
important respects seemingly hostile to it. But whatever views he
may have had on the merits of capital accumulation and the civilizing
effect of exchange, he firmly believed that the archaic feudal order
represented by the Spanish Monarchy, that 'old serpent', that 'unnatural step-mother', was past: that modern Europe–Holland,
England, and post-revolutionary France–was 'civilized, commercial, and a lover of liberty'.[19] For this reason, Venezuela, the new and
virtuous republic that Bolívar had imagined into existence in February 1819, in a town that was barely more than a village on the banks
of the Orinoco, was to dispense with the accumulated feudal liberties–monarchical concessions, not rights–with which Spaniards,
sixteenth and eighteenth-century *comuneros*, had sought to limit the
power of their kings. 'By constituting itself as a democratic republic', he said at Angostura, '[Venezuela] did away with monarchy,
with distinctions [between men], with the nobility, with local liberties [*fueros*] and privileges'. In their place came those generalized
political *iura* that the French Revolution had conferred upon all men
in virtue of their status as citizens: 'the rights of man, the freedom to
work, to think, to speak, and to write'.[20]

For the republican the appeal to the image of mythologized Indian
empires was even more disturbing than the appeal to ancient
constitutions. All the attempts to revive the political symbolism of
the Indian world had, for obvious reasons, been confined to Mexico
and Peru. But, as Bolívar was aware, they could be generalized, as
they had been by both Viscardo and Miranda, into a murky

popularizing demand for freedom in the name not of 'the people'— which meant for Bolívar very much what it had meant for Montesquieu, 'the citizens', i.e., those with sufficient standing and education to engage fully in the political process—but of the oppressed Indian and mestizo masses. What the Tupac Amarú uprising and the Hidalgo-Morelos revolt symbolized to the leaders of the Independence movement in South America was an irrational patriotism based upon an illusory and—for Bolívar had no love of noble savages—savage past, fuelled by a radical, and fanatical Catholicism. In practice it had also led to what Bolívar most feared: anarchy followed by eventual tyranny. It is true that for him the Indian could, as he could for Jefferson, become the image of a natural and unconquerable love of liberty and, even by continued resistance to European conquest, evidence that 'a people that loves independence will in the end achieve it'. But it is significant that the Indian Bolívar chose to praise was the nomadic Araucan of Chile, whose societies he characterized as 'fierce republics' precisely because they had never been fully 'reduced' by the Spaniards, rather than the Aztec or the Inca.[21] But no Indian could be the bearer of a significant past or the spiritual leader, however fictionalized, of a republican future. For the most part Bolívar thought of the Indians, when at all, as an essentially docile unpoliticizable mass that 'wishes only for rest and solitude'.[22] To his English correspondent's fascination with the liberating potential of the Mexican deity Quetzalcoatl, he replied that 'this personage is hardly known to the Mexican people'. 'Our Mexicans', he continued, 'would not follow the gentle Quetzalcoatl, even if he appeared to them in the most recognizable and favourable form, for they profess a religion that is more intolerant and exclusive than [all] the others'. Morelos, he claimed, had been lucky 'in seizing the opportunity, with the greatest firmness, by proclaiming the famous Virgin of Guadalupe...which has produced a vehement fervour for the sacred cause of liberty'. But it was clear that when that cause had triumphed the image of both Quetzalcoatl and the Virgin of Guadalupe, and with them the entire clerical presence in Spanish America, should be returned to the darkness of unreason from whence they had come.

Isolated simultaneously from an Iberian or any specifically American past, Bolívar, and those who reasoned like him, were compelled to create nations *ex nihilo*. And imagined states, the creatures always of 'the spirit of party and innovative opinions', as one hostile observer noted in 1820, will always, where the only option is a realism without a reality, be in danger of becoming 'a world that is in some way fantastic, that can be made to justify the past and authorize the hopes of the future'.[23] Bolívar was, and was conscious of being, in the full Machiavellian sense of the phrase, a 'new prince'.[24] In this respect, as both he and a large number of contemporary observers noted, Spanish America was very different from British North America. The American constitution had established a revolutionary society without Jacobinism, without the Terror, without – although Bolívar admired his military skills – Napoleon.[25] Who could resist, asked Bolívar persistently and at very considerable length, the virtues of that constitution, 'an intelligent government that at once links individual rights with general rights, to make up the common will, the Supreme Law of the General Will'.[26] But the first Venezuelan constitution, that of the cruelly but aptly named *República boba*, had been very largely a copy of the constitution of the United States, and it had resulted in chaos, indecision, and an almost immediate collapse of the political will.[27] Bolívar was, sometimes painfully, aware that British and Spanish America were culturally very distinct places. In making their revolution and in drafting their constitution the English-Americans had been able to draw on a long 'liberal' political tradition; a republicanism that, in Montesquieu's celebrated phrase, 'hides under a monarchy', as well as on an extensive experience of self-government and the political virtue which that brought with it. The South Americans, by contrast, had never had any direct experience of government, having been denied even what Bolívar referred to as 'active tyranny' – the right, granted for instance to the Chinese mandarinate, to participate in despotism – and consequently possessed no independent political identity. 'Strangers', Bolívar told the *Royal Gazette* of Kingston Jamaica in 1815, 'to the world of politics and separated from all that might, to some degree, exercise our intelligence...[we] South Americans have passed down the centuries like blindmen between colours'.[28] Preserved in a 'sort of permanent infancy with regard to public transaction',[29] they had been made into quiescent observers, the mere consumers of goods manufactured by others from the raw materials that they produced. 'Our fortune', he told the future legislators of Gran Colombia, 'is to have always been purely passive, our political existence has always been null...we were abstracted, absent from the universe'.[30] As De Pradt repeatedly told a sympathetic but puzzled European audience, all the Spanish Americans had ever known was 'three hundred years of Spanish despotism and monarchy'[31] from which they had been ruthlessly excluded, and the legacy of a conservative, fanatical, and superstitious clergy – 'the support and companion of despotism'[32] – whose hold over the people was unshakable. What Bolívar called 'the habit of obedience, a commerce of interests and of religion ...in short, all our hopes'[33] had been dictated by Spain and had, in consequence, made his fellow countrymen indifferent to 'honour and national prosperity'. They had, therefore, none of the political equipment, above all none of 'the political virtues that characterize the true republican',[34] none of the consciousness of 'being present in the universe' or, less grandiloquently, of being members of a self-governing community, which were required to transform the remains of the Spanish Empire into a federation of quasi-autonomous states on the North-American model. Any attempt to export the constitution of that 'Republic of Saints' to Venezuela would, he observed drily, be like trying to export the English constitution to Spain.[35]

The belief that their past history, and their spiritual (and hence ideological) enslavement to regal Catholicism made the Spanish Americans unsuited for representative, federal government was also shared by the North Americans; which, in part, explains their reluctance to provide the revolutionaries with the military support they requested.[36] 'Our southern brethren', priest-ridden and unlettered, wrote Jefferson to Lafayette in 1817, were not yet ready for independence, for 'ignorance and bigotry, like other inanities, are incapable of self-government'. If suddenly released from the Spanish yoke they would, he warned, 'fall under military despotism and become the murderous tools of the ambitions of their respective Bonapartes'.[37] It was a vision of the future that, in the last decade of his life, would haunt Bolívar also.

ii

The political vision that Bolívar attempted to substitute for the ideological postures provided by revived Indian empires and the ancient constitutions of Castile and Aragon was neither wholly original nor, since he lived a long active life and, as a student of Montesquieu, was always quick to adapt to changing circumstances, always consistent. But then Bolívar was not, nor claimed to be, a theoretician. The description that De Pradt gave of him, drafting constitutions with one hand, a sword in the other, catches the proper image of the man. But despite the highly pragmatic, sometimes erratic, nature of his theoretical utterances he remained, throughout his career, committed not merely to the solution of a contingent political circumstance—the need for American emancipation—but also to the vision of a new kind of society: 'the liberal nation' (la nación liberal) that was to be composed of a new kind of man: 'the good citizen' (el buen ciudadano)—a title that he claimed on more than one occasion, he would far rather have conferred upon him than 'The Liberator'.[38]

It is reasonable to assume that when Bolívar used the term 'liberal' he understood it as it was used by the framers of the Constitution of Cadiz, the 'Sacred Codex' of 1812, which very largely reflected the French constitution of 1792. That, too, although it frequently resorted to contractualist vocabularies, was a programme of reform that would transform a king whose rule, in both theory and legal practice, had been absolute, and in the eyes of many arbitrary, into a constitutional ruler beholden to 'the nation'. This would be the sole sovereign body in the state, and bound to 'protect by just and wise laws civil liberty, property, and all the other legitimate rights of those individuals of whom it is composed'.[39]

In common with this image of post-Napoleonic Spain, Bolívar's 'liberal nation' was to be a community of free men – unlike Washington, Bolívar freed his own slaves – ruled by laws that guaranteed equality before the law for all men and that were responsive to, if not dictated directly by, public opinion; a community, furthermore, that would be directed towards the happiness of its members and would be free from 'factions and parties'. In this generalized account, at least, Bolívar was echoing contemporary European liberal views: those of De Pradt, 'the sublime philosopher', who played Aristotle to his Alexander;[40] of Jeremy Bentham, who offered his services as the ideal legislator for the new state; and of Benjamin Constant, who, unperceptively perhaps, thought of Bolívar – as, seemingly, did Marx – as little more than a petty Napoleon. Where Bolívar differed radically from European liberals was in his insistence that the 'liberal nation' could be achieved only in the shape (or something very close to it) of the 'Virtuous Republic of Rousseau's *Du contrat social*.

Although the 'Sacred Codex' owed its existence to models taken from the French Revolution, and although otherwise conservative European liberals, like De Pradt, could speak of the emancipation of Spanish America as 'the most extensive result of that grand act that, in its totality, we call the [French] Revolution',[41] Bolívar, like Miranda before him, and in common with most of the other Spanish-American revolutionary leaders, looked upon the French Revolution as an example of that dismal trajectory from anarchy to despotism that was the inevitable outcome of an undirected uprising of the demos. Yet despite Bolívar's evident fear of what the revolution had produced – the 'seas of terror and anarchy' sufficient to overwhelm his own, all too fragile, ship of state – the political vision, to which all his writings refer, of the republic made virtuous by the legislative supremacy of the general will, owed everything to those

141

intellectual heroes of the Revolution: Montesquieu and Rousseau. The notion of liberty with which the 'liberal nation' was to operate was, for Bolívar, far closer to the concept of the liberty enjoyed within the ancient republics of Athens and Rome (with which he frequently compared the nascent Republic of Gran Colombia) than it was to what was described as 'modern liberty' by Benjamin Constant (whose 'The Liberty of the Ancients compared with that of the Moderns' of 1819 provides the best possible account of nineteenth-century liberal objectives). As we shall see, this disjuncture between ancient and modern liberty was to have far-reaching, and ultimately disastrous consequences.

The republic that Bolívar described in the *Discurso de Angostura*, and continued to advocate for the remainder of his political career, was very largely inspired by Rousseau's *Du contrat social*. Although Bolívar rarely mentions Rousseau by name, he left his copy of the *contrat* (which had once belonged to Napoleon – an irony that Bolívar was perhaps by 1830 in no position to appreciate) to the University of Caracas as his *testament politique*, and the language he used was clearly more heavily indebted to Rousseau than to any other single author. Rousseau himself may indeed have intended his work to be a strategy – to use Judith Shklar's telling phrase – 'to induce moral recognition in the reader', a 'yardstick' by which to test existing institutions.[42] Bolívar, however, in common with most of Rousseau's readers took it to be a programme; and, as Luís Castro has observed, his entire political project can be viewed as a flawed, and ultimately impossible attempt to transform Book III of *Du contrat social* into a constitution.[43] Rousseau's republic was, of course, modelled after the republics of the ancient world. What such societies had called 'liberty' was not the freedom of their members to pursue their own personal goals unhindered but, as Constant phrased it, 'the sharing of social power among the citizens of the same fatherland'.[44] They were wholly public communities in which the individual had no rights as an individual – despite Rousseau's own claims that every individual's *interests* would be represented – nor any socially significant identity, except *as* a citizen. Private, and what later came to be called civil, liberty was exchanged for what was held to be the superior good of political liberty. To be 'free' in such a society, and thus to be happy, was to be a fully committed member of the *respublica* which is why Rousseau could speak, in seemingly paradoxical terms, of men being 'forced to be free',[45] forced to be happy. Some of the forcing was to be achieved by demonstrating that it was in the ultimate interest of every individual that his *utilitas singlorum* should coincide in every crucial respect with that of the commonwealth (the *utilitas publica*).[46] Another more sinister, because less

142

explicit device which is set out at length in the final book of *Du contrat social* is the notion, which Rousseau took from Livy, and more directly from Machiavelli, of a 'civil religion',[47] a 'purely civil profession of faith whose articles are established by the Sovereign, not precisely, as the dogmas of a Religion are, but as sentiments of sociability without which it is impossible to be either a good Citizen or a faithful subject'.[48] Such 'sentiments of sociability' would serve to 'bind the hearts of the Citizens to the State' by making the individual's private beliefs seem identical with the political beliefs of the community. Where powerful spiritual religions were already established, as was the case in Europe, then these should be made to enforce the social doctrines of the state.

Where liberalism differed from this eighteenth-century classical republicanism – or to put it in the language used by Constant – where ancient differs from modern liberty – is over the nature of liberty itself. The virtues of the classical *respublica* lay in the cohesion of the citizen body, in that all men share the same set of political objectives, and all men participate in the political process. This guaranteed their political liberty, and in the kind of worlds they, in historical reality, were – small, belligerent, agricultural – political liberty afforded far greater pleasure than the 'peaceful enjoyment and private independence' that constituted liberty for the moderns. 'Consequently', wrote Constant, 'the ancients were ready to make many a sacrifice to preserve their political rights and their share in the administration of the state. Everybody feeling with pride that his suffrage was worthy, found in his awareness of his personal importance a great compensation'.[49] In the nineteenth-century liberal state, however, only a small fraction of the community could have access to direct political authority. The majority of the citizens were free. There were to be no parties, no factions, because although men might disagree about means, they could never do so about ends. And the opinion of all was to be respected. The liberal state provided its citizens not merely with *political* liberty, but also with civil liberty. Modern liberal societies that are large, commercial, and predominantly passive offered their members far less opportunity for direct participation in the state. Hence the importance of representation. As John Dunn has argued,

> since modern liberty differs so much from its ancient predecessor it requires a very different political articulation. In the ancient model, the more the citizens consecrated their time and energies to the exercise of their political rights, the freer they believed themselves to be. But in a modern society, the more time that the exercise of their political rights leaves available for the pursuit of

143

their private interests, the more precious for its citizens will their liberty be. Hence the necessity for the representative system.[50]

In the classical republic – and in Bolívar's plans for Gran Colombia – there was no system of representation precisely because in those republics government was shared by *all* the citizens. But in the liberal state political liberty could be sustained only by, to quote Constant again, 'an organization by means of which a nation charges a few individuals to do what it cannot or does not wish to do herself'.[51] This clearly reduced the individual's capacity for action, but it greatly enhanced his scope for personal happiness. Liberals are free because they choose to be, not because they are forced. They are free to act, but they are also free from external restraint; free, above all, from the obligation to participate in the management of the state. As Constant put it, *modern* liberty is individual liberty, which no man can be asked to sacrifice in the interests of his political liberty. It is, in terms of Isaiah Berlin's now classic dichotomy, 'negative' liberty. In Rousseau's republic, by contrast, as in Robespierre's, there could be no place for the private individual, since it is political virtue – the life of Ciceronian *negotium* – that constitutes the sole political good of the community.[52] In the liberal society a space has been made for what, in Rousseau's terms, comes close to being a contradiction, the 'private citizen'. Men may be men *and* citizens. They have access, if only as voters, to a political life, which they are denied under a monarchy, but they are not wholly subject to it. And, as Constant's own distinction between civil and political liberty suggests, the liberal republic, unlike its classical or Rousseauian predecessor, allows for – is in some sense responsible for the creation of – a visible, if still sometimes unfocused, distinction between 'civil society' and the state. The concept of an autonomous civil society was first made explicit and given theoretical definition by Hegel. But the notion of a domain in which men, and women, could share an existence as social beings independently of their roles as citizens is apparent in Locke and, more significantly for our present purposes, in Montesquieu. It is, of course, identical with what Constant calls civil liberty and it depends for its existence, and survival, upon a mutually, if also tacitly, agreed set of culturally enforced conventions. It depends, as Constant realized, but Bolívar perhaps did not, upon the existence of a compelling *image* of a community in which each private individual would wish to place his trust, trust being, as we have seen (chapter 3) the principal *vinculum societatis*, to use Locke's term. 'I do not', the argument within the head of every civil being should run, 'steal my neighbours' goods, abduct his wife, or insult his or her person, not because I am forcefully prevented from doing so (or even because my religious beliefs forbid me to so do) but because I belong to a *patria* where such things are not done'. By the end of the eighteenth century such *patriae* had come to be referred to as 'civilizations'.

iii

Bolívar's conception of the ideal republic is problematic, and ultimately muddled. In a number of crucial respects it is far closer to this liberal model than it is to that of Rousseau. He was, after all, as much indebted to De Pradt as he was to Rousseau and far closer to him in time. And, as De Pradt himself had pointed out, the distances that separated him from the pre-revolutionary world in which Raynal, and thus also Rousseau, had lived had now become immeasurable.[53] These distances were crucial. They had demonstrated, by the collapse of most of the objectives of the revolution of 1789 into either anarchy or tyranny, how fragile the virtuous republic could be, how difficult it might be in practice to force men to be consistently free. As early as 1812, despite his anger at the 'philanthropic maxims' of those 'liberal governments' which, in his view, had brought down the first Venezuelan republic, Bolívar had sworn himself 'always loyal to the liberal system' and for the most part he remained so.[54]

His conviction that the most effective contemporary model of modern liberty, the United States, was grounded in a tradition that, if not unique, was certainly not available to Spanish Americans would suggest that no form of liberalism was likely to be capable of filling the political vacuum created by the collapse of the Spanish Monarchy – as indeed proved to be the case. Yet Bolívar also saw liberalism – and continued to do so even after the experiences of 1812 – as an obvious part of another concept he had adapted from Montesquieu, the 'spirit of the age'. Liberty, he argued – modern liberty – would ultimately prove to be as irresistible as it was desirable. Even 'the apathetic Spaniards', he wrote, the last guardians of ancient despotism, 'who have also launched themselves into the political whirlwind, have made their own ephemeral attempts at Liberty'.[55] He rarely spoke, directly at least, of compelling persons to be free, and, at least until the dictatorship of 1828–30, when he attempted to re-impose Catholicism as a state religion, and to prevent Benthamite utilitarianism being taught in the universities, he never discussed the possibility of a 'civil religion'. For most of his life, in common with all liberals, he regarded religion as a purely personal matter that 'governs man in the household, in his study, within himself' and which was consequently a matter of individual choice, since only the individual 'had the right to examine his own conscience'. The laws of the republic, which a civil religion was intended to reinforce, 'by contrast regard only the surface of things; they rule only outside the citizen's home'.[56] When religion confused these two domains and sought to involve itself in the affairs of the state, as regal Catholicism had so often done, it became odious.

In many of Bolívar's political writings there are also frequent references to civil society and to civilization as prior to and distinct from the state, even if he sometimes felt that civilization, like liberty, could be too rich a food for the average American digestion.[57] In the end, as he told the Congreso Constituyente de Bolivia in the very last attempt to salvage what Luís Castro has nicely called his 'Enlightened Illusion', personal security and civil liberty guaranteed by a just administration were all that were required of a liberal state. 'The political organization matters little', he concluded, 'so long as the civil is perfect'.[58]

But despite his recognition of the need for some of the features of modernism, Bolívar's republic was predominantly, and crucially when it came to describing the non-institutional compulsions that were to hold it finally together, ancient. He does not seem to have been aware, at least not until the very end of his life when his political views degenerated into apocalyptic despair, that there were serious contradictions in such a merger of ancient with, at least some, modern notions of liberty. To Benjamin Constant, however, he seemed precisely to be an old-fashioned tyrant, masquerading as the champion of liberty while claiming absolute power in the name of universal sovereignty and drafting constitutions that were 'very defective and very little in accord with true liberty'.[59] However 'liberal' its institutional restraints might be, the end of the state was, Bolívar declared, in conventional Rousseauian terms, 'to make men good, and consequently happy'.[60] He had, too, a characteristically Rousseauian respect for the person of the 'Great Legislator', that 'superior intelligence who lives all of man's passions without experiencing any of them'.[61] All history, he told Guillermo White in 1820, had demonstrated that 'men submit only to the degree that an able legislator demands of them...If there is any just violence it is that which is employed in making men good and, in consequence, free'.[62] Every constituted society, he repeated at Angostura, must be one that is capable of producing 'the greatest possible sum of happiness, the greatest social security, and the highest degree of political stability'. And the only state capable of achieving such an end was the classical republic. This meant a political society in which 'men are born with equal rights to all the goods of society'[63] and all men are equal before the law that is always and everywhere sovereign. It meant also (despite Bolívar's plans for a hereditary senate modelled on the House of Lords,[64] a hereditary vice-presidency, and a president with the right to choose his successor[65]) a state in which every man is capable of becoming a citizen, a full, active, and educated member of the community. In republics, Bolívar argued with Rousseau, liberty is not guaranteed by rights nor protected by representative assemblies: it is constituted by virtue. 'Without republican virtue', he wrote, 'there can be no liberty in government'.[66] The republic alone could 'regenerate the character and customs that tyranny and war have bequeathed to us', and the republic alone was able to create in the rain forests 'a Moral Power, taken from the depths of antiquity and from those forgotten laws that, at one time, sustained virtue among the ancient Greeks and the Romans'. Even those most cherished instruments of public compliance in the ancient world, the Roman censors, were to be a feature of the new American republic. 'We shall', he told the legislators at Angostura in a passage that, at least as far as the sentiments it expresses, could have been taken directly from the *contrat social*,

> take from Athens the Areopagus and the guardians of customs and the laws, from Rome take the censors and the domestic tribunals, and by making a holy union of all these moral institutions we will revive in the world the idea of a people that is not content to be only free and strong, but also wishes to be virtuous. We will take from Sparta its austere establishments and by creating out of these three streams a fountain of virtue, we will give to our republic a fourth force whose strength will be the childhood and the hearts of men, the public spirit, good customs, and republican morality.[67]

This vision, he assured his listeners, was no mere 'candid delirium' but 'a thought that, perfected by experience and enlightenment, is capable of becoming very effective'.[68] To many, Sparta itself may have seemed little more than 'a chimerical invention', but Lycurgus had, in fact, produced 'real effects', effects that had sustained 'Glory, Virtue, Morality, and, in consequence, natural happiness'.[69]

This passion for the creation of an amalgam that would also be an apotheosis of the republics of the ancient world lay at the base of Bolívar's persistent objection to North-American federalism. For not merely was such a system unsuitable to 'our nascent state'[70] and unworkable by politically untutored minds – minds requiring forceful instruction in the meaning of liberty – it was also the case that the federalists had sought to replace the ideal of the small virtuous republic, dreamed up, in Madison's words, 'by theoretic politicians', with the image of a large, commercial republic based upon democratic representation, in the erroneous belief that if men could be made equal in their political rights they would also be 'perfectly assimilated in their opinions and their passions'.[71]

Bolívar's own image of the virtuous republic of Venezuela turned out, however, to be all too chimerical an invention. The failure of the various social and political groups of which Gran Colombia was so loosely composed to cohere, finally compelled Bolívar, in 1828, to create a dictatorship in the hope of preserving the republic from 'faction and party' and from final disintegration. That Bolívar's dream which, as he said himself, 'always ended in the abyss'[72] should have led to the replacement of civilian by military rule was hardly surprising; and Bolívar, a soldier who had not failed to understand the lesson of Napoleon's career (or Washington's), had always been aware of what might happen. The virtuous republic that was to have been Gran Colombia had been based on the assumption that such a society *could* be created out of a world that was racially heterogeneous,[73] economically divided, and – with the exception of the *criollo* élite – had no previous sense of itself as a community of any kind. De Pradt fully understood the significance of this. On 1 January 1829, in the *Courrier français*, Constant had chosen Bolívar, and in particular the Bolivarian dictatorship, as an example of the tyrannous excesses that could be committed in the name of ancient liberty. On 12 January, De Pradt published a lengthy reply to Constant's critique. There were, he told his adversary ('whose great fame daunts me'), 'regular' or 'formed' societies, and 'irregular or 'unformed' ones: societies where there was a substantial and resilient civilization, and societies where there was none and where the 'passions become laws in order to destroy the law'. The European states clearly belonged to the first of these categories, America to the second, and Bolívar's conduct could be judged only according to 'the assembly of circumstances in which he finds himself'. Paris might appear to those who lived in it to be 'the whole world': but it was clearly not Angostura.

'Sybarites of the civilization of Europe', he wrote,

> preachers of liberty, I would wish to see your tribunals set by the banks of the Orinoco, your benches of senators mingled with a horrible mixture of Blacks, mulattos, plainsmen [*llaneros*], creoles, of men suddenly dragged out of the depths of slavery and barbarity to be transformed into legislators and heads of state! The same blood, the same language, the same customs, a common heritage of grandeur and of talent, an advanced civilization, all these hold together all the several parts of the societies of Europe. In America all is diversity, the principles of division, an absence of civilization. In Europe one plays, in America one must create.

It is a powerful observation, but it is one whose force Bolívar seems never to have fully understood. At one level his failure can, as we have seen, be described as a failure to acknowledge fully his own tacit and faltering recognition that no modern state could adequately be founded upon the principles of ancient liberty. At another it might be characterized as a failure to perceive that, for the would-be creator of new states, the legacies of his two favoured authors, Montesquieu and Rousseau, led to two very different conclusions. Montesquieu also possessed a vision of republican liberty that was as 'ancient' as Rousseau's, in that it, too, was of a society 'moved'[74] by the virtue of its citizens. But Montesquieu's main argument—that all political arrangements must be adapted to the culture and the climate of the communities for which they are intended—showed a sensitivity, as Rousseau's seemingly did not,[75] to the degree to which even the most virtuous of societies depends for its creation and survival upon its prior cultural constitution, upon, in the language of eighteenth-century social theory, *les mœurs* of those persons of whom it is constituted. Montesquieu's was, as Constant put it, 'a less excitable and therefore more observant mind' than those of the champions of ancient republicanism. He might not have conceptualized the ancient-modern distinction quite as Constant would have liked, but he had noticed it.[76] To put it in another language, he was acutely aware of how much the purely ethical 'ought' was dependent upon the cultural 'can'. Montesquieu was also aware, as Judith Shklar has pointed out, that republics were exceptionally fragile precisely because they depended 'on the customs, habits, and attitudes of the citizens far more than on explicit legislation'.[77] Without a powerful structure of such customs, habits, and attitudes—without, that is, a civil society—already in place, it would be impossible to create a new republic, which is, perhaps, why Montesquieu himself never offered any suggestions as to how the modern Lycurgus might go about doing so.

Like every diligent reader of *De l'esprit des lois* (and he cites Montesquieu far more often than he does Rousseau), Bolívar was duly sensitive to the force of ancient custom. Any law code, he warned the legislators at Angostura, must be in accord 'with the religion of its inhabitants, its inclinations, its riches, its size and its commerce, its customs and its habits', and he chided those who thought that 'the blessings from which [the North Americans] benefit are due exclusively to the form of their government and not to the character and the customs of the citizens'.[78] A reading of Montesquieu, he told the delegates at Angostura, would teach them that every constitutional order has to be adapted to the 'customs and habits' of those for whom it is intended. *De l'esprit des lois* was 'the Codex we must consult, not Washington's.[79] And, he told his companion-in-arms General Páez in 1828, at a time when his entire project seemed in danger of disintegration, it had been precisely the tendency of the legislators of Colombia – and by implication himself – to rely 'upon foreign books, entirely alien to our things and our deeds'[80] that had reduced the nascent republic to a condition of near anarchy.

But these were only general admonitions and they are only ever expressed in generalized terms. He never identified what those customs were, because all customs have to be a product not merely of climate and environment but also of a historical process, and, in this case, of precisely that historical process from which, as we have seen, Bolívar most wished to detach his new state. For Rousseau, of course, men were very largely creatures of nature. Their social and political environment made them. They were better in Sparta, or in Alpine villages, better if breast-fed and taken on long country walks. But they were all irreducible individuals capable of being forced to be free in the truly virtuous community, no matter what their customary concerns or the conditions of their past. The 'nation' was distinct from the 'government', but it was always desirable – and clearly possible – 'to form the nation by the government'.[81] Given the constitutions that Rousseau wrote for them, Corsica or Poland could be transformed into true *respublicae*. This, too, was very largely Bolívar's view. But he was also conscious both of the Spanish legacy he was actively fighting for most of his life to overthrow, and of the divided worlds out of which he was struggling to create his 'naciones liberales'. He understood the power of the Church, and of demagogic patriotism. For him the state of nature was a real place, all too often directly encountered by the banks of the Orinoco – and he knew that men were not natural. Most of those with whom he was acquainted, in particular after three hundred years of Spanish rule, had been 'perverted by illusions of error and by noxious incentives'.[82] For such creatures, said Bolívar echoing Rousseau's judgment on the whole of mankind, both civilization and liberty would be difficult foods to digest.[83] Before men could be made into citizens, the legislators at Angostura had first to 'constitute men' out of the former vassals of the Spanish Monarchy. But although Bolívar was insistent both on the unsuitability of the American constitution and on the deleterious effect of colonial rule, he never recognized the full extent of the hold that the accumulated legacy of those 'illusions of error and noxious incentives', real or fictive, had over men's minds; that the 'Blacks, mulattos, plainsmen, creoles' of De Pradt's vivid picture were hardly likely to respond undirected to the call of the 'General Will'. What they required, in addition to the satisfaction of their own immediate interests, was an ideology – something that

Bolívar loathed as much as Napoleon[84]—that might provide the intellectual foundations for a new state. What men like Viscardo had offered his readers, however illusory in fact, had been a vivid, densely narrative past, that, unlike Bolívar's republicanism, could easily be linked to just such an ideology. The *patria* to which Viscardo, Hidalgo, and Morelos had appealed was an imaginary one, but the parts out of which it was composed were real enough. Bolívar's *patria*, on the other hand, was a political ideal, an 'Enlightened Illusion'. 'Enlightened' it clearly was, but the light had had to come wholly from within, generated by a body of texts and sustained by a language that, as De Pradt described it on the eve of the Congress of Panama, was as 'free as its arms; and under the protection of the latter, the former would compel the world to listen to a speech [*langage*] free from all deceit'.[85]

Confronted with a political language and set of political objectives that, as De Pradt enthused, constituted 'not a purely American act, but a human act', and with no specific cultural context in which to situate their liberator's objectives, it is perhaps not surprising that Bolívar's followers, in particular among the 'people' in whose interest he claimed to be fighting, should have made other contexts for him—as the defender of ancient constitutions or, in the terms of one rebel song, nothing less than the champion of the reborn Inca, the 'Inkarri', who would come one day to drive the white man from the Andes.[86]

Criollo patriotism had operated with the notion of a strong central state. The *comuneros* of 1520 had fought one monarch in the name of the representative institutions of the state. So, too, had the '*comuneros*' of 1781. The mythologized Aztec and Inca empires may have been provided with powerful representative bodies, but they were believed to have been highly centralized monarchies. The Insurgents wished simply to transplant one centralized state with another. What De Pradt called 'ambition à la Cromwell'[87] was ultimately not an option for Bolívar as it had been for Iturbide—whatever Santander's and Bolívar's later liberal critics might have said—not only because it required the continuation of the despised monarchical government, but also because such governments involved merely a transfer of power. Mexico in terms of the *Plan de Igulá*, like imperial Brazil, was merely Iberia transplanted. In every case the projected society was intended to be one composed of private individuals, not citizens.

Bolívar's mistake was to have hoped, despite himself, that men could be made into citizens by the force of constitutional arrangements alone. But constitutions (*pace* Rousseau) can be made compelling *only* when some form of civil society is already powerfully present. Hence the elaborate insistence in the Spanish constitution of

1812 on the contractual traditions of late medieval Castile and Aragon, and the attempt to describe 'liberalism' as little more than a revived form of that contractualism. But the men who gathered on the banks of the Orinoco in 1819 had necessarily cut themselves off from any such sources of community image-making. All they had left themselves with was their own self-declared legislative authority. And this, as subsequent events were to demonstrate, was hardly sufficient to construct out of the debris of such a powerful, oppressive, and archaic institution as the Spanish Monarchy, a community in which all men are freely participating members of a single polity. The move that Bolívar's republicanism involved, from the virtuous republic to the near stateless condition of the 'nación liberal', could hardly be achieved without first *creating* a state to replace the one that had been overthrown. For in a condition where all political traditions have either collapsed or have proved to be unacceptable, *only* a state will have the power to generate the conditions for civil society in the first place.

Had Bolívar pursued the logic of his own historical reflections he might have understood this sooner. For, as he told the legislators of Angostura in 1819, the Spanish Empire had collapsed, exactly as the Roman had done, into 'dismemberments' each of which 'then formed an Independent Nation according to its situation and interests'.[88] And, as he recognized, nations formed solely according to situations or interests – the vocabulary is, of course, Montesquieu's – become identity-less entities incapable of constituting themselves as 'civil societies'. It required Charlemagne to rebuild the political society that had once been Rome, and out of it to create the nations of modern Europe. The abstractions that Bolívar urged upon the various representative bodies he advised – liberty, public opinion, virtue, moral power – had no force, not even much imaginative force, outside a powerfully constituted state. And in the absence of both a civil society and a political order it is perhaps only the military that can prevent a return, to use Bolívar's language, to the state of nature.

By 1828 Bolívar himself had come to realize the full force of these observations. Only a dictatorship could save Gran Colombia from dismemberment, and from the anarchy that Bolívar feared perhaps rather more than tyranny. For Constant this move was merely further evidence that some form of despotism was ultimately 'the dismal heritage of oligarchic republics'. Bolívar had abused his privileged position as liberator, but he was also only fulfilling the inescapable political destiny of the type of society he had tried to impose upon his countrymen. America was a large unformed mass with no native political class. Its institutions had, therefore, to be provided with 'greater solidity and energy than other nations judge to be necessary'.[89] The republic could not now survive without coercion, and coercion meant the rule of the military. The emphasis in *Du contrat social* on the role of 'Great Legislators', those 'necessary beings'[90] who were capable by the force of their own vision to create new societies, and the absence of any developed individual political will could always be employed to legitimate the temporary rule of the single individual as the instantiation of the General Will.[91]

But as Bolívar himself had realized even before his own had been established, 'dictatorship is the rock on which republics founder'.[92] In the absence of a powerful central force, power – which Bolívar only ever discussed in terms of his cherished *'poder moral'* – passes to those who have the most effective instruments of coercion. Towards the end of his life, Bolívar understood full well the nature of the dangerous space he had helped to create. He had, after all, always been preoccupied with the problem of permanency, with the paradox that in historical fact, and with the exceptions of Sparta and Venice, only those states where participation, and liberty, were minimal – 'monarchies and aristocracies' – have managed to create 'at once, power, prosperity, and permanence'.[93] He himself never managed to resolve this paradox. At the end he resorted to despair. America, he declared, was 'half a world gone mad'.[94] It was, in what has, sadly, become his most famous utterance, ungovernable, and all 'those who serve a revolution plough the ocean'.

Notes

Introduction

1. For an account of *The Triumph of Spain* see Levey, 1986, pp. 261–3.
2. Botero, 1607, p. 236. See pp. 47–9 below.
3. Spinoza, 1951, p. 344.
4. Eco Haitsma Mulier, 'The language of seventeenth-century republicanism in the United Provinces: Dutch or European?', in Pagden, 1987, pp. 179–95.
5. Quoted in Chabod, 1961, p. 101.
6. Quoted in Pagden, 1986, p. 28.
7. Elliott, 1963, p. 348.
8. See Skinner, 1978, vol. I, pp. 17–18. Gattinara's attempt with the help of the Spanish humanist and imperial apologist Alfonso de Valdés, and of Erasmus, to prepare a new edition of *De Monarchia* came, however, to nothing largely because Erasmus, who distrusted all forms of universalism, refused to co-operate. See Bataillon, 1966, p. 232.
9. Montesquieu, 1951, vol. II, p. 19 (*Réflexions sur la monarchie universelle*).
10. Fletcher, 1698, pp. 55–60. It is difficult to know what to make of this text, which is written in crude but fluent Italian and claims to have been printed in Naples when it seems, in fact, to have been printed in Edinburgh for private distribution. It has been argued that it was intended as a satire. But seventeenth-century satirists are generally less equivocal about their intentions.
11. Montesquieu, 1951, vol. II, pp. 23–4 (*Réflexions sur la monarchie universelle*).
12. Montesquieu, 1951, vol. II, p. 364 (*De l'esprit des lois*, bk. VIII, ch. 21).
13. Shklar, 1987, p. 65.
14. 'An essay upon universal monarchy', in Davenant, 1771, vol. IV, p. 15. On Davenant see Hont, forthcoming.
15. Montesquieu, 1951, vol. II, p. 363 (*De l'esprit des lois*, bk. VIII, ch. 17). Botero (see pp. 47–9 below), by contrast, had argued that its extended nature was the Empire's strength since it prevented any one possession from making common cause with any other. Botero, 1956, pp. 11–12.
16. See Shklar, 1987, p. 83.
17. Montesquieu, 1951, vol. II, p. 648 (*De l'esprit des lois*, bk. XXI, ch. 22).
18. Montesquieu, 1951, vol. II, p. 248 (*De l'esprit des lois*, bk. II, ch. 4) and see Shklar, 1987, p. 83.
19. Raynal, 1780, vol. II, pp. 2–3.
20. The word means simply 'native born' but was originally a term of metropolitan abuse. See Canny and Pagden, 1987, pp. 79–80.
21. 'Aztec', which derives from the name of the mythical home of all the Central-American peoples, Aztlan, was not a term used by the inhabitants of the 'empire' that Cortés conquered, and seems to have been introduced in the eighteenth century with precisely the intention of insulating ancient from modern Indians (see Barlow, 1945). Inca, of course, refers not to

a people but to their ruler.

22. 'Memoria político instructiva, enviada desde Filadelfia en agosto 1812', in Mier, 1978, p. 204.
23. Miranda, 1929–30, vol. xv, p. 207. For the *criollo* response to the revolution in Saint-Dominique see Córdova-Bello, 1967.
24. This was Viscardo's proposal to the British government, see pp. 131–2 below.
25. See pp. 136–7 below.

Chapter 1

1. De Pradt, 1817, vol. ii, p. 174.
2. *Inter cetera* and *Eximie devotionis* (both dated 3 May) *Piis fidelium* (23 June), *Inter cetera* (28 June (?)) and *Dudum siguidem* (25 September). They are printed in Giménez Fernández, 1944, pp. 173–426.
3. Las Casas, 1951, vol. ii, p. 443.
4. For a fuller discussion see Pagden, 1987, pp. 29–65.
5. Juan López de Palacios Rubios, 'Libellus de insulanis quas vulgus Indias apelat', in Zavala, 1954, p. 27.
6. Rossi, 1972, pp. 117–222.
7. Tully, 1980, p. 69, and see Tuck, 1979, pp. 58–81. I am greatly indebted to this book for my discussion of dominium.
8. Soto, 1556, p. 280 and cf. Brufau Prats, 1960, pp. 280–4.
9. Tuck, 1979, pp. 48–9.
10. Vitoria, 1960, pp. 650–1.
11. Vitoria, 1960, pp. 650–2.
12. For these see Skinner, 1978, vol. ii, pp. 189–238.
13. Vitoria, 1960, pp. 652–5.
14. *Summa theologiae* Ia. IIae. q. 66 a.7. Parel, 1979, pp. 89–111. For a discussion of this point see Hont and Ignatieff, 1983, pp. 28–9.
15. Locke, 1970, p. 292, and see Tully, 1980, p. 114.
16. Vitoria, 1960, p. 661, 'dominium nihil aliud est quam ius utendi re in usum suum'.
17. Vitoria, 1960, pp. 663–4.
18. 'De eo ad quod tenetur homo cum primum venit ad usum rationis', in Vitoria, 1960, pp. 1307–8.
19. For a more detailed discussion of the theory of natural slavery see Pagden, 1986, pp. 27–56.
20. Vitoria, 1960, p. 651.
21. Vitoria, 1960, pp. 664–5.
22. Vitoria, 1960, pp. 723–5. For the argument that the highest moral life is one of *otium*, or pacific contemplation, see Skinner, 'Sir Thomas More's *Utopia* and the language of Renaissance humanism', in Pagden, 1987, pp. 123–157.
23. Vitoria, 1960, p. 725.
24. Vitoria, 1960, p. 706. The Spanish Thomists generally held the *ius gentium* to be a form of positive law; see, e.g., Vitoria, 1932–52, vol. iii, pp. 8–9.
25. Vitoria, 1960, pp. 705–6.
26. Vitoria, 1960, pp. 707–14.
27. Vitoria, 1960, pp. 715–21.
28. Vitoria, 1981, pp. 187–99.
29. Vitoria, 1981, p. 200.
30. Vitoria, 1960, pp. 698–9.
31. Vitoria, 1960, p. 725.
32. Cano, 1546, f. 30r.
33. For a discussion of this argument see Pagden, 1986, pp. 57–97.
34. Cano, 1546, ff. 30r–31v.
35. Cano, 1546, f. 39r.
36. Cano, 1546, f. 39v.
37. Soto, 1586, p. 423, and see Las Casas, 1969, p. 523, who insisted that to deny this was 'to fall into the heresy of Huss'.
38. The Indian law code of 1681, the *Recopilación de leyes de las Indias*, however, describes the *encomienda* in such a way as to make it clear that, in fact, it constitutes a case of limited use rights, and this is how the seventeenth-century jurist Solórzano y Pereyra interpreted it. See Solórzano y Pereyra, 1629–39, vol. i, p. 278.
39. Quoted in Boswell, 1934, vol. i, p. 45.
40. Mier, 1811, p. 61. On Mier see pp. 118–19 below.

41. Quiroga never mentions *Utopia* by name but refers to More as the author of a work on 'la república' (i.e., the state, Quiroga, 1974, p. 128), although when the *Información* was sent to Spain it was apparently accompanied by a now lost 'preámbulo y razonamiento de Utopia'.
42. See, e.g., Zavala, 1937 and 1955. For a more detailed critique of this position see Pagden, 1987a.
43. On this point see Bataillon, 1965.
44. Dealy, 1976, pp. 13–14.
45. Quiroga, 1974, pp. 141–2.
46. Sepúlveda, 1951, pp. 35–6.
47. Quiroga, 1974, pp. 144–5.
48. Quiroga, 1974, pp. 160–1.
49. Quiroga, 1974, p. 146.
50. Quiroga, 1974, p. 246.
51. Quiroga, 1974, p. 275.
52. For a discussion of this text and its reception by Cano, Soto, and Bartolomé de Carranza see Pagden, 1986, pp. 109–18.
53. Sepúlveda, 1951, pp. 83–6.
54. Sepúlveda, 1951, p. 97.
55. Sepúlveda, 1951, p. 36.
56. Sepúlveda, 1951, pp. 79–83.
57. Sepúlveda, 1951, pp. 87–90, citing *Contra Faustum*, bk. xxii, ch. 7.
58. Sepúlveda, 1951, pp. 78–9.
59. Wattell, 1820, vol. i, p. 113.
60. Sepúlveda, 1951, pp. 90–1.
61. *Jo. Genesius doctor theologus Melchiori Cano doctori theo*, in Sepúlveda, 1780, vol. iii, pp. 34–5, and see Pagden, 1986, pp. 110–13.
62. *De bello contra insulanos* and *De libertate indorum contra Sepulvedam*, parts of a commentary on the *Secunda Secundae* of Aquinas and printed in Pereña, 1982, pp. 136–393.
63. Pereña, 1982, pp. 245–9. Like Cano, Peña also accused Sepúlveda of being 'mediocriter in theologia exercitatus', ibid., p. 213.
64. Pereña, 1982, pp. 146–7.
65. Pereña, 1982, pp. 247–9.
66. Pereña, 1982, p. 261.
67. Pereña, 1982, p. 239. Soto had come to much the same conclusion with regard to the Africans enslaved by the Portuguese, Soto, 1556, p. 289.
68. In the interests of peace, which required the recovery of the well-ordered society, otherwise legitimate princes might be deprived of their goods (*bona*) and, if they continued to be unfit to rule, of their dominium. See, e.g., Suárez, 1621, p. 819.
69. Vitoria, 1960. pp. 721–2.
70. 'Sobre el titulo del dominio del rey de España sobre las personas y tierras de los indios', in Las Casas, 1969, p. 171.
71. Las Casas, 1969, pp. 33–9 and 83–5. This treatise, which was printed in Frankfurt in 1571, was the last Las Casas wrote. It relies heavily on the arguments of the work of the fourteenth-century jurist Lucas da Penna, and consequently proposes a strongly contractualist account of government which contrasts markedly with the weaker versions proposed by the Thomists in which political authority is said, in, e.g., Súarez's formulation, to be held by the people only *in fieri* and not *in conservari*, Suárez, 1613, p. 225.
72. 'Carta al maestro fray Bartolomé de Miranda sobre la perpetuidad de las encomiendas', in Las Casas, 1969, pp. 441–5.
73. Vitoria, 1960, p. 275.
74. León Pinelo, 1630, f. 95r-v.
75. Solórzano y Pereyra, 1972, p. 108. The argument that underpins this claim is set out by Vitoria himself in the prolegomenon to *De indis* (Vitoria, 1960, pp. 643–8). If someone, after due consultation with 'the most learned doctors', is convinced that an act is legitimate, then he cannot be held guilty of any offence even if those doctors are subsequently proven to be wrong. What Vitoria was not claiming, however, was that an illicit act performed in good faith could render the consequences of

that act legitimate, particularly once it was recognized that the act itself had been illicit.

76. Solórzano y Pereyra, 1972, p. 114. On Selden's *Mare clausum* see Richard Tuck, 1979, pp. 86–7.
77. Solórzano y Pereyra, 1972, pp. 112–3.
78. Mier, 1811, p. 61.
79. Nuix, 1782, p. 135. Significantly this text was first published in Italian and printed in Venice in 1780.
80. Muriel, 1791, Dist. V, Sect. 5.
81. Genovesi, 1835, p. 249.
82. Raynal, 1780, vol. II. pp. 2–7.

Chapter 2

1. Stubbe, 1670, p. 3.
2. Giannone, 1724, vol. IV, p. 296. The great eighteenth-century historian of philosophy Jacob Brucker also dismissed him as an 'enthusiast', Brucker, 1766, vol. V, p. 144.
3. The only work to provide an integrated account of all his writings is Bok, 1974, although this also pursues a Marxist version of the late-nineteenth-century vision of Campanella as a proto-revolutionary.
4. Campanella, 1636a, pp. 29–31.
5. Campanella, 1636a, p. 41.
6. Yates, 1964, p. 396.
7. La luce e una, semplice e sincera nel sole, e per se stessa manifesta, che'e di se diffusiva
e moltiplicativa,
agile, viva ed efficace ed presta;
tutto veder e veder face in sua sfera.
Canzone II, *Madrigale* I in Campanella, 1956, p. 818.
8. See Gollnitzer, 1972, vol. I, pp. 83–107.
9. See Yates, 1964, p. 376.
10. See Tuck, forthcoming, ch. 3.
11. Giannone, 1723, vol. IV, p. 303.
12. Doria, 1973, p. 38.
13. Villari, 1980, pp. 33–58.
14. Villari, 1980, p. 87, and see p. 86 below.

15. Campanella, 1640, p. 122.
16. Quoted in Amabile, 1882, vol. III, p. 26.
17. Amabile, 1882, vol. III, pp. 118–22.
18. 'Il popolo e una bestia varia e grossa
Che'ignora le sue forze...
Quoted in Villari, 1980, p. 115.
19. Quoted in Bok, 1974, p. 133.
20. Quoted in Bok, 1974, p. 140.
21. On the significance of this see Skinner, 'Sir Thomas More's *Utopia* and the language of Renaissance humanism', in Pagden, 1987, pp. 123–58.
22. Quoted in Amabile, 1882, vol. III, p. 241.
23. 'Riassunto degl'indizi contro fra. Dionisio', in Amabile, 1882, vol. III, pp. 151–2.
24. 'Riassunto degl'indizi contro fra. Dionisio', in Amabile, 1882, vol. III, pp. 151–2.
25. See the *Prima delineatio defensionum*, in Firpo, 1985, pp. 76–127.
26. The claim that it was the 'liberal' Urban VIII who secured his release and helped him to escape to France, seems to be false. For reasons that are not entirely clear he was released against the wishes of the pope. His departure from Italy then became a matter of necessity. See Amabile, 1886.
27. Quetif and Echard, 1721, vol. II, p. 508.
28. On the dating of Campanella's works see Firpo, 1940.
29. In a letter of 8 March, printed in Amabile, vol. II, p. 65.
30. Campanella, 1642, p. 31, and see De Mattei, p. 69.
31. Campanella, 1984, p. 62 and 1945, p. 45. In common with most of his contemporaries, Campanella used the term *politicus* to mean scheming and devious. See N. Rubinstein, 'The history of the word *politicus* in early-modern Europe', in Pagden, 1987, pp. 41–56. For Cam-

panella's views on Machiavelli see, e.g., Campanella, 1631, pp. 162–71, where he even claims, on one of many occasions, out of respect for 'the noble house of Machiavelli', that Niccolò must have been, literally, a bastard. Machiavelli's arguments are rejected on the familiar grounds that they are impious and based solely on human astuteness and, thus, in Campanella's terms, both morally offensive and unlikely to be effective. Campanella's shifting relationship with Machiavelli's writings is discussed in Headley, 1988 and Procacci, 1965, pp. 71–5.

32. Campanella, 1976, p. 174.
33. One of Machiavelli's failings, however, was to have relied solely on the evidence of history. 'Mirar solo l'istoria e vana dottrina e fallace, perche li tempi e costellazione sono varie', Campanella, 1945a, p. 128 and 1636a, p. 20.
34. Campanella, 1941, pp. 114–15; 1945, pp. 118–19; and 1640, pp. 3–8.
35. Campanella, 1941, pp. 189–90 and 1945b, p. 141.
36. Campanella, 1975, vol. II, p. 253. Machiavelli's astuteness (*astuzia*), when this is more than mere cunning, may also be 'in accordance...with the will', although it does not constitute knowledge. Campanella, 1941, pp. 122–3.
37. Tuck, forthcoming, ch. 3.
38. See Garver, 1987.
39. Campanella, 1956, p. 102.
40. Campanella, 1951, p. 9 and 1631a, p. 9.
41. Campanella, 1945b, p. 112.
42. Campanella, 1640, pp. 83–4.
43. Campanella, 1640, p. 82.
44. On this point see pp. 76–8 below.
45. Campanella, 1640, p. 66.
46. Campanella, 1640, p. 191.
47. Campanella, 1635a, p. 110. Cf. Botero, 1956, p. 89, who makes exactly the same point.

48. Campanella, 1941, p. 104.
49. Botero, 1956, pp. 30–5.
50. Campanella, 1956, p. 1081.
51. Campanella, 1976, p. 162.
52. Botero, 1607, p. 323.
53. Botero, 1607, p. 237.
54. Botero, 1607, p. 235.
55. Botero, 1956, p. 44.
56. Campanella, 1945, p. 14. For an extended account of the reason for the collapse of republics, see Campanella, 1941, pp. 135–42.
57. Campanella, 1945, p. 132.
58. Campanella, 1638, p. 169.
59. Campanella, 1945b, p. 112.
60. Campanella, 1945b, p. 136.
61. Campanella, 1945b, pp. 98–9.
62. Tuck, forthcoming, ch. 3.
63. Botero, 1614, pp. 5–6.
64. Botero, 1607, p. 237.
65. See Headley, 1978 and 1980. For Campanella's critique of Dante see Campanella, 1640, p. 45.
66. Campanella, 1636a, p. 21, and see Procacci, 1965, p. 71.
67. 'Discorsi universali del governo ecclesiastico per far una gregge e un pastore', in Campanella, 1956, p. 1121.
68. Campanella, 1640, pp. 93–4.
69. Campanella, 1956, pp. 1101–3.
70. Campanella, 1635a, pp. 300–1.
71. Campanella, 1960, p. 36.
72. 'Discorsi universali del governo ecclesiastico per far una gregge e un pastore', in Campanella, 1956, p. 1121.
73. Campanella, 1640, pp. 93–4 and 1635a, pp. 300–1.
74. Campanella, 1945b, pp. 126–9 and 1976, pp. 172–6.
75. Campanella, 1945b, pp. 134–5.
76. Campanella, 1945b, pp. 93–6.
77. Set out in Campanella, 1945, pp. 145–6.
78. Campanella, 1976, p. 178.
79. Campanella, 1640, pp. 18–19.
80. Campanella, 1640, p. 21 and 1955, p. 36.
81. Campanella, 1640, pp. 16–17.
82. Campanella, 1640, pp. 18–34.
83. Campanella, 1640, pp. 22–3.
84. Campanella, 1941, p. 117.

85. Campanella, 1941, p. 110.
86. This passage appears in the Vatican mansucript of the Italian text of the *De Monarchia hispanica*, Vat. Barb. Lat. 5198, f. 17r and cf. 'Discorsi universali del governo ecclesiastico per far una gregge e un pastore', in Campanella, 1956, p. 1119.
87. See pp. 27–30 above.
88. Campanella, 1635a, p. 319.
89. Campanella, 1640, p. 58.
90. Campanella, 1960, p. 91.
91. Campanella, 1976, p. 180 and 1633, p. 85.
92. Campanella, 1960, pp. 86–9.
93. Campanella, 1633, p. 90.
94. Campanella, 1633, p. 86 and 1955, p. 142.
95. Campanella, 1954, p. 104.
96. Campanella, 1640, p. 100.
97. Botero, 1607, p. 232.
98. Botero, 1607, p. 236.
99. Campanella, 1656, title.
100. Campanella, 1640, p. 101 and 1941, p. 110.
101. 'Discorsi universali del governo ecclesiastico per far una gregge e un pastore', in Campanella, 1956, p. 1123.
102. Campanella, 1640, p. 101.
103. See Campanella, 1632, pp. 186–7 and 1635b, pp. 292–3. What he does have to say on economics is discussed in De Mattei, 1928, pp. 121–34.
104. See, e.g., Campanella, 1941, pp. 102–4.
105. Campanella, 1941, p. 110 and 'Discorsi universali del governo ecclesiastico per far una gregge e un pastore', in Campanella, 1956, p. 1122.
106. 'Discorsi universali del governo ecclesiastico per far una gregge e un pastore', in Campanella, 1956, p. 1125.
107. 'Discorsi universali del governo ecclesiastico per far una gregge e un pastore', in Campanella, 1956, p. 1122.
108. Campanella, 1640, p. 124.
109. Cf. Botero, 1956, p. 51, 'novelty is always hated and any change in old customs arouses resentment'.
110. Campanella, 1941, pp. 103–4.
111. Cf. Botero, 1956, p. 49.
112. Campanella, 1640, p. 37.
113. Vat. Barb. Lat. 5198, f. 19r and Campanella, 1941, pp. 122–3. Cf. Botero, 1956, p. 49n.
114. Campanella, 1640, p. 35.
115. Campanella, 1941, p. 102.
116. Campanella, 1640, pp. 103–4.
117. Campanella, 1635a, p. 318 and see Campanella, 1633a, pp. 186–7 and repeated in 1635b, p. 111.
118. Campanella, 1945, p. 74.
119. Campanella, 1640, p. 101.
120. Botero, 1956, p. 98.
121. Francisco de Medina in the introduction to his edition of the poems of Garcilaso de la Vega, quoted in Guitarte, 1986, p. 131.
122. Campanella, 1967, vol. III, p. 254.
123. Campanella, 1967, vol. I, pp. 135–8; vol. II, pp. 61–2; and pp. 142–6. The fullest account of Campanella's metaphysics is still Di Napoli, 1947.
124. Campanella, 1640, p. 37.
125. Campanella, 1640, pp. 199–200.
126. Campanella, 1945a, p. 74.
127. 'Discorsi universali del governo ecclesiastico per far una gregge e un pastore', in Campanella, 1956, p. 1125.
128. Botero, 1956, p. 66.
129. Campanella, 1640, p. 41.
130. Campanella, 1640, p. 93 and cf. Botero, 1956, p. 66.
131. Campanella, 1640, pp. 43–4.
132. Campanella, 1640, p. 101, refuting Machiavelli, 1960, p. 279 (*Discorsi*, bk. II, ch. 2).
133. See Tuck, forthcoming ch. 3.
134. Campanella, 1976, p. 178.
135. Campanella, 1640, pp. 47–8.
136. Campanella, 1635a, p. 300–1.
137. Campanella, 1640, p. 51.
138. Campanella, 1640, p. 87.
139. Campanella, 1640, pp. 68–70, cf. Campanella, 1975, vol. II, pp. 491–2, more generally on the role of women within the household.
140. Campanella, 1640, p. 138.

141. 'Il mondo e il libro dove il Senno eterno scrisse i propri concetti...' Campanella, 1956, p. 791.
142. Campanella, 1640, pp. 437–8.
143. Campanella, 1984, p. 60.
144. Campanella, 1659, f. A2v.
145. Campanella, 1640, pp. 93–4.
146. Campanella, 1640, p. 442.
147. Campanella, 1640, pp. 93–4.
148. Campanella, 1640, p. 96.
149. Campanella, 1640, pp. 98–100.
150. Campanella, 1659, f. A2v.
151. Campanella, 1960, p. 36.
152. Campanella, 1635, pp. 69–70.
153. Campanella, 1640, pp. 101–2.
154. 'I do not know', he wrote to Francesco Barberini in 1634, 'what shocking things I have done to make me so odious to the Spaniards. I wrote *Della Monarchia di Spagna* for them, the *Panegirico ai principi d'Italia* for that monarchy, and the *Articuli profetali*; and they have these and use them in Spain'. There is no evidence of the truth of the last statement. Campanella, 1956, p. 1001.
155. Tuck, forthcoming, ch. 3.

Chapter 3

1. Giannone, 1753, vol. IV, p. 374.
2. Conventionally described by one seventeenth-century political theorist as 'the most chosen, rich, and virtuous who live civilly without engaging in sordid or mechanical activities'. Imperato, 1604, pp. 35 and 57. For an analysis of the uses of the term see Conti, 1984.
3. *Pubblico editto et manifesto per tutto il Fed. Mo regno di Napoli*, in Conti, 1983, p. 32.
4. Giannone, 1753, vol. IV, p. 391.
5. Coleras, 1731, p. 43.
6. Villari, 1985, p. 124.
7. Quoted in Galasso, vol. II, p. 534. On the Accademia see Conti, 1975 and 1978.
8. See Nuzzo, 1984, p. 46.
9. Genovesi, 1962, pp. 572–3.
10. In the dedicatory preface to *De antiquissima Italorum sapientia*, Vico, 1971, p. 61.
11. See R. Bellamy, '"Da metafisico a mercante"–Antonio Genovesi and the development of a new language of Commerce in eighteenth-century Naples', in Pagden, 1987, p. 278; and Ferrone, 1982, pp. 501–15 and 525–45.
12. Galasso 1982, vol. I, p. xi.
13. Doria, 1852, pp. 283 and 365–6.
14. Doria, 1972, pp. 106–7.
15. Doria, 1852, p. 97. Doria, however, is also certain that not all absolute monarchies are tyrannies, since a monarchy that is 'assoluta in quanto a se, interamente legata in quanto al'onesto e in quanto a Dio' would be a true *respublica*. It is only those like Spain where public duties have been subsumed by private interests that become a 'dominio despotico', ibid., pp. 99–100.
16. For the significance of these crucial terms see Skinner, 'Sir Thomas More's *Utopia* and the language of Renaissance humanism', in Pagden, 1987, pp. 123–58.
17. Doria, 1852, p. 352. For an account of the theoretical underpinnings of Doria's work, which in the psychology and the metaphysics it employs is markedly different from that of Genovesi and Filangieri, see Nuzzo, 1984.
18. Genovesi, 1803, p. 70.
19. Quoted in Dunn, 1985, p. 35, which provides by far the best account of the place of trust in Locke's thinking.
20. Genovesi, 1758, f. 276v.
21. Genovesi, 1803, p. 119.
22. Genovesi, 1803, p. 89.
23. Genovesi, 1803, p. 68.
24. Genovesi, 1803, p. 88.
25. Dunn, 1985, p. 36.
26. Genovesi, 1835, p. 454.
27. See the excellent account in Pii, 1984, p. 139. Genovesi's critiques of both Puffendorf and Cumberland are in Genovesi, 1763, vol. IV, pp. 91–107.

28. See Hont, 'The language of sociability and commerce: Samuel Puffendorf and the theoretical foundations of the "Four-Stages Theory"', in Pagden, 1987, pp. 253–76.
29. Genovesi, 1835, p. 23.
30. Genovesi, 1835, p. 454.
31. Genovesi, 1803, p. 72.
32. Genovesi, 1803, pp. 71–2.
33. Genovesi, 1758, f. 277r.
34. Genovesi, 1758, f. 277r.
35. Genovesi, 1803, p. 94. This also, of course, distinguishes this use of *fede* from simple faith.
36. Genovesi, 1803, pp. 72–3.
37. Doria, 1852, p. 153.
38. Cf. the discussion in Genovesi, 1835, p. 453.
39. See, e.g., Genovesi, 1803, pp. 69–71, and Doria, 1852, pp. 353–4.
40. Weber, 1925, vol. i, pp. 201–4.
41. Doria, 1852, p. 154. Cf. Genovesi, 1835, p. 453, where *virtù* is defined in what are, for Genovesi, characteristically Rousseauian terms are 'quell' affezione del cuore umano per cui c'interessiamo nel ben pubblico, e preferiamo quello al ben nostro privato'.
42. Genovesi, 1758, f. 107v–8v. He also argues that what he calls 'internal luxury' is more important for a community – since it stimulates not only internal trade but also internal communication, on which *fede pubblica* depends – than 'external luxury' which requires the importation of foreign goods.
43. Doria, 1973, pp. 21–2.
44. Doria, 1935, p. 175.
45. *Relatione del stato di Napoli*, quoted in Villari, 1980, p. 166.
46. Doria, 1973, p. 26.
47. Doria, 1973, pp. 30–2.
48. Doria, 1973, pp. 26–7.
49. Genovesi, 1758, f. 44r, 'le leggi senza il costume poco o nulla giovano a migliorare negli uomini', and Genovesi, 1777, pp. 68–70.
50. Montesquieu, 1951, vol. ii, p. 564 (*De l'esprit des lois*, bk. xix, ch. 14).
51. Doria, 1972, p. 22.
52. Doria, 1972, pp. 42–3.
53. Genovesi, 1777, p. 62.
54. Quoted in Maffei, 1710, p. 16.
55. Pitt-Rivers, 1977, pp. 7–9.
56. Mandeville, 1971, p. 43.
57. 'Considérations sur les moeurs de ce siècle', in Duclos, 1820, vol. i, p. 56. Duclos also notes that 'today' the term has come to mean nothing more than self-respect (pp. 61–3); a piece of wishful thinking.
58. Genovesi, 1777, p. 65.
59. Genovesi, 1803, p. 109.
60. Filangieri, 1819, vol. vi, p. 21.
61. 'Vera religio est homini necessaria atque utilis', Genovesi, 1763, vol. ii, p. 105 f. and 1803, p. 80; and see Pii, 1984, pp. 131–63. This is the theological analogue to the Grotian equation between what is right, *honestum*, with what is required for human survival, *utile*.
62. Mark Goldie, 'The Civil Religion of James Harrington', in Pagden, 1987, p. 199, and see p. 143 below.
63. Doria, 1852, p. 135.
64. Quoted in Dunn, 1985, p. 43. Cf. Doria's observation that religious belief had the effect of creating in people 'un sommo timore de' giuramenti ed un orrore senza misure verso gli spergiuri' Doria, 1852, p. 136.
65. Doria, 1972, pp. 33–4.
66. Genovesi, 1803, p. 78.
67. Genovesi, 1803, p. 77n.
68. Carli, 1780, vol. i, pp. 183–4. Carli is speaking of the 'free' Inca Empire. The account of the natural fear all despotates feel for public festivities is a reference to the Spanish attempts to abolish Inca ceremonial practices. See pp. 103–4 below.
69. Doria, 1972, pp. 32–3.
70. Doria, 1972, pp. 33–4.
71. Doria, 1756, pp. 422–3.

72. Doria, 1972, pp. 55–6.
73. For the association of *douceur* with conversation between the sexes and with both the commercial and the 'noncommercial' uses of the term commerce, see Hirschman, 1977, pp. 61–3.
74. Genovesi, 1835, pp. 427–8.
75. Montesquieu, 1951, vol. II, p. 563 (*De l'esprit des lois*, bk. XIX, ch. 12).
76. Doria, 1973, pp. 48–53.
77. Doria, 1973, p. 56.
78. *Il Politico moderno*, quoted in Doria, 1973, p. 56.
79. Doria, 1973, pp. 26 and 48. On the additional, and crucial relationship between tyranny and the servitude of women, see Tomaselli, 1985, pp. 113–14.
80. Schelling, 1984, p. 208.
81. Genovesi, 1803, pp. 111–15.
82. Doria, 1953, p. 163.
83. Genovesi, 1803, pp. 113–16.
84. Doria, 1953, pp. 184–5.
85. Filangieri, 1819, vol. II, p. 77.
86. Doria, 1852, p. 283.
87. Doria, 1953, p. 162 and cf. Doria, 1973, pp. 41–2.
88. See Nicolini, 1950.
89. Montesquieu, 1951, vol. II, pp. 651–2 (*De l'esprit des lois*, bk. XXII, ch. 2).
90. Genovesi, 1803, pp. 102–9.
91. Doria, 1953, p. 180.
92. Doria, 1953, p. 264.
93. Genovesi, 1803, pp. 70–1.
94. See Villari, 1980, pp. 67–8, and Doria's observations in 1953, p. 170.
95. Delumeau, 1959, vol. II, p. 557, and Villari, 1980, pp. 67–8. See also p. 41 below.
96. Doria, 1953, p. 203.
97. Doria, 1973, p. 37.
98. Doria, 1852, pp. 134–6.
99. 'si puo avere più credito in una repubblica che in una monarchia', Genovesi, 1803, pp. 57–8.
100. Genovesi, 1835a, pp. 260–1. He also claimed, however, that Montesquieu's contention that, in his own terms, monarchies were not

made for 'la forza diffusiva' was 'falso e pericoloso'.
101. Genovesi, 'Discorso sopra il vero fine delle lettere e delle scienze' (1753), in Genovesi, 1984, p. 248.
102. Doria, 1825, p. 353.
103. Doria, 1953, p. 222.
104. Doria, 1852, pp. 95–102.
105. Machiavelli, 1960, pp. 177–82 (*Discorsi* bk. I, chs. 17–18) and see Wind, 1961. I am grateful to James Hankins for bringing this article to my attention.
106. See Conti, 1984, pp. 25–6.
107. Skinner, 1974 and 1974a.
108. Weber, 1951, p. 237.

Chapter 4

1. This was the view presented by Francisco Falcón before the Second Council of Lima in 1567. Quoted in Góngora, 1975, p. 80.
2. See the comments in Cervantes de Salazar, 1963, p. 66.
3. Anderson, 1983, p. 63.
4. Quoted in Eguiara y Eguren, 1944, p. 483. The only full account of Sigüenza y Góngora's life and works is still Leonard, 1929.
5. Sigüenza y Góngora, 1928, p. 13.
6. Sigüenza y Góngora, 1928, p. 50.
7. Sigüenza y Góngora, 1928, pp. 33–4.
8. For a more detailed account of Sigüenza y Góngora's role in the creation of a *criollo* identity in Mexico see Canny and Pagden, 1986, pp. 72–5 and 85–8.
9. See Sigüenza y Góngora, 1683, f. 5v on the duty of the University of Mexico to make known the virtues of Mexican culture.
10. See Sigüenza y Góngora, 1962.
11. Sigüenza y Góngora, 1928, p. 72.
12. Sigüenza y Góngora, 1983, f. 4r.
13. Sigüenza y Góngora, 1928, p. 17.
14. The best account of this is Gliozzi, 1977, and see Pagden, 1986, pp. 193–7.
15. Grotius, 1642, and see Gliozzi, 1977, pp. 446–64, on the dispute

between Grotius and Johannes de Laet.

16. Sigüenza y Góngora, 1928, pp. 18–19. If Nephtuhim had been, indeed, the founder of Carthage, then this would lend weight to the claim, put forward by Ovideo among others, that the Amerindians were, in fact, the descendants of a former Carthaginian colony. Sigüenza y Góngora himself, however, was sceptical of this claim; 'to tell the truth', he confessed, 'this tale of Carthaginian sailors has never been to my liking', ibid., p. 29.

17. Sigüenza y Góngora, 1928, pp. 29–30.

18. Sigüenza y Góngora, 1928, p. 31.

19. Sigüenza y Góngora, 1928, pp. 30–1.

20. Sigüenza y Góngora, 1928, p. 32.

21. Sigüenza y Góngora, 1928, pp. 33–4.

22. Sigüenza y Góngora, 1928, p. 16.

23. Sigüenza y Góngora, 1928, p. 35.

24. Sigüenza y Góngora, 1932.

25. For Clavigero's reliance on Sigüenza y Góngora's 'museum' see, however, Burrus, 1959.

26. The best account of Clavigero's life, though it is analytically weak, is Ronan, 1977.

27. Viscardo, 1792, p. 189.

28. For the activities of the Jesuit exiles see Battlori, 1966.

29. Clavigero, 1944, p. 397.

30. The original Spanish version was discovered and published by Mariano Cuevas in 1945 (Clavigero, 1964). I have used the Italian text because it was the one known to Clavigero's contemporaries and because, in making his translation, Clavigero introduced a number of changes that make it the definitive version.

31. Clavigero, 1780–1, vol. I, p. 2.

32. Gibbon, 1972, p. 318.

33. Clavigero, 1780–1, vol. IV, p. 31.

34. I would like to thank Sabine MacCormack for pointing this out to me. The imaginative role of the Devil in America will be discussed by her in a forthcoming book.

35. Clavigero, 1780–1, vol. IV, pp. 5–6.

36. Clavigero, 1780–1, vol. IV, pp. 216–17.

37. See Cline, 1960.

38. See Ronan, 1977, p. 189.

39. Clavigero, 1780–1, vol. I, p. 15.

40. Hervas, who was also in exile in Italy, was the author of the anti-revolutionary tract, *Causas de la revolución de Francia en el año 1789*, Madrid, 1807. See Javier Herero, 1988.

41. Quoted in Battlori, 1953, p. 106.

42. Clavigero, 1780–1, vol. I, p. iv.

43. Cortés, 1986, pp. 85–6 and 98–9.

44. Clavigero, 1780–1, vol. III, pp. 80–3.

45. See Cortés, 1986, pp. 467–8, n.42, for a further analysis of these texts.

46. This has been discussed at length in Lafaye, 1974.

47. Clavigero wrote a treatise on the Virgin of Guadalupe, *Breve ragguaglio della prodigiosa e rinomata immagine della Madonna di Guadalupe del Messico*, Cesena, 1782.

48. Muñoz, 1984, p. 47.

49. Quoted in Canny and Pagden, 1987, p. 68.

50. Clavigero, 1780–1, vol. I, p. 123. This claim was, in part, a response to the Spanish assertion that whatever injustices the Indians may have suffered, they had suffered them at the hands of the *criollos*. See Costeloe, 1986, pp. 24–5.

51. Cf. Humboldt, 1811, vol. I, p. 157, 'If all that remained of the French or German nation were a few poor agriculturalists, could we read in their features that they belonged to nations that had produced a Descartes and Clairaut, a Kepler and a Leibnitz?'.

52. Carli, 1780, vol. I, pp. 118–19.

53. Montesquieu, 1951, vol. II, p. 490 (*De l'esprit des lois*, bk. xv, ch. 1).

54. Quoted in Muñoz, 1984, p. 50.

55. On the term 'Aztec' see Barlow, 1945. Anahuac (*Atl-Nahuac*) or 'Near the Water') was the name originally given to the coastal regions, and to the lands around the lake system of central Mexico, but by the early sixteenth century seems to have become a metonym for the whole of the Aztec domain. Insurgent writers such as Mier and Bustamante (see pp. 118–19 and 129–30 below) used the term to describe New Sapin. They also attempted to persuade the new independent republic to adopt the name, but failed.

56. See Pagden, 1986, pp. 146–209.

57. De Pauw, 1777, vol. II, pp. 138–40.

58. Buffon, 1853, vol. I, p. 336 and II, p. 285–6.

59. Robertson, 1831, pp. 782–3 (*History of America*, bk. IV).

60. Feijóo, 1777, vol. VIII, pp. 101–25.

61. Clavigero, 1780–1, vol. IV, pp. 4–5.

62. Sahagún, 1938, vol. III, p. 82.

63. For these supposed attributes of *criollo* behaviour see Canny and Pagden, 1987, pp. 80–2.

64. De Pauw, 1777, vol. II, p. 139.

65. De Pauw, 1777, vol. II, p. 140.

66. Quoted in Canny and Pagden, 1987, pp. 81–2.

67. Clavigero, 1780–1, vol. IV, p. 8.

68. See Pagden, 1986, pp. 146–97.

69. Clavigero, 1780–1, vol. IV, p. 39.

70. In 1691, for instance, Leibnitz wrote to La Loubere, 'it would be important if we could have quite old and original histories of these countries on the extremity of Asia. As also if we could gain some knowledge of the language of all the eastern Indies. For it is by this means that we can best make conjectures on the orgins of nations'. Quoted in Aarsleff, 1982, p. 99, n.39.

71. Clavigero, 1780–1, vol. IV, pp. 21–2.

72. Pocock, 1977, p. 243.

73. See Pagden, 1986, pp. 198–209.

74. Clavigero, 1780–1, vol. IV, p. 18.

75. Carli, 1780, vol. II, pp. 82–5.

76. Clavigero, 1780–1, vol. IV, pp. 13–14.

77. See Clavigero, 1780–1, vol..IV, p. 13.

78. Clavigero, 1780–1, vol. IV, p. 14.

79. Carli, 1780, vol. I, p. 21. Clavigero, however, reverses Carli's argument which is to demonstrate that as, in his view, the tools, weapons, and musical instruments of the Indian and the Ancients are similar, there must have been, at one time, a reciprocal communication between the ancients of both the New and the Old world.

80. Dr. Ortíz de Hinojosa, quoted in Pagden, 1986, p. 183.

81. Quoted in Aarsleff, 1982, p. 99 n.39.

82. Robertson, 1831, p. 797 (*History of America*, bk. IV).

83. La Condamine, 1745, pp. 53–4.

84. De Pauw, 1777, vol. II, pp. 137–8.

85. Molina, 1782, pp. 13–14.

86. See Clavigero, 1789, vol. I, pp. 16–17.

87. Clavigero, 1780–1, vol. IV, pp. 241–2. Clavigero also wrote a Nahuatl grammar, but this contains no discussion of the quality of the language. Clavigero 1974.

88. Clavigero, 1780–1, vol. IV, pp. 242–3.

89. Quoted in Mannheim, 1984, p. 297.

90. De Pauw, 1777, vol. II, p. 138.

91. Clavigero, 1780–1, vol. IV, p. 243.

92. Buffon, 1852, vol. I, p. 22 and II, p. 200. Buffon's argument is, in fact, that the total number of words in any Indian language is far less than the total number of words in–in the example he gives–Greek, and that 'cette abondance des mots, cette richesse d'expressions nettes et précises

ne supposent elles pas la même abondance d'idées et connaissances?'.

93. Clavigero, 1780–1, vol. IV, p. 247.
94. Montesquieu, 1951, vol. II, p. 536 (*De l'esprit des lois*, bk. XVIII, ch. 9).
95. Clavigero, 1780–1, vol. IV, p. 239.
96. Clavigero, 1780–1, vol. IV, p. 212.
97. Pernety, 1770, p. 95. On Pernety see Mannucci, 1988, pp. 96–132.
98. Clavigero, 1780–1, vol. IV, p. 211.
99. Buffon, 1852, vol. I, p. 22, quoted in Clavigero, 1780–1, vol. IV, p. 214.
100. See Robertson, 1831, pp. 909–11 (*History of America*, bk. VII), cited by Clavigero, 1780–1, vol. IV, p. 225.
101. De Pauw, 1777, vol. II, p. 158, and Clavigero, 1780–1, vol. IV, pp. 212–13.
102. Clavigero, 1780–1, vol. IV, pp. 224–5. Robertson, in fact, makes the not dissimilar observation (which Clavigero does not mention), that Mexican picture writing had progressed so far that they 'approach to the plain or simple hieroglyphic, where some principal part or circumstance in the subject is made to stand for the whole'. Robertson, 1831, pp. 910 (*History of America*, bk. VII).
103. De Pauw, 1777, vol. II, p. 156.
104. Montesquieu, 1951, vol. II, p. 585 (*De l'esprit des lois*, bk. XX, ch. 2), and on the non-commercial aspects of exchange see Hirschmann, 1977, p. 60.
105. Clavigero, 1780–1, vol. IV, p. 205, quoting Montesquieu, 1951, vol. II, p. 539 (*De l'esprit des lois*, bk. XVIII, ch. 15).
106. Clavigero, 1780–1, vol. IV, pp. 206–7.
107. Clavigero, 1780–1, vol. IV, pp. 293–7.
108. Viscardo, 1797, p. 305.

Chapter 5

1. Clavigero, 1944, p. 397.
2. Battlori, 1953, pp. 104–6.
3. For Viscardo's activities in London see Vargas Ugarte, 1971, pp. 31–5; Lynch, 1969; and Waddell, 1983.
4. Viscardo, 1801, pp. 2–3.
5. See Góngora, 1965, and Brading, n.d., pp. 41–2; and on Mier, Brading, 1973, pp. 70–3.
6. *Jamaica Letter*, September 1815, in Bolívar, 1950, vol. I, p. 166.
7. Palacios Fajardo, 1817, p. 5.
8. Mier, 1944, p. 63.
9. Mier, 1813, vol. II, p. 554.
10. Mier, 1811, p. 21. Their true political status might, however, as Viscardo pointed out (see p. 123 below), be thought of as analogous to that of the colonies of the ancient world, which were also self-governing autonomous bodies.
11. Mier, 1813, vol. II, p. 555, and 'Memória Político instructíva, enviada desde Filadelfia en agosto 1812 a los jefes independientes del Anahuac llamado por los españoles Nueva España', in Mier, 1978, p. 204, where he argues that the, by then conventional, comparison between Mexico and the United States was not only inappropriate but also insulting.
12. Mier, 1813, vol. II, p. 611. Given the wider powers granted to the 'people' under the legendary Aragonese constitution, the fact that the viceroyalty was an Aragonese institution was not without political significance.
13. Mier, 1813, vol. II, p. 595. All that Solórzano says is that 'Although the dominium, government, and protection of all the extended provinces of the New World belong to our Catholic kings of Spain...it was always the royal will that those Indian communities (*pueblos*) in which there was some form of polity...should be governed and ruled by the kings and captains

they had had in the times of their infidelity'. Solórzano y Pereyra, 1972, pp. 405–6. And cf. Mier, 1944, p. 63, on Solórzano's reading of the *Leyes de las Indias*.

14. Mier, 1813, vol. II, pp. 596–7, 'Memoria político instructíva', Mier, 1978, pp. 215–16, 'and the King of Castile could use the title of Emperor of the Indies only to protect in them the preaching of the Gospel', citing Las Casas. This is, of course, not so far removed from Vitoria's conclusion on the subject of dominium (see pp. 18–22 above).

15. Mier, 1944, pp. 63–6 and 1813, vol. II, p. 602. The claim that it was the Habsburgs who had begun the systematic erosion of the power of the *Cortes*, and hence undermined the ancient 'Gothic' contract between king and people, is also made by the Constitution of Cadiz of 1812 with which Mier, who refers to it scathingly as little more than an instantiation of Rousseau's *Contrat social*, was familiar. See Constitución, 1812, p. 6.

16. Viscardo, 1801, p. 53. See Halperín Donghi, 1961, p. 142, who aptly describes Viscardo as 'el modernizador y defensor de la *thèse nobiliaire*'.

17. Viscardo, 1801, p. 27.
18. Viscardo, 1801, pp. 24–5.
19. Viscardo, 1801, p. 4.
20. Viscardo, 1801, p. 23.
21. Viscardo, 1979, pp. 291–2. One proof of this, in Viscardo's opinion, was the relative economic prosperity of the Basque country, 'that corner of Spain where the survivors of ancient liberty had taken refuge', ibid., p. 321. Viscardo was himself of Basque origin.
22. Viscardo, 1801, p. 2.
23. Viscardo, 1801, pp. 8–9.
24. Viscardo, 1801, p. 388.
25. See Cárdenas Acosta, 1960.
26. Viscardo, 1792, p. 199.

27. Viscardo, 1801, p. 29.
28. On these see Canny and Pagden, 1987, pp. 54–6.
29. *Manifesto al mundo. La justicia y la necessidad de la independencia de la Nueva España*, Puebla, 1821, pp. 7–8. Signed 'M de B'.
30. Viscardo, 1801, p. 35.
31. Viscardo, 1797, p. 342.
32. Viscardo, 1797, pp. 323 and 340.
33. Viscardo, 1801, p. 36.
34. Canny and Pagden, 1987, pp. 64–5.
35. Viscardo, 1801, p. 34.
36. Viscardo, 1797, p. 343.
37. Viscardo, 1797, p. 286.
38. Viscardo, 1797, p. 287. Viscardo's views on the nature of exchange and on the evils of monopolies are derived from *The Wealth of Nations*. See, e.g., Smith, 1976, p. 164 (bk. I, ch. 11, b), and pp. 628–31 (bk. IV, ch. 7, c).
39. Viscardo, 1797, p. 290 .
40. Viscardo, 1797, p. 307.
41. Smith, 1979, p. 631 (bk. IV, ch. 7, c). Smith also claimed that it was precisely Portugal's neglect of Brazil, because of its poverty in precious metals, that had led to it becoming a 'great and powerful colony'. (Smith, 1976, p. 569, bk. IV, ch. 7, b.)
42. Viscardo, 1797, p. 288.
43. Cf. Miranda, 'three centuries of oppression are sufficient to teach us our rights. These are: personal security, liberty, and property; so essential to men who live in society', 'Proclama de Miranda', undated, in Miranda, 1959, p. 150.
44. Viscardo, 1797, p. 333.
45. The claim that Quechua played a dominant role in securing cultural and political unity in Tawantinsuyu is probably a fabrication of the Spanish administration in search of a lingua franca, similar to Nahuatl in Mexico. See Mannheim, 1984.
46. Algarotti, 1757, vol. II, pp. 122–5.

47. Quesnay, 1888, pp. 558 and 562.
48. Walton, 1814, p. 41.
49. Viscardo, 1801, pp. 11–12.
50. Viscardo, 1801, p. 7.
51. Viscardo, 1801, p. 37.
52. 'Copia de la carta que se cogio a un indio...', British Museum ADD. MS. 13, 976, ff. 197v–198.
53. Viscardo, 1792, p. 195.
54. Quoted in Fisher, 1966, p. 135.
55. Viscardo, however, pointed out in one of his more sober moments that 'nothing demonstrated so clearly the degree of displeasure that reigns among Spaniards than that so many of them should have made common cause with the Indians, and have chosen to place themselves under a chieftain of a nation that they despise', Viscardo, 1792, pp. 197–8. On the objectives of the revolt see Rowe, 1954. After its defeat all uses of Inca imagery and Quechua theatre and poetry were banned.
56. Viscardo, 1792a, p. 243.
57. See Flores Galindo, 1986; and on the Tupamaros, Szeminski, 1984.
58. Mier, 1812, p. 601.
59. Cárdenas Acosta, 1960, vol. I, p. 125.
60. Printed in Cárdenas Acosta, 1960, vol. I, p. 125.
61. Anon, 1820, pp. 12–19.
62. Viscardo, 1792a, p. 241.
63. Letter to John Udney from Massacarrara, September 30, 1781, printed in Battlori, 1953, p. 206.
64. Viscardo, 1792a, pp. 231–3.
65. Mannheim, forthcoming, and Colin, 1966, p. 143.
66. See Brading, n.d., pp. 42–3.
67. Bustamante, 1826, *Introducción*.
68. Mier, 1811, p. 18.
69. Address to the Congreso constituyente 15 July 1822, in Mier, 1978, p. 238 and, at greater length, in 'Memoria político instructíva', Mier, 1978, p. 209.
70. 'Memoria político instructíva', Mier, 1978, p. 217.
71. Mier had, for this reason, no time for Rousseau. 'I consider', he wrote, 'the "social contract" of [Rousseau], as did Voltaire, to be an *anti-social contract*'. Mier, 1813, vol. II, p. 570.
72. 'Profecía del doctor Mier sobre la fundación mexicana', delivered on 13 December 1822, in Mier, 1978, p. 292.
73. Viscardo, 1791, pp. 169–70.
74. Quoted in Robertson, 1929, vol. I, p. 151. He added, however, 'with the difference that he is not mad'. Cf. Pardo de Leygonier, 1962.
75. See Battlori, 'William Pitt y los projectos constitucionales de Miranda y Viscardo', in Battlori, 1966, pp. 621–5.
76. In another fragment, the 'Esquisse de gouvernment federale' of May 1810, which repeats some of the features of the 'Projet', Miranda spoke of *two* Incas, responsible to the nation for all their actions, and 'malgré que leurs personnes soient sacrées et invioables pendent le temps de la magistrature, ils pourront cependent être recherché après par devant la haute cours nationale', Miranda, 1959, p. 75, which suggests that their role was much closer to that of the presidency of the United States. It is unlikely that Miranda knew that the Inca state had, in fact, been divided into an upper (*Hanan*) and a lower (*Urin*) moiety, each ruled by a separate Inca. For this division see Mannheim, forthcoming.
77. 'Projet de constitution por les colonies hispano-américaines', Public Record Office (London), PRO 30/8/345, pt. I, p. 147r-v.

Chapter 6

1. The best account of Bolívar's education under the legendary polymath, Simón Rodríguez, and his experiences in Europe is still

the rather dreary narrative of Masur, 1969, pp. 33–44. Bolívar's reading was extensive. His favourite authors, and the ones who most clearly influenced his political thinking, were Rousseau, Montesquieu, and Voltaire; but he makes occasional references to Raynal and his library contained copies of Helvetius, Filangieri (with Constant's commentary), and Du Tracy. See Pérez Vila, 1960.

2. De Pradt, 1817, vol. I, p. xvii.
3. *Jamaica Letter*, in Bolívar, 1950, vol. I, p. 160.
4. Bolívar, 1950, vol. III, pp. 729–30, *Mi delirio sobre el Chimborazo*. There has been some doubt expressed about the authenticity of this document, but both the language, and the sentiments, are fully in keeping with Bolívar's most effusive moments.
5. Castro Leiva, 1985, p. 36.
6. *Discurso de Angostura*, 15 February 1819, in Bolívar, 1950, vol. III, pp. 684–5. On Britain he asked, following Montesquieu, 'in truth can one call a monarchy a system that recognizes popular sovereignty, the division and balance of powers, the civil liberties of conscience, the press, and all that is sublime in politics?'.
7. *Jamaica Letter*, in Bolívar, 1950, vol. I, p. 165.
8. *Discurso de Angostura*, in Bolívar, 1950, vol. III, p. 682.
9. The constitutional argument had also been employed in Spain itself by moderate reformers such as Gaspar de Jovellanos and figures prominently in the otherwise more radical constitution of 1812.
10. Letter to General O'Leary, 13 September 1829, in Bolívar 1950, vol. III, p. 315.
11. See, e.g., Mier, 'Memoria político instructíva', in Mier, 1978, p. 198, criticizing De Pradt for wishing 'to give us kings from his dynasty', a futile enterprise since, 'before our

marked propensity for republican government, the image of regalism vanishes altogether'.
12. Lisson, 1867, p. 16. As De Pradt noted, 'in the number of American constitutions that have come to my notice, there has not been one that included a single word referring to royalty. On the contrary, all are marked by a strong dye of republicanism and incline more to the institutions of the United States than to those of Europe'. De Pradt, 1817, vol. I, pp. xii–xiii.
13. 26 September 1822, in Bolívar, 1929–30, vol. III, p. 98.
14. *Discurso de Angostura*, in Bolívar, 1950, vol. II, p. 692.
15. *Mensaje a la Convención de Ocaña*, May 1828, in Bolívar, 1950, vol. III, p. 789.
16. Letter to Cristóbal Mendoza, Bogotá, 28 August 1828, in Bolívar, 1950, vol. III, p. 951, repeating the arguments of bk. IV, ch. 1, *Du contrat social*.
17. *Discurso de instalación del Consejo de Estado de Angostura*, 1 November 1817, in Bolívar, 1950, vol. III, p. 656.
18. 25 May 1826, in Bolívar, 1950, vol. III, p. 767.
19. *Jamaica Letter*, in Bolívar, 1950, vol. I, pp. 160 and 162.
20. *Discurso de Angostura*, in Bolívar, 1950, vol. III, p. 679.
21. *Jamaica Letter*, in Bolívar, 1950, vol. I, p. 172.
22. September (?) 1815, Kingston, Jamaica, in Bolívar 1950, vol. I, pp. 179–80.
23. Anon., 1820, p. iv.
24. *Discurso al congreso constituyente de Bolivia*, 25 May 1826, in Bolívar, 1950, vol. III, pp. 765–7.
25. See Bolívar, 1950, vol. II, p. 437, referring, with evident embarrassment, to De Pradt's comparisons between him, Washington, and Napoleon (De Pradt, 1825, pp. 82–90, described Napoleon as 'l'homme de l'immensité').
26. *Discurso de Angostura*, in Bolívar,

1950, vol. III, p. 681.

27. On the constitution of 1811 see Fortoul, 1930, vol. I, pp. 217–40.
28. Bolívar, 1950, vol. I, p. 176.
29. *Jamaica Letter*, in Bolívar, 1950, vol. I, p. 165.
30. *Discurso de Angostura*, in Bolívar, 1950, vol. III, p. 677.
31. De Pradt, 1825, p. 82.
32. *Proclama a los Venezolanos*, in Bolívar, 1950, vol. III, p. 605.
33. *Jamaica Letter*, in Bolívar, 1950, vol. I, p. 160.
34. *Memoria dirigida a los ciudadanos de la Nueva Granada por un caraqueño*, 15 December 1812, in Bolívar, 1950, vol. III, p. 544.
35. *Discurso de Angostura*, in Bolívar, 1950, vol. III, p. 681. Experience strengthened this view. On 13 September he told O'Leary that federalism was merely 'regulated anarchy' and that 'it would be better for America to adopt the Koran than the government of the United States, even though that is the best in the world', Bolívar, 1950, vol. III, p. 315.
36. See Frankel, 1977, pp. 38–50.
37. Jefferson, 1984, p. 1408. I would like to thank Malcolm Sylvers for having drawn this passage to my attention.
38. 'I prefer', he wrote, 'the title of Citizen to that of Liberator, because whereas the latter derives from war, the former derives from the Laws', *Discurso ante el Congreso de Colombia*, 3 October 1821, in Bolívar, 1950, vol. II, p. 1178.
39. Constitución, 1812a, Article 4, pp. 5–6.
40. 'More fortunate than Alexander, I have a sublime philosopher for my historian, in place of that lying poet Quintus Curtius'–Bolívar's classical learning was wide if erratic–Bolívar, 1950, vol. II, p. 339, in a letter of 21 March 1826. On 15 November 1824 he had offered De Pradt a pension of 3000 pesos, ibid., vol. II, p. 45.
41. De Pradt, 1817, vol. I, p. ix. De

Pradt, however, was expressing the widely held view that even if the excesses of the revolution were to be deplored and never to be repeated, it had released Europe from the twin burdens of feudalism and absolutism. Without it the restored constitutional and liberal monarchy would have been impossible.
42. Shklar, 1969, pp. 2 and 17.
43. Castro Leiva, 1985, p. 55.
44. 'The Liberty of the Ancients compared with that of the Moderns', Constant, 1988, p. 317.
45. 'Quinconque refusera d'obéir à la volonté générale y sera contraint par tout le corps: ce qui ne signifie autre chose sinon qu'on le forcerá d'être libre', Rousseau, 1964, vol. III, p. 364 (*Du contrat social*, bk I, ch 7).
46. *Lettre à C. de Beaumont*, in Rousseau, 1964, vol. IV, p. 937, and see Viroli, 'The concept of *ordre* and the language of classical republicanism in Jean Jacques Rousseau', in Pagden, 1987, p. 170.
47. See pp. 79–80 above.
48. Rousseau, 1964, vol. III, pp. 464–5 (*Du contrat social*, bk. IV, ch. 8).
49. 'The Liberty of the Ancients compared with that of the Moderns', in Constant, 1988, p. 316.
50. Dunn, forthcoming.
51. 'The Liberty of the Ancients compared with that of the Moderns', in Constant, 1988, p. 325.
52. Cicero, *De Officiis*, I.6.19, 'all the praise of virtue derives from action'.
53. De Pradt, 1817, vol. I, p. v. Raynal, claimed De Pradt, 'would not recognize the world his writings introduced us to'.
54. *Memoria dirigida a los ciudadanos de la Nueva Granada por un caraqueño*, in Bolívar, 1950, vol. III, pp. 541–2.
55. *Discurso de Angostura*, in Bolívar, 1950, vol. III, pp. 684–5.
56. *Discurso al Congreso constituyente de Bolivia*, 25 May 1826, in Bolívar,

1950, vol. III, pp. 769–770.

57. Letter to General Robert Wilson, 7 February 1828, in Bolívar, 1950, vol. II, p. 768.
58. Bolívar, 1950, vol. III, p. 768.
59. Quoted in Pardo de Leygonier, 1963, p. 68.
60. Letter to Guillermo White, 26 March 1820, in Bolívar, 1950, vol. I, p. 442.
61. Rousseau, 1964, vol. III, p. 381. (*Du contrat social*, bk. II, ch. 7)
62. Bolívar, 1950, vol. I, pp. 442–3.
63. *Discurso de Angostura*, in Bolívar, 1950, vol. III, p. 681.
64. *Discurso de Angostura*, in Bolívar, 1950, vol. III, pp. 686–7.
65. *Discurso al congreso constituyente de Bolivia*, 26 May 1826, in Bolívar, 1950, vol. III, pp. 765–6. By this time, however, Bolívar was seeking for ways of establishing continuity for the new states without resorting to either a monarchy or a dictatorship. Though, as the critics of the constitution of Bolivia pointed out, it was difficult to see what distinguished his tri-cameral solution from a true monarchy.
66. Letter to Guillermo White, 26 March 1820, in Bolívar, 1950, vol. I, p. 442.
67. *Discurso de Angostura*, in Bolívar, 1950, vol. III, p. 692.
68. *Discurso de Angostura*, in Bolívar, 1950, vol. III, pp. 693–4.
69. *Discurso de Angostura*, in Bolívar, 1950, vol. III, pp. 683–4.
70. *Memoria dirigida a los ciudadanos de la Nueva Granada por un caraqueno*, in Bolívar, 1950, vol. III, p. 543.
71. Madison, Hamilton, Jay, 1987, p. 126.
72. Letter to Castillo Rada, 24 April 1828, in Bolívar, 1950, vol. II, p. 836.
73. Bolívar, however, had frequently claimed that this racial diversity, and the even greater cultural diversity which that implied, was no threat to the project of a single American republic, since all 'the children of Spanish America, of whatever colour and condition, preserve a reciprocal and fraternal affection for one another'. Kingston, September (?) 1815, Bolívar, 1950, vol. I, p. 181.
74. *Avertissement de l'auteur*, Montesquieu, 1951, vol. II, p. 228 and cf. ibid., pp. 239–44 (*De l'esprit des lois*, bk. II, ch. 2).
75. *Du contrat social*, bk III, ch. 7 ('Que toute forme de gouvernement n'est pas propre a tout pays') does consider this question. But Rousseau is wholly concerned with climatic and environmental questions, rather than cultural disposition. The lessons (that, for instance, 'in every country customs are an integral part of the constitution of the state') of the fragment, *Des moeurs*, were not, of course, available to Bolívar. See Rousseau, 1964, vol. III, pp. 554–60.
76. 'The Liberty of the Ancients compared with that of the Moderns', in Constant, 1988, p. 319.
77. Shklar, 1987, p. 79.
78. *Discurso de Angostura*, in Bolívar, 1950, vol. III, p. 681.
79. *Discurso de Angostura*, in Bolívar, 1950, vol. III, p.689.
80. Letter of 26 August, in Bolívar, 1950, vol. II, p. 957.
81. *Projet de constitution pour la Corse*, in Rousseau, 1964, vol. III, p. 901.
82. *Discurso de Angostura*, in Bolívar, 1950, vol. III, p. 678.
83. Letter to General Robert Wilson, 7 February 1828, in Bolívar, 1950, vol. II, p. 768.
84. Letter to Santander, 8 July 1826, in Bolívar, 1950, vol. II, pp. 427–9.
85. De Pradt, 1825, p. 44.
86. 'Salta el Inca de la tumba / y se lanza presuroso / tras del heroe generoso/ que su stirpe va a vengar.' Quoted in Marie-Danielle Demalay, 'Une reponse du berger a la bergere: les creoles andins entre l'Amérique et l'Europe au XIX siècle', in Benassy, 1981–2, vol. I, p. 125. On the multiple uses to which the popular image of Bolívar has

been put since his death see Salas de Lecuna, 1987.

87. De Pradt, 1825, p. 87.
88. *Discurso de Angostura*, in Bolívar, 1950, vol. III, p. 676.
89. Letter to General O'Leary, 13 September 1829, in Bolívar, 1950, vol. III, p. 315.
90. The phrase is De Pradt's, *Courrier français*, 1 January 1829.
91. See Shklar, 1969, pp. 157–8, and Riley, 1982, p. 107. Rousseau's 'Great Legislator' does not, however, operate through the presence of the military as Bolívar did.

92. Letter to Robert Wilson, 30 April 1827, in Bolívar, 1950, vol. II, p. 617.
93. *Discurso de Angostura*, in Bolívar, 1950, vol. III, p. 679.
94. Letter to General Briceno, 15 May 1828, in Bolívar, 1950, vol. II, p. 862.

Bibliography of Works Cited

For ease of reference, no distinction has been made between manuscripts, printed books, or articles, nor between primary and secondary sources.

Aarsleff, Hans, 1982. *From Locke to Saussure. Essays on the study of language and intellectual history*, Minnesota.

Algarotti, Francesco. 1757. 'Saggio sopra l'impero degli incas', in *Opere varie*, Venice, vol. II, pp. 120–37.

Amabile, Luigi. 1882. *Fra. Tommaso Campanella, la sua congiura, i suoi processi e la sua pazzia*, 4 vols (2 of texts, 2 of documents), Naples.

——. 1886. 'L'andata di fra Tommaso Campanella a Roma dopo la lungha prigionia di Napoli'. *Atti dell'accademia di scienze morali e politiche di Napoli*, no. 20.

——. 1887. *Fra Tommaso Campanella ne'castelli di Napoli e Roma*, 2 vols, Naples.

Anderson, Benedict. 1983. *Imagined communities. Reflections on the origin and spread of nationalism*, London.

Anon. 1820. *Reflexiones sobre el estado actual de la América, o cartas al Abate de Pradt escritas en frances por un natural del América del Sur*, Madrid.

Barlow, R.H. 1945. 'Some remarks on the term "Aztec Empire"'. *The Americas*, vol. I, pp. 345–6.

Bataillon, Marcel. 1965. 'Vasco de Quiroga et Bartolomé de las Casas', In *Études sur Bartolomé de las Casas*, Paris.

——. 1966. *Erasmo y España*, 2nd Spanish edn, Mexico.

Battlori, Miguel. 1951. 'Las maquinaciones del abate Godoy en Londres en favor de la independencia de hispanoamerica'. *Archivium historicum Societatis Jesu*, no. 21, pp. 85–107.

——. 1953. *El Abate Viscardo. Historia y mito de la intervención de los jesuitas en la independencia de hispanoamérica*, Caracas.

——. 1966. *La cultura hispano-italiana de los jesuitias expulsos 1767–1814*, Madrid.

Benassy, Marie-Cecile, et al., eds. 1981–3. *Études sur l'impact culturel du nouveau monde. Séminaire interuniversitaire sur l'Amérique espagnole colonial*, Paris.

Bok, Gisela. 1974. *Thomas Campanella: Politisches Interesse und philosophische Spekulation*, Tubingen.

Bolívar, Simón. 1929–30. *Cartas del Libertador*, ed. Vicente Lecuna, 11 vols, Caracas.

———. 1950. *Obras completas*, ed. Vicente Lecuna, 2nd edn, 3 vols, Havana.

Boswell. 1934. *Boswell's life of Johnson*, ed. G.B. Hill, 2 vols, Oxford.

Botero, Giovanni. 1605. *Relatione della republica venetiana*, Venice.

———. 1607. *Discorso dell'eccelenza della monarchia*, in *I Capitani del signor Giovanni Botero Benese*, Turin.

———. 1614. *Discorso della lega contra il Turco*, Viterbo.

———. 1956. *The reason of state*, trans. P. J. and D. P. Waley, London.

Brading, D.A. 1973. *Los orígenes del nacionalismo méxicano*, Mexico.

———. n.d. *Prophecy and myth in Mexican history.* Cambridge Latin-American Miniatures, no. 1, Cambridge.

Brucker, Jacob. 1766. *Historia critica philosophiae*, Leipzig.

Brufau Prats, F. J. 1960. 'El pensamiento político de Domingo de Soto'. *Acta salamanticensis*, no. 4, pp. 280–4.

Buffon, Le Clerc, Georges, Comte de Buffon. 1853. *Oeuvres complètes de Buffon*, ed. M. Florens, 12 vols, Paris.

Burrus, E.J. 1954. 'Jesuit exiles, precursors of Mexican independence'. *Mid-America*, no. 36, pp. 160–75.

———. 1959. 'Clavigero and the lost Sigüenza y Góngora manuscripts'. *Estudios de Cultura Nahuatl*, no. 1, pp. 59–90.

Bustamante, Carlos María de. 1826. *Tezcoco en los últimos tiempos de sus antiguos reyes, o sea relación tomada de los manuscritos inéditos de Boturini; redactados por El Lic.D. Mariano Veytia. Publicalos con notas y adiciones para estudio de la juventud mexicana, Carlos María de Bustamante*, Mexico.

Campanella, Tommaso. 1631. *Atheismus triumphatus seu reductio ad religionem per scientiarum veritates*, Rome.

———. 1631a. *Risposte alle censure del 'ateismo triunfato'*, ed. L. Firpo, Florence, 1951.

———. 1633. *Discorsi della libertà e della felice soggezione allo stato ecclesiastico*, Iesi.

———. 1633a. *Monarchia Messiae*, Iesi.

———. 1635. *Documenta ad gallorum nationem*, in *Opusculi inediti*, ed. L. Firpo, Florence, 1951.

———. 1635a. *Le monarchie delle nationi*, in Amabile, 1887, vol. ii, pp. 299–347.

———. 1635b. *Consultationes aphoristicae (An Monarchia Hispanorum sit in augumenta, vel in status, vel in decremento)*, in *Opusculi inediti*, ed. L. Firpo, Florence, 1951.

———. 1636. *Ludovico iusto XIII Regi Christianissimo ad Christianae rei patrocinium dedicat Fr. Thomas Campanella*, Paris.

———. 1636a. *De gentilium philosophia praesertim peripatetica*, Paris.

———. 1640. *De Monarchia hispanica discursus*, Amsterdam.

———. 1642. *De libris propriis et recta ratione studendi syntagma*, Paris.

———. 1659. *Thomas Campanella an Italian friar and second Machiavel. His*

173

advice to the King of Spain for attaining the universal Monarchy of the World, trans. with a prefatory epistle by William Prynne, London.

————. 1937. *The defence of Galileo* (1616), trans. Grant McColley. *Smith College Studies in History*, vol. xxii, nos. 3–4.

————. 1939. *Epilogo magno*, ed. Carmelo Ottaviano. *Reale Accademia d'Italia studi e documenti*, Rome, vol. x.

————. 1941. *Aforismi politici* (1601), ed. L. Firpo, Turin.

————. 1945. *Discorso di Fra. Campanella circa il modo come i Paesi Bassi, volgarmente detti di Fiandra, si possono ridurre sotto l'obedienza del re di Spagna* (1594), ed. L. Firpo, Turin.

————. 1945a. *Antiveneti* (1606), ed. L. Firpo, Florence.

————. 1945b. *Discorsi ai principi d'Italia* (1607), ed. L. Firpo. Turin.

————. 1951. *Opusculi inediti*, ed. L. Firpo, Florence.

————. 1955. *Per la conversione degli ebrei*, in *Quod reminiscentur III et convertentur ad Dominum universi fines terrae*, ed. Romano Amerio.

————. 1956. *Opere di Giordano Bruno e di Tommaso Campanella*, eds. Augusto Guzzo and Romano Amerio. *La letteratura italiana. Storia e testi*, Milan-Naples, vol. xxxiii.

————. 1960. *Appendix ad messiae monarchiam. Sermo de iuribus Regis Catholici super novum Haemispherium, aliaque Regna Infidelium*, printed in facsimile in *Monarchia messiae con due 'Discorsi della libertà e della felice suggezione allo Stato ecclesiastico'*, ed. L. Firpo, Turin.

————. 1967. *Metafisica*, ed. Giovanni di Napoli, 3 vols, Bologna.

————. 1975. *Opera latina Francoforti impressa annis 1617–1630* (facsimile), ed. L. Firpo, Turin.

————. 1976. *Articuli prophetales* (1609), ed. Germann Ernst, Florence.

————. 1984. *Liber apologeticus contra impugnantes institutum scholarium piarum* (1631–2), intro. and trans. by K. Jensen and A.K. Liebreich, *Archivum Scholarium Piarum*, no. 8, pp. 29–76.

Campillo y Cosío, José. 1789 (but written in 1743). *Nuevo sistema de gobierno económico para la América*, Madrid.

Canny, Nicholas and Anthony Pagden, eds. 1987. *Colonial identity in the Atlantic world. 1500–1800*, Princeton.

Cano, Melchor. 1546. 'De dominio indorum', Biblioteca Vaticana MS. Lat. 4648.

Cárdenas Acosta, Pablo E. 1960. *El movimiento comunal de 1781 en el Nuevo Reyno de Granada*, 2 vols, Bogota.

Carli, Giannrinaldo. 1780. *Delle lettere americane*, 2 vols, Cosmopoli.

Castro Leiva, Luís. 1984. 'El historicismo político bolivariano'. *Revista de estudios políticos*, no. 42, pp. 71–100.

————. 1985. *La Gran Colombia, una ilusión ilustrada*, Caracas.

————. 1987. 'El historicismo bolivariano: un intento de puntualización'. *Boletin americanista*, no. 36, pp. 5–27.

Cervantes de Salazar. 1963. *México en 1554 y túmulo imperial*, ed. E. O'Gorman, Mexico.

Chabod, F. 1961. *Storia di Milano nell'epoca di Carlo V*, Milan.

Clavigero, Francisco Javier. 1780–81. *Storia antica del Messico cavata da'migliori storici spagnuoli, e da' manoscritti, e dalle pinture antiche degl' indiani*, 4 vols, Cesena.

———. 1789. *Storia della California, opera postuma del Nob. Sig. Abate D. Francisco Saverio Clavigero*, Venice

———. 1944. *Proyectos útiles para adelantar el comercio de la Nueva España*, in *Tesoros documentales de México siglo*, Mexico, vol. XVIII.

———. 1964. *Historia antigua de México*, ed. R. P. Mariano Cuevas, Mexico.

———. 1974. *Reglas de la lengua méicana*, ed. Arthur J. O. Anderson, Mexico.

Cline, Howard F. 1960. 'A note on Torquemada's native sources and historiographical methods'. *The Americas*, no. 25, pp. 372–86.

Coleras, J. 1731. *Vie de Spinosa*, Brussels.

Colin, M. 1966. *Le Cuzco's à la fin du xviie et au début du xviiie siècle*, Caen.

Constant, Bejamin. 1822. *Commentaire sur l'ouvrage de Filangieri. Oeuvres de Gaetano Filangieri*, Paris, vol. VI.

———. 1988. *Political writings*, ed. Biancamaria Fontana, Cambridge.

Constitución 1812. *Discurso preliminar leido en las Cortes al presentar la comission de constitución el proyeto de ella*, Cadiz.

Constitución 1812a. *Constitución política de la Monarquía Española promulgada a Cadiz a 19 Mayo de 1812*, Cadiz.

Conti, Vittorio. 1975. 'Paolo Mattia Doria e l'Accademia di Medinacoeli'. *Pensiero politico*, no. 8, pp. 203–18.

———. 1978. *Paolo Mattia Doria, della repubblica dei togati all repubblica dei notabili*, Florence.

———. 1983. *Le leggi di una rivoluzione. I bandi della repubblica napoletana dall'ottobre 1647 all'aprile 1648*, Naples.

———. 1984. *La rivoluzione repubblicana a Napoli e le strutture rappresentative (1647–1648)*, Florence.

———. 1985. 'Vita civile e governo civile', in *Paolo Mattia Doria fra rinnovamento e tradizione. Atti del covegno di Studi Lecce, 4–6 novembre 1982*, Lecce. pp. 213–26.

Córdova-Bello, Eleazar. 1967. *La independencia de Haití y su influencia en Hispanoamérica*, Mexico-Caracas.

Cortés, Hernán, 1986. *Hernán Cortés. Letters from Mexico*, ed. and trans. Anthony Pagden, 2nd edn, New Haven-London.

Costeloe, Michael P. 1986. *Responses to revolution. Imperial Spain and the Spanish American revolutions, 1810–1840*, Cambridge.

Davenant, Charles. 1771. *The political and commerical works of that celebrated writer Charles D'Avenant LL. D.*, 5 vols, London.

Dealy R. 1976. *The politics of an Erasmian lawyer: Vasco de Quiroga*, Malibu.

Delumeau, J. 1959. *Vie économique et sociale de Rome dans la seconde moitié du xvie siècle*, Paris.

De Mattei, Rodolfo. 1928. *La politica di Campanella*, Rome.

———. 1969. 'Note sul pensiero politico di T. Campanella'. *Accademia nazionale dei Lincei. Quaderno* no. 126, pp. 67–107.

De Pauw, Cornelius. 1777. *Recherches philosophiques sur les Américains, ou mémoires intéressants pour servir à l'histoire de l'espèce humaine*, 2 vols, Berlin.

De Pradt, Dominique Dufour. 1817. *Des colonies et de la révolution actuelle de l'Amérique*, 2 vols, Paris.

_____. 1817a. *Des trois derniers mois de l'Amérique méridionale et du Brésil*. 2nd edn, Paris.

_____. 1825. *Congrès de Panama*, Paris.

Di Napoli, Giovanni. 1947. *Tommaso Campanella, filosofo della restaurazione cattolica*, Padua.

Doria, Paolo Mattia. 1756. *Ragionamenti di Paolo Mattia Doria...ne'quali si dimostra la donna, in quasi che tutte le virtù più grandi, non essere all'uomo inferiore*, Frankfurt.

_____. 1852. *Della vita civile*, Turin.

_____. 1953. 'Del commercio del regno di Napoli', in E. Vidal, *Il Pensiero civile di Paolo Mattia Doria negli scritti inediti*, Milan.

_____. 1973. *Massime del governo spagnuolo a Napoli*, ed. Vittorio Conti, Naples.

Duclos, Charles. 1820. *Oeuvres complètes*, 4 vols, Paris.

Dunn, John. 1985. '"Trust" in the politics of John Locke', in *Rethinking modern political theory. Essays 1979–83*, Cambridge.

_____. Forthcoming, 'Liberty as a substantive political value', in *Interpreting political responsibility*.

Eguiara y Eguren, Juan José de. 1944. *Prólogos a la biblioteca méxicana*, ed. Augustín Millares Carlo, Mexico.

Elliott, J.H. 1963. *Imperial Spain*, London.

Feijóo, Benito Gerónimo. 1777. *Theatro crítico universal e Discursos varios en todo genero de materias para desengaño de errores comunes*, 8 vols, Madrid.

Ferrone, Vincenzo. 1982. *Scienza natura religione. Mondo newtoniano e cultura italiana nel primo Settecento*, Naples.

Filangieri, Gaetano. 1819. *La scienza della legislazione*, 6 vols, Philadelphia.

Firpo, Luigi. 1940. *Bibliografia degli scritti di Tommaso Campanella*, Turin.

_____. 1985. *Il suplizio di Tommaso Campanella*, Rome.

Fisher, Lillian Estelle. 1966. *The last Inca revolt, 1780–1783*, Norman.

Fletcher, Andrew. 1698. *Discorso delle cose di Spagna scritti nel mese di luglio 1698*, Edinburgh.

Flores Galindo, A. 1986. *Europa y el país de los Incas: la utopía andina*, Lima.

Fortoul, José Gil. 1930. *Historia constitucional de Venezuela*, 2nd edn, 3 vols, Caracas.

Frankel, Benjamin A. 1977. *Venezuela y los Estados Unidos (1810–1888)*, Caracas.

Galasso, Giuseppe. 1982. *Napoli Spagnola dopo Masaniello*, 2 vols, Florence.

Garver, E. 1987. *Machiavelli and the history of prudence*, Wisconsin.

Genovesi, Antonio. 1758. *Elementi del commercio*, Biblioteca Nazionale, Naples, MS. xiii, B. 920.

_____. 1763. *Elementa metaphysicae mathematicum in morem adornata*, 5 vols, Naples.

_____. 1769. *Lettere accademiche su la questione se sieno più felici gl'ignoranti che gli scienziati*, Naples.

_____. 1774. *Lettere familiari dell'Abate Antonio Genovesi*, 2 vols, Naples.

_____. 1777. *Spirito delle leggi del Signore di Montesquieu con le note dell'Abate Genovesi*, 4 vols, Naples.

_____. 1803. *Lezioni di economia civile. Scrittori classici italiani di economia politica. Parte Moderna*, Milan, vols. VII–IX.

_____. 1835. *Della diceosina o sia della filosofia del giusto e dell'onesto*, Milan.

_____. 1835. *La logica per li giovanetti. Classici italiani di economia politica*, Milan, vol. CCCLVIII.

_____. 1962. *Autobiografia, lettere e altri scritti*, ed. Gennaro Savarese. Milan.

Gerbi, Antonello. 1983. *La disputa del nuovo mondo. Storia di una polemica: 1750–1900. Nuova edizione a cura di Sandro Gerbi*, Milan-Naples.

Giannone, Pietro. 1723. *Dell'istoria civile del regno di Napoli*, 4 vols, Naples.

Gibbon, Edward. 1972. *The English essays of Edward Gibbon*, ed. Patricia B. Craddock, Oxford.

Giménez Fernández, Manuel. 1944. 'Nuevas consideraciones sobre la historia y el sentido de las letras alejandrinas de 1493 referentes a las Indias'. *Anuario de estudios américanos*. vol. I, pp. 173–429.

Gliozzi, Giuliano. 1977. *Adamo e il nuovo mundo*, Florence.

Gollnitzer, Heinz. 1972. *Geschichte des weltpolitischen Denkens*, 2 vols, Gottingen.

Góngora, Mario. 1965. 'Pacto de los conquistadores con la corona y antigua constitución indiana: dos temas ideológicos de la época de la independencia'. *Revista del Instituto de historia de derecho R. Levene*, no. 16, pp. 11–30.

Guitarte, Guillermo L. 1986. 'La dimensión imperial del español en la obra de Aldrete: sobre la aparición del español de América en la lingüística hispánica', in *The history of linguistics in Spain*, ed. Antonio Quilis, *Amsterdam studies in the theory and history of linguistic science*, Amsterdam/Philadelphia, S. III, vol XXXIV.

Halperín Donghi, T. 1961. *Tradición política española e ideología revolucionaria de mayo*, Buenos Aires.

Headley, John M. 1978. 'The Habsburg world empire and the revival of Ghibellinism'. *Medieval and Renaissance Studies*, Chapel Hill, no. 7, ed. S. Wenzel, pp. 93–127.

_____. 1980. 'Gattinara, Erasmus and the imperial configurations of Humanism'. *Archiv für Reformationsgeschichte*, no. 71, pp. 64–98.

_____. 1988. 'On the rearming of heaven: The Machiavellism of Tommaso Campanella'. *Journal of the History of Ideas*, no. 49, pp. 387–404.

Herero, Javier. 1988. *Los orígenes del pensamiento reaccionario español*, 3rd edn, Madrid.

Hirschman, Albert. 1977. *The passions and the interests. Political arguments for capitalism before its triumph*, Princeton.

Hont and Ignatieff. 1983. 'Needs and justice in the *Wealth of Nations*', in *Wealth and virtue. The shaping of political economy in the Scottish Enlightenment*, eds Istvan Hont and Michael Ignatieff, Cambridge, pp. 1–44.

Hont, Istvan. Forthcoming, *Power, plenty and virtue*, Princeton.

Humboldt, Alexander von. 1811. *Political essay on the Kingdom of New Spain*, trans. J. Black, 4 vols, London.

Imperato, F. 1604. *Discorso politico intorno al regimento delle Piazze della città di Napoli*, Naples.

Iturri, Francisco. 1789. *Carta crítica sobre la historia de América del señor D. Juan Bautista Muñoz*, Rome.

Jefferson, Thomas. 1984. *Writings* (Library of America), Cambridge.

La Condamine, Charles de. 1745. *Relation abrégée d'un voyage fait dans l'intérieur de l'Amérique méridionale*, Paris.

Lafaye, Jacques. 1974. *Quezalcoatl et Guadalupe. La formation de la conscience nationale au Méxique. 1531–1813*, Paris.

Las Casas, Bartolomé de. 1951. *Historia de las Indias* (1527), ed. Augustín Millares Carlo, 3 vols, Mexico.

———. 1958. *Tratado de las doce dudas*, in *Biblioteca de autores españoles*, Madrid, vol. CX.

———. 1969. *De regia potestate*, ed. L. Pereña et al., Madrid.

Léon Pinelo, Antonio. 1630. *Tratado de confirmaciones reales*, Madrid.

Leonard, Irving. 1929. *Don Carlos de Sigüenza y Góngora. A Mexican savant of the seventeenth century*, Berkeley.

Levey, Michael. 1986. *Giambattista Tiepolo*, New Haven-London.

Lissón, Carlos. 1867. *La república en el Perú y la cuestión peruana*, Lima.

Locke, John. 1970. *The two treatises on government*, ed. Peter Laslett, Cambridge.

Lynch, John. 1969. 'British policy and Spanish America, 1783–1806'. *Journal of Latin-American Studies*, vol. I, pp. 1–30.

Machiavelli, Niccolò. 1960. *Il principe. Discorsi sopra la prima deca di Tito Livio*, ed. Sergio Bertelli. Milan.

Madison, James; Alexander Hamilton; and John Jay. 1987. *The Federalist papers* (1788), ed. Isaac Kramnick, Harmondsworth.

Maffei, Scipio. 1710. *Della scienza chiamata cavalleresca*, Rome.

Mandeville, Bernard. 1971. *An inquiry into the origin of honour and the usefulness of Christianity in war* (1732), ed. M.M. Goldsmith, London.

Mannheim, Bruce. 1984. '*Una nación acorralada*: Southern Peruvian Quechua language planning and politics in historical perspective'. *Language and Society*, no. 13, pp. 291–309.

———. Forthcoming. *The language of the Inka since the European invasion*, Texas.

Mannucci, Erica Joy. 1988. *Gli altri lumi. Esoterismo e politica nel settecento francese*, Palermo.

Masur, Gerhard. 1969. *Simón Bolívar*, Albuquerque.

Mier, Servando Teresa de. 1811. *Carta de un Americano al Español sobre su numero* XIX, London.

———. 1812. *Segunda carta de un Americano al Español sobre su numero* XIX. *Contestación a su repuesta dado en el numero* XXIV, London.

———. 1813. *Historia de la revolución de Nueva España antiquamente Anahuac,* 2 vols, London.

———. 1821. *Carta de despedida a los Mexicanos,* Puebla.

———. 1944. *Escritos inéditos de Fray Servando Teresa de Mier,* ed. J.M. Miquel i Verges and Hugo Díaz Thomé, Mexico.

———. 1978. *Ideario político,* ed. Edmundo O'Gorman, Caracas.

Miranda, Francisco de. 1929–30. *Archivo del General Miranda,* 24 vols, Caracas.

———. 1959. *Textos sobre la independencia. Estudio preliminar por José Nucete-Sardi,* Caracas.

Molina, Giovanni Ignazio. 1782. *Saggio sulla storia naturale del Chili,* Bologna.

Montesquieu, Charles de Secondat, Baron de. 1951. *Oeuvres complètes,* ed. Roger Caillois, Bibliothèque de la Pléiade, 2 vols, Paris.

Muñoz, Juan Bautista. 1984. *Las polémicas de Juan Bautista Muñoz. Cargos hechos por el S.or D. Juan Bautista Muñoz contra el Abate Filiberto de Parri Palma o sea el Abate D. Ramon Diosdado Caballero sobre la Historia antiqua de México por el Abate D. Francisco Xavier Clavigero,* ed. Carlos W. Onis, Mexico.

Muriel, Domingo (Cyriaco Morelli). 1791. *Rudimenta iuris naturae et gentium,* Venice.

Nicolini, F. 1950. 'Falsa moneta a Napoli alla fine del seicento'. *Bolletino dell'Archivio storico del Banco di Napoli,* pp. 57–65.

Nuix, Juan. 1782. *Reflexiones imparciales sobre la humanidad de los españoles en las Indias, contra los pretendidos filósofos y políticos, para ilustrar las historias de MM. Raynal y Robertson,* Madrid.

Nuzzo, Enrico. 1984. *Verso la 'Vita civile'. Antropologia e politica nelle lezioni accademiche di Gregorio Caloprese e Paolo Mattia Doria,* Naples.

Pagden, Anthony. 1986. *The fall of natural man. The American Indian and the origins of comparative ethnology,* 2nd edn, Cambridge.

———. 1987. *The languages of political theory in early-modern Europe* (ed.), Cambridge.

———. 1987a. 'The humanism of Vasco de Quiroga's "Información en derecho"', in *Humanismus und Neue Welt. Mitteilung* XV *der Kommission fur Humanismusforschung,* pp. 133–42, Bonn.

Palacios Fajardo, Manuel. 1817. *Outline of the revolution in Spanish America,* London.

Pardo de Leygonier, G. F. 1963. 'Bolívar, L'Abbé De Pradt et Benjamin Constant'. *Revue de l'Institut Napoleon,* no. 86, pp. 62–8.

Parel, Anthony. 1979. 'Aquinas's theory of property', in *Theories of property: Aristotle to the present,* eds A. Parel and T. Flanagan, Calgary, pp. 89–111.

Pereña, L. 1982. *De bello contra insulanos,* ed. L. Pereña et al., Madrid.

Pérez Vila, Manuel. 1960. *La biblioteca del Libertador*, Caracas.

Pernety, A. J. (Dom). 1770. *Dissertation sur l'Amérique et les Américains contre les Recherches philosophiques de Mr. de P*, Berlin.

Pii, Eluggero. 1984. *Antonio Genovesi dalla politica economica alla 'politica civile'*, Florence.

Pitt-Rivers, Julian. 'The anthropology of honour', in *The fate of Schechem, or the politics of sex. Essays in the anthropology of the Mediterranean*, Cambridge.

Pocock, J.G.A. 1977. *Politics, language and time*, New York.

Procacci, Giuliano. 1965. *Studi sulla fortuna del Machiavelli*, Rome.

Quesnay, François. 1767. 'Analyse des Incas du Perou', in *Oeuvres économiques et philosophiques de F. Quesnay*, ed. Auguste Oncken, Paris, 1988, pp. 555–62.

Quetif, Jacques; and Echard, Jacob. 1721. *Scriptores Ordinis Praedicatorum recensiti notis historicis et criticis illustrati ad annum 1700*, Paris.

Quiroga, Vasco de. 1974. *Información en derecho*, ed. Paulino Castañeda Delgado, Madrid.

Raynal, Guillaume Thomas. 1780. *Histoire philosophique et politique des établissemens et du commerce des Européens dans les deux Indes*, 4 vols, Geneva.

Riley, P. 1982. *Will and political legitimacy. A critical exposition of social contract theory in Hobbes, Locke, Rousseau, Kant and Hegel*, Harvard.

Robertson, William. 1831. *The works of William Robertson, D. D.*, London.

Robertson, William. 1929. *The life of Miranda 1750–1816*, 2 vols, Chapel Hill.

Ronan, Charles E. 1977. *Francisco Javier Clavigero, S.J. (1731–1787), figure of the Mexican Enlightenment: his life and works*, Rome-Chicago.

Rossi, Paolo. 1972. 'La proprietà nel sistema privatistico della seconda scolastica', in *La seconda scolastica nella formazione del diritto privato*, ed. Paolo Rossi, Milan, pp. 117–222.

Rousseau, Jean Jacques. 1964. *Oeuvres complètes, édition publiée sous la direction de Bernard Gagnebin et Marcel Raymond*, Bibliothèque de la Pléiade, 4 vols, Paris.

Rowe, John H. 1954. 'El movimiento nacional inca del siglo XVIII', *Revista universitaria* (Cuzco) no. 107, pp. 17–47.

Sahagún, Bernardino de. 1938. *Historia de las cosas de la Nueva España*, 5 vols, Mexico.

Salas de Lecuna, Yolanda, 1987. *Bolívar y la historian en la conciencia popular*, Caracas.

Salcedo Bastardo, J. L. 1973. *El primer deber con el acervo documental de Bolívar sobre la educación y la cultura*, Caracas.

Schelling, T. C. 1984. 'Strategic analysis and social problems', in *Choice and Consequence*, Cambridge, Mass.

Sepúlveda, Juan Ginés de. 1780. *Joannis Genesii Sepulvedae cordubensis opera*, 4 vols, Madrid.

———. 1951. *Demócrates segundo, o de las justas causas de la guerra contra los indios*, ed. Angel Losada, Madrid.

Shklar, Judith. 1696. *Men and citizens. A study of Rousseau's social theory*, Cambridge.

——. 1987. *Montesquieu*, oxford.

Sigüenza y Góngora, Carlos de. 1683. *Triumpho parthénico que en gloria de María Santissima immaculadamente concebida, celebró la Pontificia Imperial y Regia Academia Méxicana*, Mexico.

——. 1928. *Theatro de virtudes políticas que constituyen a un principe, advertidas en los monarchos antiguos del México imperial*, in *Obras*, ed. Francisco Pérez Salazar, Mexico.

——. 1931. *Poemas*, ed. Irving A. Leonard, Madrid.

——. 1932. *Alboroto y motín de México del 8 junio de 1692, relación de Don Carlos de Sigüenza y Góngora en una carta al almirante Don Andrés de Pez*, ed. Irving A. Leonard, Mexico.

——. 1962. *Piedad heroica de Don Fernando Cortés*, ed. Jaime Delgado, Mexico.

Simmons, Merle. 1983. *Los escritos de Juan Pablo Viscardo y Guzmán precursor de la independencia hispanoaméricana*, Caracas.

Skinner, Quentin, 1974. 'The principles and the practice of opposition: the case of Bolingbroke versus Walpole', in *Historical perspectives: studies in English thought and society in honour of J. H. Plumb*, ed. N. MacKendrick, London.

——. 1974a. 'Some problems in the analysis of political thought and action', *Political theory*, no. 2, pp. 277–303.

——. 1978. *The foundations of modern political thought*, 2 vols, Cambridge.

Smith, Adam. 1976. *An inquiry into the nature and causes of the wealth of nations*, ed. W.B. Todd, 2 vols (with continuous pagination), *The Glasgow Edition of the Works and Correspondence of Adam Smith*, Oxford, vol. II.

Solórzano y Pereyra, Juan de. 1629–39. *Disputationem de Indiarum jure sive de justa Indiarum occidentalium inquisitione acquisitione et retentione*, 2 vols, Madrid.

——. 1972. *Política indiana sacada en lengua castellana de los dos tomos del derecho i govierno municipal de las Indias*, in *Biblioteca de autores españoles*, Madrid, vol. CCLII.

Soto, Domingo de. 1556. *De iustitia et iure*, Salamanca.

Spinoza, Benedict de. 1951. *A theologico-political treatise and a political treatise*, trans. and ed. R.H.M. Elwes, New York.

Stubbe, Henry. 1670. *Campanella revived or an enquiry into the history of the Royal Society*, London.

Suárez, Francisco. 1613. *Defensio fidei catholicae et apostolicae adversus anglicanae sectae errores*, Coimbra.

——. 1621. *Disputatio XII. De bello*, in *Opus de triplici virtute theologica. Fide spe et charitate*, Paris.

Szeminski, Jan. 1984. *La utopía tupamarista*, Lima.

Tomaselli, Sylvana. 1985. 'The Enlightenment debate on women'. *History Workshop*, no. 20, pp. 101–24.

Tuck, Richard. 1979. *Natural rights theories: their origin and development*, Cambridge.

———. Forthcoming. *Philosophy in government*, Cambridge.

Tully, James. 1980. *A discourse on property. John Locke and his adversaries*, Cambridge.

Vargas Ugarte, R. *La Carta a los Españoles-Americanos de Don Juan Pablo Viscardo*, Lima.

Vico, Giambattista. 1971. *Opere filosofiche*, ed. Paolo Cristofolini, Florence.

Villari, Rosario, 1980. *La rivolta antispagnola a Napoli. Le origini 1585–1647*, Bari.

Viscardo, Juan Pablo. 1791. *Projet pour rendre l'Amérique independente*, in Simmons, 1983, pp. 165–72.

———. 1792. *Suite de precedent projet et Essai historique des troubles de l'Amérique Meridionale dans l'an 1780*, in Simmons, 1983, pp. 173–204.

———. 1792a. *Esquisse politique sur l'état actuel de l'Amérique Espagnole et les moyens d'adresse pour faciliter son independence*, in Simmons, 1983, pp. 205–53.

———. 1797 *La Paix et le bonheur du siècle prochain. Remontrance adressée à tous les peuples libres ou qui veulent l'être par un Américain Espagnol*, in Simmons, 1983, pp. 282–384.

———. 1801. *Carta dirijida a los Españoles-Americanos por uno de sus compatriotas*, London.

Vitoria, Francisco de. 1932–52. *Comentarios de la Secunda Secundae de Santo Tomas (1534–7)*, ed. V. Beltran de Heredia, 6 vols, Salamanca.

———. 1960. *Obras de Francisco de Vitoria*, ed. Teofilo Urdanoz, Madrid.

———. 1981. *Relectio de iure belli*, eds. L. Perena et al., Madrid.

Waddell, D.A.G. 1983. *Gran Bretaña y la independencia de Venezuela y Colombia*, Caracas.

Walton, William. 1814. *An exposé of the dissensions of Spanish America...intended as a means to induce the mediatory interference of Great Britain*, London.

Washburn, W.E. 1962. 'The meaning of "discovery" in the fifteenth and sixteenth centuries'. *The American Historical Review*, no. 68, pp. 1–19.

Wattell, Emerich de. 1820. *Le droit de gens ou principe de la loi naturelle*, 2 vols, Paris.

Weber, Max. 1925. *Wirtschaft und Gesellschaft*, 2 vols, Tubingen.

———. 1951. *The religion of China: Confucianism and Taoism*, Glencoe.

Wind, Edgar, 1961. 'Platonic tyranny and the Renaissance Fortuna. On Ficino's reading of Laws IV, 709A–712A', in *De artibus opuscula* XL. *Essays in honour of Erwin Panofsky*, ed. Millard Meiss, 2 vols, vol. I, pp. 491–96.

Yates, Frances A. 1964. *Giordano Bruno and the hermetic tradition*, London.

Zavala, Silvio. 1937. *La utopía de Tomás Moro en la Nueva Espana*, Mexico.

———.1954. *De las islas del Mar Océano*, Mexico.

———. 1955. *Sir Thomas More in New Spain*, London.

Index of Names

Accursius, Florentinus, 17
Acosta, José de, 99, 100, 104–5, 107
Alcedo y Bexerano, Antonio de, 105
Alegre, Francisco Javier, 98
Alexander the Great, 24, 51, 61, 141
Alexander III, Pope, 34
Alexander VI, Pope, 14, 33
Alfonso V, King of Naples, 47
Alfonso X, 'The Wise', King of Castile, 61
Algarotti, Francesco, 126, 130
Almain, Jean, 18
Alva, Duke of, 44, 47
Ammirato, Giovanni, 49
Anahuac, see Aztec
Anderson, Benedict, 91
Aniello, Tommaso, ('Masaniello'), 65–6, 69, 87
Aquinas, St Thomas, 17, 37
Arawak, 28
Aristotle, 20, 23, 27, 28, 31, 61, 77, 111, 113, 141
Augustine, St Augustine of Hippo, 29
Aztec, 26, 28, 31, 92, 93, 94, 96, 97, 102, 104, 106,
   108, 109, 112, 113–16, 125, 138, 151

Bellarmine, Robert (Cardinal and St Roberto
   Bellarmino), 33–4
Bentham, Jeremy, 141
Berlin, Isaiah, 144
Bolívar, Simón, 12, 13, 118, 122, 125, 129, 130,
   131, 132, 133–53
Borgia, Cesare, 57
Botero, Giovanni, 2, 47, 48, 49, 54, 55, 56, 57, 59
Bruno, Giordano, 37
Buffon, Georges Le Clerc, Comte de, 105, 106, 112,
   113, 114, 115
Bustamante, Carlos Maria, 129–30

Caballero, Ramon Diosdado, 104
Caesar, Julius, Emperor of Rome, 55, 58
Calvin, Jean, 18, 51
Campanella, Tommaso, 5, 6, 7, 8, 27, 37–63, 66,
   70, 73, 74, 75, 79
Cano, Melchor, 22–4, 30
Capito, Marcantonio, 42
Carli, Gianrinaldo, 74, 80, 99, 103–4, 105, 108, 109,
   115, 130
Carranza, Bartolomé de, 33
Castro Leiva, Luís, 134, 142, 146
Cavo, Andres, 98
Cerdá y Aragon, Count of Paredes, Marqués de la
   Laguna, Viceroy of New Spain, 92–3, 94
Cervantes de Salazar, Francisco, 93
Charlemagne, Roman Emperor and King of the
   Franks, 50, 59, 152
Charles V, Holy Roman Emperor and King of
   Spain, 2, 3, 4, 5, 6, 27, 32, 68, 102, 121
Charles III, King of Spain, 1, 98, 123
Chateaubriand, François René, Vicomte de, 136
Cicero, Marcus Tullius, 112, 113
Clavigero, Francisco Xavier, 10, 11, 97–116, 117,
   118, 119, 125, 130

Columbus, Christopher, 1, 13, 47, 54, 62
comuneros, 121, 122, 127–8, 131, 137, 151
Constant, Benjamin, 141–4, 146, 148, 149, 152
Constantine the Great, Emperor of Rome, 92
Constitution of 1812, 2, 11, 141, 152
Córdoba, Gonzalo de ('The Great Captain'), 47
Cortés, Hernán, 13, 25, 32, 62, 96, 102, 123, 129
Cortés, Martín, 123
Cortese, Giulio, 42
Covarrubias, Sebastián de, 54
Cumberland, Richard (Bishop of Peterborough), 71
Cyrus II, King of Persia, 50, 51, 52, 53, 54, 60, 83

D'Ailly, Pierre, 18
D'Andrea, Vincenzo, 65–6
Dante, Alighieri, 6, 7, 49
Davenant, Charles, 8
De la Court, Johan and Pieter, 4
De Pauw, Cornelius, 104–6, 107, 111–12, 113–15
De Pradt, Dominique Dufour, 13, 133, 139, 140,
   141, 145, 148–9, 150, 151
Descartes, René, 370–8, 43, 99
Díaz del Castillo, Bernal, 102
Di Pizzoni, Giovanni Battista, 42
Doria, Paolo Mattia, 5, 8, 9, 40, 41, 56, 68–89, 91
Duclos, Charles, 77
Dunn, John, 71, 143–4

Elliott, John, 5
Ezekiel, 51

Feijóo, Benito Gerónimo, 105, 106
Ferdinand II, King of Aragon, 5, 14, 15, 33, 53, 119
Filangieri, Gaetano, 5, 8, 36, 69, 73, 74, 79, 84, 85,
   91, 119
Fletcher, Andrew, 7
Fontenelle, Bernard le Bovier de la, 99
Fox Morcillo, Sebastián, 3
Friedrich The Wise, Duke of Saxony, 59
Furió Ceriol, Federico, 3

Galileo Galilei, 38, 44, 60
Garcilaso de la Vega, 'El Inca', 11, 129
Gassendi, Pierre, 99
Gattinara, Mercurio de, 4, 6, 49
Genoino, Giulio, 76
Giannone, Pietro, 37, 40, 65, 66, 68, 69
Gibbon, Edward, 99
Genovesi, Antonio, 5, 8, 9, 36, 68–89, 91
Gerson, Jean Charlier de, 26
Gonzalo de Castañeda, José, 103, 106
Gorky, Maxim, 38
Grotius, Hugo, 4, 16, 17, 29, 34, 38, 53, 95, 107
Guise, Duc de, 66

Hegel, Georg Wilhelm Friedrich, 144
Henry VIII, King of England, 31, 59
Herodotus, 83
Hérvas y Panduro, Lorenzo, 101
Hidalgo, Miguel, 10, 132, 134, 138, 151
Hobbes, Thomas, 72, 73

Humboldt, Alexander von, 118
Huss, John (Jan Hus), 18
Hutchinson, Thomas, 66

Inca, 28, 85, 92, 108, 121, 125, 126, 127, 128–9, 131, 138, 151
Inés de la Cruz, Sor Juana, 92
Isabella, Queen of Castile, 1, 14, 33, 119
Iturbide, Augustín, Emperor of Mexico, 12, 130, 136, 151

Jefferson, Thomas, 138, 140
Johnson, Dr Samuel, 24
Josephus, 95

La Condamine, Charles de, 103, 104, 107, 111
Lafayette, Marie Paul Joseph, Marquis de, 140
Lafitau, Joseph François, 105, 108
Las Casas, Bartolomé de, 15, 24, 25, 30, 32, 33, 116
Leibnitz, Gottfried Wilhelm, 99, 100
León Pinelo, Antonio, 34
Lipsius, Justus, 3, 46
Livy, Titus Livius, 143
Locke, John, 19, 24, 70, 71, 73, 80, 110, 144
Louis XIII, King of France, 43, 63
Louis XIV, King of France, 2
Lucian, 25, 27
Luther, Martin, 18, 50, 59

Machiavelli, Niccolò, 5, 45, 46, 51, 55, 57, 58, 59, 69, 87, 143
Madison, James, 147–8
Major, John (Johannes Maior), 20, 28
Mandeville, Bernard, 71, 74, 77, 82
Marsilius of Padua, 50
Marx, Karl, 141
Masaniello, see Aniello, Tommaso
Maximilian, Ferdinand Maximilian Joseph of Habsburg, Emperor of Mexico, 12
Mazarin, Cardinal (Giulio Mazzarini), 5
Medinaceli, Duke of, 68
Mersenne, Marin, 37
Mexía, Pedro de, 6
Mexica, see Aztec
Mexicans, see Aztec
Mier Noriega y Guerra, José Servando Teresa de, 11, 25, 35, 118–19, 122, 127, 130, 132
Miranda, Francisco de, 11, 12, 117, 118, 130, 131–2, 133, 134, 137, 141
Moctezuma, 26, 32, 96, 102, 103, 129
Molina, Juan Ignacio, 98, 105, 111
Molina, Luís de, 16, 17, 105
Montesinos, Antonio de, 14, 15
Montesquieu, Charles de Secondat, Baron de, 7–8, 9, 11, 36, 69, 77, 78, 82, 85, 99, 104, 113, 115, 119, 122–4, 138–40, 142, 144, 145, 149, 150
More, St Thomas, 25
Morelos, José María, 10, 129, 132, 134, 138, 151
Muñoz, Juan Bautista, 100, 102
Muriel, Domingo (Cyriaco Morelli), 35, 26

Napoleon Bonaparte, Emperor of France, 131, 139, 141, 142, 148, 151
Nebrija, Antonio de, 57
Neptune (Nephtuhim), 95, 96
Newton, Isaac, 73
Nuix, Juan, 35
Numa, Pompilius, King of Rome, 57, 61

Páez, José Antonio, 150
Palacio Fajardo, Manuel, 118
Palacios Rubios, Juan López de, 15, 17
Pascal, Blaise, 72
Paz, Matías de, 15
Peña, Juan de la, 30–2
Peñalver, Fernando, 136
Pernety, Antoine Joseph, 113
Philip II, King of Macedonia, 61–2

Philip II, King of Spain, 33, 68, 85, 112, 119
Pitt, William, 117, 131
Pizarro, Francisco, 13, 62
Plato, 37, 42, 103, 125
Pocock, J.G.A., 108
Pomponazzi, Pietro, 27
Prynne, William, 55, 61
Puffendorf, Samuel, 17, 29, 35, 71
Purchas, Samuel, 97, 101, 107
Pythagoras, 57

Quesnay, François, 126, 130
Quetzalcoatl, 96, 102, 103, 138
Quiroga, Vasco de, 25–7, 28

Raynal, Guillaume Thomas, 9–10, 35, 36, 124, 145
Richelieu, Cardinal Armand Jean Du Plessis, Duc de, 38, 76
Robespierre, Maximilien François, 144
Robertson, William, 35, 105, 106, 107, 111, 114
Rousseau, Jean Jacques, 78, 87, 130, 137, 141, 143, 144, 145, 147, 149, 150

Sahagún, Bernardino de, 102, 106
Sánchez, Francisco, 110
Schelling, Thomas, 83
Sciarra, Marco, 41, 86
Selden, John, 34
Sepúlveda, Juan Ginés de, 6, 18, 26–30, 31–2, 53
Serra, Antonio, 85
Shaftesbury, Anthony Ashley Cooper, Third Earl of, 71, 73
Shklar, Judith, 142, 149
Sigüenza y Góngora, Carlos de, 10, 92, 93–7, 100, 101, 102, 103, 107, 116
Sixtus V, Pope, 86
Smith, Adam, 74, 124, 125
Solórzano y Pereyra, Juan de, 33, 34–5, 119
Soto, Domingo de, 17, 20, 24, 25, 29, 30, 53, 54
Spinoza, Benedict de, 3, 4, 66
Stigola, Antonio, 42
Suárez, Francisco, 16, 17, 31, 63

Tacitus, Publius Cornelius, 69
Taino, 28
Tawantinsuyu, the 'Inca Empire', 92, 125, 127 and see Inca.
Telesio, Bernardino, 37, 40, 62
Thomas, St, Apostle of Malabar, 102–3
Tiepolo, Giambattista, 1, 2
Tocqueville, Alexis de, 29
Toledo, Francisco de, Viceroy of Peru, 126
Torquemada, Juan de, 100
Tuck, Richard, 17, 40
Tupac Amarú, Inca, 126
Tupac Amarú, José Gabriel, 10, 92, 121, 127, 138

Udney, John, 128

Valdés, Alfonso de, 6, 49
Valla, Lorenzo, 58
Vernaleone, Giovanni Paolo, 42
Vespucci, Amerigo, 62
Vico, Giambattista, 68, 69
Viscardo, Juan Pablo, 11, 98, 116, 117–32, 137, 151
Vitoria, Francisco de, 5, 16, 18–22, 23, 24, 25, 32, 33, 35, 36, 53, 63

Wallenstein, Albrect Wenzel von, 47
Walton, William, 126
Washington, George, 141, 148, 149
Wattell, Emerich de, 28
Weber, Max, 74, 88, 89
White, Guillermo, 146
Wycliff, John, 18, 19

Zumárraga, Juan de, 25
Zúñiga, Antonio de, 112

With the discovery and conquest of America in the early sixteenth century, Spain became the largest and most powerful of the European monarchies. By the early nineteenth century it had collapsed into little more than a dependency of its own American colonies. Throughout this period it was regarded as a unique social and political community, the most exalted, the most feared, finally the most despised, and always the most discussed since the Roman Empire. In this book Anthony Pagden examines the nature of that discussion in Spain's European possessions, in the American colonies, and in Spain itself. At first, he argues, the Spanish Empire seemed to many in Catholic Europe to be a new universal monarchy, the only agent capable of providing a sure defence against the growing threat of the Ottoman Turks and of putting an end to the religious wars in Europe itself. By the early eighteenth century, however, when these threats had passed, the Empire came increasingly to be seen as a corrupt and corrupting despotate, a menace to growing internationalism, and the very antithesis of the new commercial societies that were to dominate the modern world.

Pagden begins by analyzing the discussion over the legitimacy of the conquest of America and its place in a new Spanish imperialism. He then traces the changing response to Spanish rule in Italy, the richest and politically the most sophisticated of Spain's European dominions, from the most daring and comprehensive project for the Spanish universal empire, that of the Neapolitan philosopher and utopian political theorist Tommaso Campanella, to the critique of Spanish despotism and Spanish corruption by the political economists of the Italian Enlightenment. In the concluding chapters he discusses the